EFFECTS OF THE
HARE KRSNA MAHA MANTRA
ON STRESS, DEPRESSION, AND THE THREE GUNAS
A Doctoral Dissertation Using Modern Methods to Study an Ancient Practice

By
DAVID BRIAN WOLF

Appreciation for Effects of the Hare Krsna Maha Mantra on Stress, Depression, and the Three Gunas

Bhaktivedanta Swami profoundly contributed to humanity's understanding of the nature of consciousness. A primary method by which he achieved this is through his elucidation of the precepts underlying the practice of chanting the Maha Mantra. Dr. Wolf's research provides, in the context of rigorous, modern empirical methodology, strong support for the Vedic philosophical paradigm on which Maha Mantra chanting is based, and for the efficacy of the practice itself, for substantially enhancing well-being. I am personally grateful for this research, as it has formed for me a substantial part of the basis of my efforts to develop a mathematical model of guna psychology, and to enrich and expand understanding of decision-making processes.

— **Mauricio Garrido, PhD, Physics**

In his book, *Effects of the Hare Krsna Maha Mantra on Stress, Depression, and the Three Gunas*, Dr David Wolf effectively presents an ancient spiritual practice through the lens of the modern scientific approach, making it fascinating and relevant to anyone seeking relief from the pressures of modern life. This scholarly presentation offers practical understanding of Mantra Meditation from both the original Vedic perspective and current modern research. This gives the reader impetus to live a more meaningful and content life and provides a scientifically backed method of achieving it. My daily Maha Mantra Meditation has significantly decreased my everyday stress as well as given me a deep sense of peace and well-being. I encourage anyone seeking a spiritual practice or technique to read and carefully consider the wisdom and research contained herein

— **Sajana Allin, D.M.D.**

This research offers facts and numbers that confirm what I've experienced for twelve years, and thousands of individuals have been experiencing for much longer than that, experimenting with this ancient Mantra. As a teacher I see that students from a very young age show higher focus, longer concentration span and sharpened intelligence for their learning when exposed to this Mantra. Also, they show high interpersonal and intrapersonal skills. As a coach I observe that clients who chant the Maha Mantra as a daily spiritual practice implement and include their insights from the coaching process into their character and lives more effectively and naturally than others who do not follow a spiritual practice.

For me personally, the Maha Mantra supports me in connecting with a place of clarity from which I live my daily life, managing to more and more align thoughts, feelings and actions with my values. All these experiences contribute to a deep sense of joy, abundance and meaning that accompany me daily.

— Annette Bonomo, Primary School Teacher,
Transformational Coach, Coach Instructor

Mantra meditation has been a standard way of beginning each day for conscious living since antiquity. It is a simple and practical portal to minding the mind - that pivots on the effects of Divine Name Audible Repetition (DNAR) on fundamental properties underpinning our temperament and psychic personality. The psychological milieu of every individual is perceived by the most ancient systems of knowledge, the Vedas, as gunas - omni substances, or qualities, at work at the subconscious level that can be changed to our advantage by the password key of specific sound vibrations.

Dr. Wolf is someone ahead his time, whose pioneering efforts include developing the Vedic Personality Inventory (VPI), a scale that measures the gunas, those intangible but perceptible constituents of the human psychological system. It is perhaps the best tool I know that foretells our capacity to self-regulate at any given time. This book is a magnificent read for anyone who is committed to advance human well-being. It provides a vast avenue for future research on mechanisms of conscious activation of our inbuilt higher gear by simple attention to the Hare Krsna mantra. The implications of this can dramatically, and in a very practical way, transform mental health and spiritual health - at low cost, towards making the art of Medicine great again.

— Venugopal Damerla, M.D., Prabhupada Research Institute
for Integrative Medicine: Founding President and Medical Director

Upon reading *Effects of the Hare Krsna Maha Mantra*, a research study by David B. Wolf, PhD., I am reminded of a quote from Albert Einstein. "Science without religion is lame, religion without science is blind." David B. Wolf is making a link between ancient wisdom tradition and modern science and thus he enables us to find values in religion without needing to blindly follow. I consider his research as credible, innovative, scientific and statistically valid, and I regard *Effects of the Hare Krsna Maha Mantra* as a doorway to the possibilities of finding gems in the heritage of ancient sources of knowedge.

— Helena Pokorová, Doctor of Veterinary Medicine, Author-
Equine Psychosomatic

David Wolf's 1999 dissertation, *Effects of the Hare Krsna Maha Mantra on Stress, Depression, and the Three Gunas*, is an important work exploring clinically measurable positive effects of mantra meditation. In his research, Wolf categorizes various personality types in a system he describes as the Vedic Personality Inventory, based on Vedic guna theory, an analysis subsequently featured in a number of essays published in peer reviewed journals:

Wolf, D. (1999). "A Psychometric Analysis of the Three Gunas," *Psychological Reports*, 84, 1379-1390.

Wolf, D. & Abell, N.(2003). "Examining the Effects of Meditation Techniques on Psychosocial Functioning," *Research on Social Work Practice*, 13, 27-42.

Stempel, H.S., Cheston, S.E., Greer, J.M., & Gillespie, C.K. (2006). "Further exploration of the Vedic Personality Inventory: Validity, reliability and generalizability," *Psychological Reports*, 98,261-273.

These publications in turn inspired Marricio Garrido, PhD (Physics), of the Bhaktivedanta Institute for Higher Studies, in areas of consciousness and decision-making studies. Garrido presented his own research, in good part influenced by Wolf's work, at three major conferences:

"Modes of Material Nature: A mathematical model of consciousness based on Eastern philosophical traditions", presented at the 2016 Science of Consciousness Conference.

"Environment-Induced Dynamics in Decision Making", presented at the 2018 Science of Consciousness Conference.

"Effects Induced on the Dynamics of Decision Making by the External Environment", presented at the 2018 Society for Judgment and Decision Making, 39th Annual Conference.

I anticipate the publication of Wolf's dissertation will prove relevant for other scholars as well, exploring research in the growing field of consciousness studies.

— **Barbara Sutton, Secretary/Treasurer**
for the Bhaktivedanta Institute for Higher Studies

Dr. Wolf has combined psychological insights, sociological theory and ancient wisdom in a compact package which must intrigue even the most skeptical of us about the power of mantras. He is above all a scholar and has researched a topic that takes us into a new realm while keeping true to the highest academic standards. His peer reviewed work is earning citations, as it must. Wolf has provided both a method for raising our consciousness and the metrics to determine if we succeed.

— **Robert Cohen, Geologist**

I am delighted that Dr. David Wolf is publishing his important dissertation, *Effects of the Hare Krsna Maha Mantra on Stress, Depression, and the Three Gunas*. In this groundbreaking work, Dr. Wolf provides convincing scientific evidence that the "great mantra," or Mahamantra, actually delivers the positive, life-changing benefits that sacred tradition has ascribed to it for thousands of years. In our overstressed, dangerously conflicted world, this simple, powerful, time-tested method to elevate our consciousness is most valuable and welcome.

— **Howard Resnick, Ph.d. (Hridayananda das Goswami)**

Dr. Wolf provides a sound theoretical basis and convincing empirical evidence for the effects of the genuine ancient meditation process in the form of Hare Krishna chanting. His work is instrumental to establish this chanting as an accepted method that reignites our inner life and takes us to step out of the daily drama of the modern lifestyle. When practicing this process, popularized in the West by A. C. Bhaktivedanta Swami, my clients and myself experience the results reported in the study. Moreover, a common experience includes decreased hankering for transitory and ultimately self-defeating pleasures, while approaching the true purpose of human life whispered by the soul.

— Jindrich Pokora, Economist, Executive Coach

Dr Wolf's dissertation focuses on a group experiment on the efficacy of chanting the hare krsna maha mantra on mental ailments. The empirical evidence provided by this experiment establishes the efficacy of the maha mantra from a scientific perspective to the world community. Although the chanting has been emphasized in the Vedic scriptures, the benefits of this spiritual practice are for the first time presented for a rational mind. Dr Wolf's work on guna theory was of great help in my own dissertation, namely "Behavioral Transformation on Practitioners of Bhakti Yoga According to Bhagavad-Gita". His invaluable work is widely being quoted and referred to in presentations in the field of mantra meditation and spiritual practice, guiding thousands towards Vedic spiritual practices.

— Ninad Gandhi, Ph.d.

Srila Prabhupada gave the ultimate gift to the whole world, the chanting of Maha Mantra. I am immensely benefitted by this mantra meditation. As a neurologist, I see depression, anxiety, Alzheimer's diseases, and other chronic diseases on the rise. In the modern era, every practice should be evidence-based to reach more people. Dr. Wolf's research is timely and profound, showing the positive effects of Maha Mantra on our gunas, stress, and depression. This work is key in inspiring more people around the world to practice maha-mantra chanting, which is beneficial physically, emotionally, psychologically and spiritually. This process will open doorways to the ultimate purpose of life. This work will inspire the next generation of scientists to pursue further studies on Hare Krishna maha-mantra."

— Dr. Prasanna Tadi, M.D, Stroke Neurologist,
Creighton University/CHI Health

**Effects of the Hare Krsna Maha Mantra
on Stress, Depression, and the Three Gunas**
David Brian Wolf
davidbwolf@satvatove.com
P.O. Box 1694
Alachua, Florida 32616 USA

ISBN-978-0-9984843-4-1

Library of Congress Control Number: 2019917942

Design & Layout by:
Bhīṣmadeva Dāsa / HoofprintMedia.com

The original doctoral dissertation, Effects of the Hare Krsna Maha Mantra on Stress,
Depression, and the Three Gunas, was published in 1999.

Introduction

Twenty years ago a dissertation committee, consisting of professors Neil Abell, Walter Hudson and Bruce Bullington, approved Effects of the Hare Krsna Maha Mantra on Stress, Depression, and the Three Gunas. The Abstract of the thesis states, "The author suggests that the *maha mantra* has potential for utilization in clinical areas similar to those where other interventions of Eastern origin have been successful, such as treatment of stress, depression, and addictions. Further, it is recommended that the *maha mantra* be integrated into a spiritual approach to client care in social work and related fields."

The Florida chapter of the National Association of Social Workers invited me to conduct a workshop, Mantra Meditation and Social Work Practice, at its annual conference, in Orlando, Florida, in June, 2019. In fulfillment of the vision of the Maha Mantra dissertation, a few days ago I facilitated this workshop, with several dozen members of the social work community experiencing Hare Krsna maha mantra japa chanting, and learning to share this process with their clients.

Carl Rogers wrote, "A personal subjective choice made by man sets in motion the operations of science, which in time proclaims that there can be no such thing as a personal subjective choice." Certainly it was my personal subjectivity that led me to choose to study the effects of chanting Hare Krsna, and I thank my major professor, Neil Abell, for this. I was thinking to research some topic for my dissertation, "just to get the degree", so to speak. But Dr. Abell insisted, "No, I won't support you in that. I'll support you only if you study some subject that you're passionate about." I thought for a few moments, and we looked at each other. Then he said, "I've seen you walking around campus, holding a cloth bag, chanting something....you seem enthused about that. Why don't you research that practice for your dissertation." Clearly higher powers were speaking through Dr. Abell, and thus began this project.

Rogers' quote is particularly relevant to the study of Maha Mantra meditation. Since my involvement in the human potential movement in the late 1970s I've noticed two primary approaches to transformation. One I'll call the blank slate approach. The idea is that, at the core, we are nothing, and on the foundation of that nothingness, we can invent any possibility we choose. "Blank slate" is not the philosophical foundation of mantra yoga as described in the Vedas.

The other approach, consistent with the Vedic paradigm, is what I'll call the diamond model of transformation. At the core, we're not nothing. Rather, we are an irreducible quanta of consciousness- metaphorically, a diamond. A diamond is always strong, radiant and effulgent. And, a diamond can be covered by dust, or dirt, or thick mud. In the diamond approach, transformation of consciousness is a process of uncovering what is naturally there, a process of cleansing the diamond. The coverings of the non-physical entity that is the self, consist of the *gunas*, or three modes of material nature, which are described in some depth in this dissertation, and in a few related articles, including several of those listed at the end of this publication, in the section entitled A Selection of Articles Related to the Maha Mantra Studies.

Guna means "rope". Thus the *gunas* are ropes that bind the non-physical entity that is the self, to the material energy. As one engages in the process of diamond-cleansing, the self frees itself to authentically express. Living is transformed from reacting, based on the pulling of the *gunas*/ropes, to consciously responding, based on inspiration, joy and purpose. Life experience transforms from mechanistic, reductionist, and deterministic, to genuinely spontaneous and voluntary. Ancient wisdom traditions assert, and modern research confirms, that practices such as vibrating mantras that are intrinsically transcendent to the *gunas*, is a most powerful way to cleanse the diamond, and thus experientially realize that there is in fact such a thing as a personal subjective choice.

A few years ago I facilitated a workshop for the staff of a Veterans Administration Medical Center in Colorado. Attendees included medical personnel, including the director of the hospital. At the start of the presentation I asked, "Suppose someone comes to you and says, 'I hurt my finger.' In that phrase, 'my finger', there are two entities; the finger, and the owner of the finger. So, who are you treating? The finger, or the owner of the finger?"

The director, representing the effect on many in the room, expressed, "That's a simple question... But, you know, we've never really thought about it..."

I continued, "Well, it's important, because the finger, essentially, is made of the same stuff as, for example, this chair - it's dead matter. There's no healing force in the finger. The healing power is in the owner of the finger, the non-physical entity that animates the body."

This for me, personally, highlights my inspiration for studying the Maha Mantra. Through the practice of chanting the Hare Krsna Maha Mantra, since the early 1980s, I've increasingly experienced myself as different than dead matter, as a vibrant non-physical entity that animates the body, and that is imbued with consciousness and volition.

Below is a slightly edited version of Establishing Maha Mantra Japa Chanting as Evidence-Based Practice, a paper I wrote for the Conference Proceedings of the Bhaktivedanta Institute for Higher Studies conference that took place in Gainesville, Florida in January, 2019. That is followed by the dissertation itself, published in 1999.

Establishing Maha Mantra Japa Chanting
as Evidence-Based Practice
by David Wolf

Abstract: Two weeks ago a university professor invited me to participate in a panel of speakers, for her graduate class on trauma therapy and crisis counseling. A primary topic was "evidence-based practice". I presented about my doctoral dissertation, Effects of the Hare Krsna Maha Mantra on Stress, Depression, and the Three Gunas, and articles published in scholarly journals based on that thesis. The panel members, professors and students were inspired to hear about the efficacy of mantra meditation as a healing modality. In 2017 the Association for Coach Training Organizations (ACTO) invited me to give a keynote workshop in Toronto at its annual international conference. The workshop was entitled Mantra Meditation and Transformative Coaching. As part of the workshop dozens of founders and directors of coach training schools worldwide learned the Vedic-based philosophy underpinning the science of mantra, and they learned to chant mahā-mantra japa, as we all chanted a round in unison. Many of them expressed enthusiasm to integrate this meditation practice into their lives, and to train their coaches and clients in implementing it.

These are two amongst many examples of effectively introducing *mahā-mantra japa* to professional populations. With the research and scholarly publications that already exist, providing strong evidence for the auspicious effects of *mahā-mantra japa* on reducing stress and depression, and enhancing life satisfaction, as well as the more recent research and publication of Damerla et. al., indicating the healthful effects of *mahā-mantra japa* on the heart, there is abundant opportunity for students, researchers and practitioners in mental health, social services and medical fields to integrate *mahā-mantra japa* chanting, on an increasingly evidence-based foundation, into their practices and studies, as has already been done in recent decades with other meditation methods. [end of Abstract]

The primary method for transformation of consciousness, for inspiring the self to turn towards itself in self-awareness, emphasized by A. C. Bhaktivedanta Swami, the founder of the Bhaktivedanta Institute, is chanting and hearing the *Hare Kṛṣṇa mahā-mantra- hare kṛṣṇa hare kṛṣṇa kṛṣṇa kṛṣṇa hare hare hare rāma hare rāma rāma rāma hare hare.* Bhaktivedanta Swami's distinctive contributions to the world centrally relate to his insights on the nature of consciousness itself, and particularly to the possibilities available to human consciousness. Therefore, towards a scientific presentation of Kṛṣṇa consciousness, it makes sense for scientifically-minded followers of Bhaktivedanta Swami to be interested to investigate, in the context of modern science, the practice of *mahā-mantra* chanting, which the Vedas assert to be a powerful technique for change of consciousness.

In 1999 I published my doctoral dissertation, Effects of the Hare Kṛṣṇa Mahā Mantra on Stress, Depression, and the Three Guṇas. A major element of my literature review was researching studies that had already been conducted on the effects of meditation, including mantra meditation. As expected, even by the late 90s, extensive research had been done on a diversity of meditative and prayerful approaches to well-being and healing, including varieties of mantra meditation, and this body of research is extensively cited in Effects of the Hare Kṛṣṇa Mahā Mantra on Stress, Depression, and the Three Guṇas.

Filling A Gap in the Research Literature

A conspicuous gap in the research literature was the lack of any systematic, scholarly study on the effects of chanting the *Hare Kṛṣṇa mahā-mantra*. Conspicuous, considering that the Vedas assert the *mahā-mantra* as the most efficacious means for self-realization in the present age (Prabhupada, 1975; Sri-Caitanya-caritamrta Adi-lila 3.40 purport). With intention to begin to fill this lacuna, I set about the *mahā-mantra* studies, first with a single-system design, and then a group design.

The group design included three groups, with the prime independent variable of interest being the *mahā-mantra*. The dependent variables were stress, depression, and effects on the three *guṇas- sattva, rajas and tamas*. Control variables included gender and age. Each dependent variable was measured with a suitable scale with strong psychometrics. For the three *gunas*, this scale was the Vedic Personality Inventory (Stempel, et al. 2006; Wolf, 1999). Results of the study largely confirmed Vedic hypotheses regarding chanting the *Hare Kṛṣṇa mahā-mantra*, and have been published in various journals, including Research on Social Work Practice (Wolf and Abell, 2003).

Impact of Mahā-mantra Research and Publication

The *mahā-mantra* and Vedic Personality Inventory (VPI) research and publications have inspired and influenced researchers and practitioners worldwide in their direction of study and choice of practice technique. For example, Dr. Jill Bormann, a leading researcher in the field of mantra meditation who has been working for many years with veterans diagnosed with PTSD, has, as a result of the *Hare Kṛṣṇa mahā-mantra* studies and publications, added the *Hare Kṛṣṇa mahā-mantra* to her list of possible mantras for veterans to chant (personal correspondence from Dr. Bormann to the author, January 30, 2017). Even Oprah magazine (August, 2016) published an article about the *Hare Kṛṣṇa mahā-mantra* japa studies conducted by Wolf (right next to an article entitled "Your thighs are gonna thank you").

Damerla et al. (2018) recently published a study on the beneficial effects on heart health of chanting *Hare Kṛṣṇa mahā-mantra japa*. A few weeks ago, while visiting family, I mentioned about this study, to a dentist relative of mine, whom I overheard speaking about his less than satisfying experiences with various types of meditation. Being medically-trained, the heart-rate variability (HRV) research especially interested him. He asked me to show him how to chant *Hare Kṛṣṇa mahā-mantra japa*, and he has integrated this practice into his life.

A main reason that the Association for Coach Training Organizations (ACTO) invited me to their annual international conference, as mentioned in the Abstract of this article, to give a keynote workshop entitled Mantra Meditation and Transformative Coaching, was the research and literature base that already exists in regards to the auspicious effects of chanting *Hare Kṛṣṇa mahā-mantra japa*. There are abundant opportunities, with even the current relatively limited research and publication that has been done, for practitioners in diverse fields to introduce *Hare Kṛṣṇa mahā-mantra japa* chanting. This can be done, by those with an inspiration and intention to do it, in all the fields where other forms of meditation are already prominent, including rehabilitation centers, hospitals, prisons, the military, the corporate sector, schools, and practically all fields connected with therapy, well-being, experiential education, and healing.

Lifetimes of Research Agendas

At least equally exciting, for intrepid spiritual scientists, are limitless opportunities, constituting lifetimes of research agendas, for expanding *Hare Kṛṣṇa mahā-mantra* research. Effects on diverse dependent variables, ranging from school performance to marital satisfaction, from severity of symptoms related to various psychological disorders, to speed of addiction recovery, could be investigated, with respect to how they're affected by *Hare Kṛṣṇa mahā-mantra* chanting. And of course numerous control variables, such as race, nationality, and economic status, can be considered, to enhance the rigor of the studies. And similarly, dozens and hundreds of studies can be designed and implemented to further test the effects of *Hare Kṛṣṇa mahā-mantra* chanting on dependent variables of a physiological nature.

An Empirical Basis for Happiness

The paradigm of the three *guṇas* constitutes, from the Vedic perspective, an empirical basis for happiness, and inner-security, peace, and all of the qualitative interior experiences that are commonly sought. That is, the Vedas assert that cultivation of world views and life habits that are predominated by *sattva*, will positively correlate with fulfillment, joy, healthy non-attachment, and all the life experiences for which living entities strive. Research on the *guṇas* (Stempel, 2006; Wolf, 1999; Wolf, 1998) provides strong evidence for this Vedic assertion. We can understand this in light of a statement attributed to St. Francis, "We are searching for what is searching". That essential experience we tend to seek through action and external attainment, is intrinsic to the self.

Of the *guṇas*, *sattva guṇa* is closest to the original consciousness, or state of being, of the self. Therefore, *sattvic* mental and behavioral habits inspire the inner experiences we seek. The *Hare Kṛṣṇa mahā-mantra* is purported in Vedic science to consist of śuddha-sattva, or unadulterated *sattva*, and thus is identical with the original, non-material consciousness of the atomic unit of sentience that is the actual self. Research projects investigating the veracity of Vedic claims can focus on studies on the effects of sattvic habits and world views, and on śuddha-sattva practices such as *Hare Kṛṣṇa mahā-mantra* chanting.

Epistemological Considerations

"Bhaktivedanta" indicates realized knowledge acquired through devotion to the Absolute. Such a method for obtaining knowledge begins and descends from a source untainted by the material modes of nature and by the intrinsic incompleteness of material senses, mind and intellect.

Also it's true that effects of practices that spring from transcendent origin may be evaluated with reference to epistemologies founded in empirical perception and inference, keeping in mind of course the shortcomings intrinsic to empiric methodologies. *Bhakti* śāstra asserts that the precepts and effects of *bhakti-yoga*, while not dependent on material sensory perception, are empirically verifiable, and not merely metaphysical or abstract. Actual knowledge in *bhakti* translates to "direct perception of the self by realization" (Bhagavad-gita As It Is, 9.2).

Some, or many, practitioners of *bhakti-yoga* and *mantra-yoga*, with their distinctive epistemological commitments, may understandably not be especially personally interested in positivist approaches to the study of the effects of *mantra* meditation. And simultaneously, such empirical studies, carefully aligned with the most rigorous practices of modern scientific research, can fulfill the purport of "Bhaktivedanta".

References

Damerla, V., Goldstein, B., Wolf, D., Madhavan, K., and Patterson, N. (2018). Novice Meditators of an Easily Learnable Audible Mantram Sound Self-Induce an Increase in Vagal Tone During Short-term Practice: A Preliminary Study. Integrative Medicine: A Clinician's Journal, 17 (5), 20-28.

Prabhupada, A. C. B. S. (1972). Bhagavad-gita As It Is. Hong Kong: Bhaktivedanta Book Trust.

Prabhupada, A. C. B. S. (1975). Sri Caitanya-caritamrta. Los Angeles: The Bhaktivedanta Book Trust.

Stempel, H. S., Cheston, S., Greer, J. M., Gillespie, C. K. (2006). Further exploration of the Vedic Personality Inventory: Validity, reliability and generalizability. Psychological Reports, 98 (1), pgs. 261-273.

Wolf, D. (1999). Effects of the Hare Krsna Maha Mantra on Stress, Depression and the Three Gunas, Doctoral dissertation, Florida State University, 1999.

Wolf, D. (1999). A Psychometric Analysis of the Three Gunas, Psychological Reports, 84, 1379-1390.

Wolf, D. B. (1998). The Vedic Personality Inventory: A Study of the Gunas. Journal of Indian Psychology, 16(1), 26-43.

Wolf, D. and Abell, N. (2003). Examining the Effects of Meditation Techniques on Psychosocial Functioning. Research on Social Work Practice, 13 (1), 752-766.

I would also like to thank Bhismadeva dasa (HoofprintMedia.com) for designing and laying out this publication.

THE FLORIDA STATE UNIVERSITY

SCHOOL OF SOCIAL WORK

EFFECTS ON THE HARE KRSNA MAHA MANTRA ON STRESS,

DEPRESSION, AND THE THREE GUNAS

By

DAVID BRIAN WOLF

A Dissertation submitted to the
School of Social Work
in partial fulfillment of the
requirements for the degree of
Doctor of Philosophy

Degree Awarded:
Summer Semester, 1999

The members of the Committee approve the
dissertation of David Brian Wolf defended on
June 8, 1999.

Neil Abell
Professor Directing Dissertation

Bruce Bullington
Outside Committee Member

Walter Hudson
Committee Member

This dissertation is dedicated to A. C. Bhaktivedanta Swami Prabhupada, who introduced the Hare Krsna maha mantra in the Western world.

Acknowledgements

I would like to acknowledge the dedicated and skilled guidance given in this project by my Major Professor, Dr. Neil Abell. Also, I thank Dr, Walter Hudson, whose valuable input into this dissertation despite trying circumstances was a constant source of inspiration. In addition I wish to express my gratitude to my Outside Committee Member, Dr. Bruce Bullington, for sacrificing his time and providing thoughtful and attentive comments at each stage of this endeavor. My thanks also go to Alice Allen for her counsel and assistance with statistics. I want to express my appreciation to Ijya dasa (Mr. Eric Johnson) for his patience and competence as a research assistant, and also to my wife, Maha Laksmi dasi (Miriam Wolf), for her ceaseless support as well as her service as a research assistant.

Table of Contents

List of Tables

Abstract

EFFECTS OF THE HARE KRSNA MAHA MANTRA ON
STRESS, DEPRESSION, AND THE THREE GUNAS

Name: David Brian Wolf

Department: School of Social Work

Major Professor: Dr. Neil Abell

Degree: Doctor of Philosophy

Term Degree Awarded: Summer, 1999

The author conducted a 3-group study on the effects of chanting the *hare krsna maha mantra* on stress, depression, and the three modes of nature- *sattva*, *rajas*, and *tamas*- described in the Vedas as the basis for human psychology. Sixty-two subjects, self-selected through newspaper advertisements in a Southeastern university town, completed the study. Average age was 24.63 years, with 31 males and 31 females participating. Stress was measured with the Index of Clinical Stress, depression was measured with the Generalized Contentment Scale, and the modes of nature, or *gunas*, were measured with the Vedic Personality Inventory. Subjects were tested at pretest, posttest, and followup, with testing times separated by four weeks. Participants were randomly assigned to a *maha mantra* group, an alternate mantra group, and a control group. Subjects in each of the chanting groups chanted their mantra approximately 25 minutes each day. The researcher concocted a mantra as the alternate mantra, though subjects in the alternate group thought it was a genuine Vedic mantra. Primary hypotheses of the study were based on Vedic theory, and stated that the *maha mantra* group would increase *sattva*, and decrease stress, depression, *rajas* and *tamas*, significantly more than the other two groups. ANCOVA results, controlling for gender and age, supported these hypotheses at $p<.05$ for all dependent variables except *rajas*, with effect sizes (eta^2) for the four variables whose results supported the hypothesis ranging from .21 to .33. The author suggests that the *maha mantra* has potential for utilization in clinical areas similar to those where other interventions of Eastern origin have been successful,

3

such as treatment of stress, depression, and addictions. Further, it is recommended that the *maha mantra* be integrated into a spiritual approach to client care in social work and related fields. Suggestions for further research include applying path analysis to the data of this study to ascertain causal relationships, and application of Hierarchical Linear Models to the data to combine single-system analysis and group analytical methods for extracting the maximum amount of information. Additionally, further studies on the *maha mantra* are warranted, with various populations and in various settings.

CHAPTER 1

THEORETICAL BACKGROUND

This dissertation focuses on a group experiment that was conducted on the effects of chanting the *hare krsna maha mantra* a mantra emphasized in the literature from ancient India for its efficacy in relieving stress, depression, and other mental health disturbances (Prabhupada, 1976). Therefore, chapter 1 presents some basic theoretical concepts, derived from the Eastern Vedic literatures, necessary for understanding the process of chanting mantras. chapter 2 contains a review of the literature on spiritual interventions, a term which will be defined in chapter 1. The Vedas describe the Hare Krsna *maha mantra* as a spiritually-based intervention for psychological upliftment (Prabhupada), and therefore it is appropriate to study related theory and literature on spiritual approaches to mental health improvement.

Considering the person-in-environment orientation of the social work profession, spirituality and religion must be acknowledged and respected by social workers, as these factors are an integral part of practically every human culture, and they frequently play a central role in the lives of many people. Canda (1988) emphasizes the importance for social workers to take into account the spiritual needs of clients so that the fullness of the clients' human dignity and potential is recognized and respected in all helping situations. He asserts that spirituality is a basic aspect of human experience, both within and outside the context of religious institutions, and that it therefore should be explored more fully through social work practice, research, and theory building. In the United States, Gallup Poll data consistently show that approximately 95% of the population believes in God, and about half the population is actively religious on at least a weekly basis (Paloutzian

& Kirkpatrick, 1995). As the following literature review will show, religious and spiritual dimensions are among the most important cultural factors structuring human experience, beliefs, values, behavior, and illness patterns. It is justifiable, therefore, for helping professionals to consider the religious and spiritual components of clients' lives in attempts to serve the client population.

Bullis (1996) writes "Traditionally, social work literature has reluctantly addressed religion's or spirituality's impact on clinical practice" (p. 6). He attributes this to the historic rift between the religious and psychoanalytic movements, the alleged atheistic orientation of social workers, and economic, political, and professional competition between religious professionals and secular social workers. Bullis continues "For the most part spirituality in social work literature is conspicuous only by its absence" (p. 6).

If a multicultural perspective is to be more than a facade for social workers, the phenomena of religion and spirituality must be genuinely appreciated. The term "genuinely appreciated" is emphasized herein, since Western approaches to diversity sometimes involve a patronizing pseudo-respect meant to veil a proselytizing mission that seeks to undermine long-held spiritual and religious beliefs and replace them with a relativistic viewpoint. Bellah et al. (1991) relate excerpts from a talk given a few years ago by a student speaker at a Harvard University graduation:

> There is one experience that I believe we have all acquired during our career at this fine institution, and that, ladies and gentlemen, in a word, is confusion. The freedom of our day is the freedom to devote ourselves to any values that we choose, on the mere condition that we don't believe them to be true. (pgs. 43-44)

So, for social workers, whose profession has roots in spiritual and religious humanitarianism (Dolgoff, Feldstein, & Skolnik, 1993), it may be a good idea to objectively examine the literature on spirituality as it relates to the many facets of social work. To reject such literature as being non-scientific due merely to its content, without consideration of its methodology and substantive results, may be considered dogmatism.

Literature Categorization

This paper will address the topic of spiritually-based interventions in the helping professions, with a focus on the relevance of such interventions to the field of social work. Writings in this area will be classified into the following categories: general relevance of spirituality and religiosity to the helping professions; measurement of spirituality; and spiritual interventions. General relevance of spirituality and religiosity to the helping professions includes research pieces that investigate correlations between spiritual and religious factors and variables such as delinquency, management of HIV/AIDS, hospice work, depression, self-esteem, and alcohol and drug use. Most of these studies incorporate quantitative designs, though there are a few qualitative pieces and some articles that primarily provide commentary on the topic. Measurement of spirituality includes research articles that attempt to define and measure the construct of spirituality utilizing psychometric procedures. The spiritual interventions section contains studies and literature reviews that examine the effects of an intervention that is purported to be spiritual in nature. These studies focus on spirituality as a specific intervention that produces effects on pre-defined dependent variables, whereas the general relevance articles deal only with correlative relationships. The general relevance of spirituality and religiosity to the helping professions category will be subdivided into two major sections- commentary and empirical research. The spiritual interventions category will also be subdivided into three sections- empirical quantitative studies, empirical qualitative studies, and literature reviews. This classification scheme is presented in Figure 1, and will be further explained in the section entitled summary of literature classification.

General relevance and measurement articles are presented as supportive material to illustrate the importance and practicality of the spiritual component to the helping professions. Articles in the spiritual interventions category will be comprehensively analyzed and presented in Appendix A. Components of these research articles, such as theory, design, measurement and results, will be summarized and synthesized, and the literature in the field will be reviewed and integrated with attention to gaps in the research.

Spirituality and Religiosity

Bullis (1996) states that "spirituality refers to the inner feelings and experiences of the immediacy of a higher power" (p. 2), while religion refers to the "outward form of belief including rituals, dogmas and creeds, and denominational identity" (p. 2). Thus, the concepts are related, though not interchangeable.

To further explain, we will refer to Vedic philosophy, which constitutes the orientation of the author, as well as the basis for several of the interventions described in this paper. According to the Vedas, "spiritual" refers to an energy that is transcendental to gross and subtle forms of matter. Matter has gross forms, such as earth, water, air, and space, and subtle forms, including mind and intelligence. Spiritual energy is distinct from all these forms of matter. "Religion" refers to rituals, procedures, or institutions that are meant, at least in principle, to facilitate access to spiritual experience. Obviously, there are religious adherents who are not very spiritual, and spiritual persons who do not manifest religious observance (Prabhupada, 1976).

Though religion is not synonymous with spirituality- some might claim it is antonymous- studies on religiosity are included in this work because in the literature and in theory it is closely connected with spirituality and spiritual interventions. According to the *Srimad-Bhagavatam* (Prabhupada, 1976), religion is meant to elevate one to a platform of spirituality, beyond sectarian conceptions that are based in worldly designations. An example of such a conception is nationality. According to the Vedas, the self is a spiritual particle that is encased in a subtle and gross material body. If this body is born in America, then one may think "I'm American", if born in Australia, one may think "I'm Australian", etc. However, these designations have no inherent connection with the spiritual self, only with the material covering. To further explain, if I'm riding in a Toyota, it would be a mistake to therefore conclude that I'm Japanese. Tomorrow I may ride in a Volkswagen, and then, based on bodily misidentification, I'd consider myself German. Similarly, our bodies are material vehicles that have a purpose and should be cared for properly, though it is illusion to consider the body to be the self. For further clarification of the distinction between the body and the non-material self, one may ask oneself "Who is it that is thinking 'I am the body' or 'I am an American'"? The entity that is thinking is different than the body.

Clearly, much of what passes as religion in the world today does not qualify as religion based on the definition of *Srimad-Bhagavatam*. Still, religious institutions and practices continue to serve as a major vehicle for people to achieve spirituality. In the literature review that follows, this will become more evident. Therefore, many findings correlating religiosity and attributes of well-being are included in this paper.

Bullis (1996) writes that "social workers are just beginning to define the nature of spirituality in interventions" (p. 17), and reports that many conventional religious practices, such as prayer and scriptural reading, are used by social workers and other mental health professionals as interventions. For purposes of this dissertation, spiritual interventions refer to religious practices or other observable techniques designed to impact one's spiritual experience.

Epistemological Justification for Empirical Study of Spiritual Interventions

Dawson (1997) asserts that spirituality cannot rightly be subsumed under empirical science. That is, spirituality should not be reduced to a conception that is subject, for instance, to the laws of thermodynamics, or is contingent on Einstein's equation that relates energy and matter. This would be scientism, whereby spirit loses its transcendence to matter and becomes subservient to empirical epistemologies. Dawson maintains that spirituality is a type of energy, but one not subject to empirical laws.

Since this paper examines spiritual interventions, and the author does not view spirituality as merely a component of material science, it may be questioned why we are investigating positivist research on spiritual topics, and why such research has been and should be conducted. In response, it should be understood that science consists of knowledge that can be reliably verified by systematic procedures of observation. Science is not necessarily limited to material subject matters. There are procedures employed in spiritual interventions that yield results that can be reliably assessed, and these procedures can be conceived as the basis for a spiritual science (Prabhupada, 1976). Empirical methods can be, and have been, extensively applied in the evaluation of spiritual science and the effects of religious practice on psychosocial well-being. In fact, according to Levin, Larson, and Puchalski (1997), writing on the field of medicine, research on spiritual and religious factors is as sophisticated as any other area within epidemiology, and findings have been subjected to greater scrutiny than most research.

Material Science and the Vedas

Keefe (1996) comments "In the last thirty years, meditation began its marriage to the rational-empirical tradition of Western science. In this most recent alliance it is being tested, objectified, stripped of its mystical trappings, and enriched with empirical understanding" (p. 434). Most of the meditative methods that are being tested, and that will be analyzed in this paper, are based in Vedic theory and practices. This illustrates how a spiritual theory with concomitant praxes can be dovetailed with empirical science. Empirical support for these methods, in areas such as decreasing depression, stress and substance abuse, may strengthen the scientific basis of Vedic theory.

Though the ultimate goal of Vedic science is realization of our spiritual nature, there is a vast material component in Vedic science. Vedic material science is based on the three *gunas*, or modes of nature- *sattva*, *rajas*, and *tamas*. Characteristics of each mode are extensively described in Vedic literature, and these descriptions form operational definitions for experimental science. For instance, a characteristic of *tamas guna* is depression, whereas *sattva guna* is symptomized by a feeling of happiness (Dasgupta, 1961). According to Vedic theory, practice of a meditative process, such as chanting of certain sound vibrations, will diminish the effects of *tamas*, and augment the influence of *sattva*. Thus, *guna* theory is conducive for empirical investigation, in this case by standardized psychometric tools for assessment of depression and happiness. Much work needs to be done, however, to further operationalize Vedic concepts and formulate and implement research designs.

Assumptions Derived from Vedic Theory

Before concluding the introduction it is appropriate to elaborate on Vedic theory, especially as it relates to social science, because this is the world view of the author, and the reader will therefore be better equipped to critique and understand this paper with an appreciation of Vedic concepts. This presentation is not meant to be a comprehensive defense of Vedic assertions. The main purpose is to acquaint the reader with the beliefs of the author, and to prepare the reader for what follows. This explication of Vedic philosophy will use as a framework Burrell's and Morgan's (1979) four criteria for assessing a social science theory. These criteria are ontology, epistemology, human nature and methodology.

Ontologically, social science approaches can be placed on a continuum with realism and nominalism at the extremes. Nominalists deny that social structures are real, and assert that reality is a subjective phenomena, while realists insist that social structures exist as empirical entities (Burrell & Morgan, 1979). For Vaisnavas, adherents of Vedic philosophy and culture, creation, consisting of material and spiritual aspects, is real. This realism is countered, however, by the understanding that persons in material consciousness, who comprise almost everyone in this world, falsely perceive reality according to the illusory conceptions that pervade their mind and intelligence. The Vaisnava social scientist, therefore, acknowledges the importance of subjectivity in studying and interacting with people, since subjective understandings are the subtle force that drives human interaction. Another caveat to regarding Vaisnavas as realists is the theological notion that reality is a manifestation of the consciousness of God. In this sense, Vaisnavas may be considered as radical subjectivists (Prabhupada, 1975).

Epistemologically, social scientists can be placed on the continuum from anti-positivism to positivism. Positivist epistemologies, which dominate the natural sciences, search for regularities and causal relationships in the social world. Anti-positivists prefer to view social science as a subjective undertaking, and concentrate on comprehending the experience of the individual, rather than discovering objective laws governing interaction (Burrell & Morgan, 1979). Vedic epistemology includes a branch, called *anumana*, that is equivalent to the process of modern empirical science. *Anumana* involves acquiring knowledge through sensory observations that are then processed, analyzed, and organized into theories by the mind and intelligence. These theories are then tested by further observations. Though the Vedas accept this as a possible approach to knowledge, they also describe the shortcomings of this system. A major drawback of this method is that it is based on the mind and senses, which are imperfect in several ways. For instance, our senses make mistakes, and thus we have erasers on pencils. The senses are susceptible to illusion, and therefore we may confuse a rope for a snake. Additionally, our senses are very limited. Though we can't see what's happening two inches behind our head, and have a difficult time remembering what we were doing at this time two weeks ago, we conjecture, based on empiric data, what happened thousands of light years away, billions of years ago (Gosvami, 1977).

The Vedas describe knowledge as innate to the self. This knowledge is covered, and Vedic social science seeks to extricate the self from this covering. Towards this goal, positivist and anti-positivist approaches may be used, though utilization does not negate inherent flaws of a method (Prabhupada, 1975).

With regards to this dissertation, there is no internal contradiction in studying and discussing Vedic concepts and methods using positivist approaches. Empirical methods are condoned by the Vedas, though the Vedas also critique them. Several other epistemological systems, along with their uses and deficiencies, are also elaborated in the Vedic literatures. Exposition of these systems is beyond the scope of this paper, and this short presentation is included to justify the use of empirical methodologies within a Vedic context.

Voluntarism versus determinism forms another debate amongst social science theorists. Voluntarists accept the free will of the human being, whereas determinists believe that a person's actions are caused by environmental factors (Burrell & Morgan, 1979). Vaisnavas view the self as possessing free will. However, the capacity for self-determination, which stems from the spiritual entity that is the actual self, is covered by the material energy. To the extent that the self is covered by the modes of material nature, or *gunas*, free will cannot manifest. Thus, the human situation involves a mixture of deterministic and voluntaristic forces. Circumstances of birth provide boundaries, within the material sphere of activities, for the self, though free will remains active. A Vedic social worker assists the self to make the best choices from available options (Prabhupada, 1976).

Methodologically, social science research techniques include qualitative and quantitative methods. Quantitative techniques tend to be compatible with realist, positivist and determinist approaches (Heineman, 1981). From the Vaisnava vantage point, quantitative techniques are increasingly useful as the object of study possesses less consciousness. Thus, a positivist, quantitative research design would be more effective studying rocks than animals, and less effective when studying human beings, due to the relatively high degree of consciousness in humans. Consciousness means free will, and consciousness is considered to be a symptom of the spiritual energy. When free will enters the equation, predictive capacity of the scientist decreases. Hence, social sciences are less exact than hard sciences such as chemistry and physics. Still, material nature covers the free will of humans to a large extent, and therefore the Vaisnava social scientist can utilize quantitative methods for researching social interaction and the activities of the mind and intelligence (Prabhupada, 1976). By employing quantitative approaches, the social scientist is implicitly expressing deterministic assumptions about the person(s) being studied. The following section examines selection and classification procedures for analysis of research articles on spiritual topics.

Scope of the Present Study

Considering the concepts described above, we will study the effects of the *maha mantra* on variables such as stress, depression, and the three *gunas*. Prior to discussing the experiment on the *maha mantra*, there will be a literature review on correlations between spiritual and religious factors with indicators of mental and physical health, and on the effects of spiritual and religious interventions. This literature review will also include a discussion of the literature on psychometric attempts to measure spirituality. After the literature is reviewed and synthesized, the methodology for the group experiment on the *maha mantra* will be discussed. Then, in chapter 4, results from the *maha mantra* study will be analyzed, with regards to differential effects on dependent variables between persons who chanted the *maha mantra* and persons who chanted an alternate mantra, as well as with persons who did not chant any mantra. Additionally, a single-system design pilot study of the *maha mantra*, which was conducted prior to the group experiment, will be described in the appendices. Chapter 5 will discuss the results of the group study, especially as they relate to the theoretical presentations of this chapter, and the literature review of chapter 2.

CHAPTER 2

LITERATURE REVIEW AND SYNTHESIS

Selection Procedures

Four databases- PsychInfo, Medline, PsycLIT, and Sociofile- were searched for this systematic research synthesis. In these databases, the following keywords, alone and in combinations, were used: meditation, mantra, prayer, faith, spirituality, religion, health, stress, anxiety, depression, and social work.

Klein and Bloom (1994) delineate five major types of articles in the social work literature- empiricism, technology, conceptualization, valuation and commentary. Of these, the empiricism, technology, and commentary categories are relevant to the classification system of this paper. Empiricism, according to Klein and Bloom (1994):

refers to activities of engaging the world and people in it by means of the five basic senses. The empirical component includes planned actions to observe and measure social events in laboratories, clinics, or community settings- what would be termed 'research' or 'evaluation' in the current literature. (p. 422)

The categorization scheme of Klein and Bloom (1994) will be further described in the categorization overview section of this chapter. For now, the categories are introduced to help the reader understand the discussion of selection procedures that follows.

For the general relevance of spirituality and religiosity to the helping professions category (see Figure 1), commentary and empirical research articles that examined the importance of spirituality and religiosity to fields such as social work, mental health and medicine were sought. There are many such articles, and the 43 pieces chosen for inclusion in this section are by no means exhaustive. The main point of the general relevance section is to demonstrate that spirituality and religiosity are considered important factors for helping professionals. Therefore, variety in articles was stressed to illustrate the pervasive nature of these factors. If several articles covered the same topic, the most recent ones were chosen for inclusion. The main criterion for inclusion was diversity, with respect to population and professional area. For example, the studies selected examine the role of spiritual and religious factors in areas such as chronic illness, life satisfaction, attributes of caregivers in Alzheimer's disease, death depression and anxiety, predictors of mortality, alcohol and drug use, management of HIV/AIDS, depression, delinquency, self-esteem, crime, hospice work, coping with war, general well-being, coping with a chronically ill child, resolving childhood abuse issues, suicide, and dealing with illnesses such as cancer and heart disease. Populations studied include adolescents, African Americans, elderly, long-term hospital inpatients, burn patients, mental health clients, suicidal persons, and hospice workers.

Not all articles in this section provide evidence for the potential importance of spirituality and religiosity, though the great majority of them do. Selection of empirical research articles in this category was based on title, to check for substantive area and population, and date, as described above. That is, results were not analyzed prior to selection. This methodology was incorporated to reduce selection bias. Commentary articles in this category were selected after the empirical research articles, in order to provide some theoretical framework that bridged a variety of fields, including social work, nursing, medicine, psychology, and psychiatry. Though more than the eight commentary articles included herein were found, none of these articles argued for the unimportance of spirituality and religiosity, and thus the tenor of the commentary articles can also be considered representative of the literature.

Articles in the measurement of spirituality section (see Figure 1) focus on quantitative empirical research on the measurement of spirituality. These studies focus on attempts to directly measure spirituality, rather than correlates of spirituality, such as general well-being. Three spirituality instruments are analyzed.

The Spiritual Well-Being Scale (SWBS) is the most widely researched and utilized tool in the field, and is based on Judeo-Christian psychological theory (Ellison & Smith, 1991). Based on Vedic *guna* theory, the Vedic Personality Inventory (VPI) is the *guna* scale that has been most extensively analyzed with psychometric methods (Wolf, 1998). Hatch, Hellmich, Naberhaus, and Berg (1995) have developed the Spiritual Involvement and Beliefs Scale (SIBS), which is an attempt, derived from dissatisfaction with the SWBS, to assess spirituality without Western bias.

Articles in the spiritual interventions category (see Figure 1) constitute the main topic of this literature review. Included are articles that examine interventions that purport to be spiritual in nature, with regard to their effects on dependent variables such as depression, stress, and substance abuse recovery. This review focuses on the content of the interventions, as well as the methodological rigor of the studies. The prime selection criteria was diversity that reflects the heterogeneity of interventions and methodologies. Using this criteria, articles investigating the effects of Western-style prayer, Alcoholics-Anonymous non-sectarian spirituality, social work community interventions, and Eastern-style meditation were chosen. Only in the area of Eastern-style meditation were there many articles, necessitating further selection criteria. Delmonte (1983) and Delmonte and Kenny (1985) conducted literature reviews on Eastern-style spiritual interventions, and these reviews are included in this analysis as a summary of research in this area prior to 1985. For research on Eastern-style interventions since 1985, selections included studies with a variety of research techniques, especially with regards to qualitative and quantitative approaches, and studies that investigated a range of interventions, such as mantra-based, Buddhist, and physical yoga techniques.

Categorization Overview

Except for the commentary articles in the general relevance category, all literature classified in Figure 1 fits the definition for empiricism given by Klein and Bloom (1994), which is presented above in the section on selection procedures. For the specific purposes of this paper, general relevance, spiritual interventions, and measurement of spirituality categories have been differentiated. For the general relevance category, commentary and empirical research sub-categories have been created, and for the spiritual intervention category, empirical quantitative, empirical qualitative, and literature review sub-categories have been created. In the measurement category, all pieces are quantitative and meet the criteria for technology pieces, as defined by Klein and Bloom (1994). "Technologies may be mechanisms or procedures that extend empiricism in a research sense... or the tools that one may bring to bear in a given practice setting." (p. 422). According to Klein and Bloom, quantitative empirical articles use standardized empirical methods such as descriptive research and bivariate and multivariate analysis, and qualitative empirical studies include case studies, ethnographic methods, and community case illustrations. The literature reviews in the Spiritual Interventions section examine empirical studies, and have been placed in a separate sub-category. Commentary articles refer to:

> statements that describe, critique, or comment on empirical, technological, conceptual, or valuational activities....Commentary represents participation in public discussion of the issues of the day. These discussions provide the foundation on which to develop other components of the applied social science. (p. 423)

The articles in the commentary section of the general relevance category fit this description.

In the general relevance of spirituality and religiosity to the helping professions category there are 8 commentary articles and 35 empirical research articles (see Figure 1). Each category is divided into sections according to field of practice, such as social work, medicine, and mental health. All these pieces address the influence of spirituality and religiosity on the helping professions in a wide variety of fields and populations, as described above. Social workers are active in all of the environments and with all the populations included in these articles. Therefore, social work researchers, administrators and practitioners will benefit by noting the contents of these articles. For example, several articles deal with health care, a field in which many social workers are employed. With an understanding of the spiritual and religious factors common to this setting, social workers will be better equipped to assist clients in coping with their situation. Similarly, studies on the correlation between spirituality and religiosity and delinquency can help social workers in case management, on individual, familial, and communal levels, with families and communities that struggle with juvenile delinquency.

In the measurement of spirituality category there are five articles (see Figure 1), all technology pieces, presenting various psychometric strategies for measurement of spirituality according to different orientations (e.g., Vedic, Western). These articles are included because it is sometimes suggested that spirituality is not the domain of science, since spirituality cannot be operationalized or measured. Here, however, are attempts at such operationalization and measurement, following accepted psychometric procedures.

There are 15 spiritual intervention pieces (see Figure 1). Among these, there are nine quantitative studies, four qualitative studies, and two literature reviews. The literature reviews deal with Eastern-style interventions, such as mantra chanting and meditation, as do five of the quantitative pieces and three of the qualitative articles. One quantitative study evaluates prayer to the Judeo-Christian God, and two quantitative articles examine effects of a 12-step program. There is one quantitative study that investigates a variety of spiritual and religious interventions, and one qualitative investigation presents a model for social work with religious and spiritual communities. These 15 pieces are the focus of this literature review, and will be analyzed in appendix A.

Figure 1: Literature Classification for Spiritual Interventions

GENERAL RELEVANCE OF SPIRITUALITY AND RELIGIOSITY TO THE HELPING PROFESSIONS (43 ARTICLES)

Commentary (8 Articles)

Social Work- Canda (1988), Keefe (1996)

Medicine- Hudson (1996), Levin, Larson, & Puchalski (1997), McKee, & Chappel (1992), Peri (1995)

Mental Health- Lukoff, Lu, & Turner, R. (1995), Templeton (1994)

Empirical Research (35 Articles)

Social Work- Joseph (1988)

Medicine- King, & Bushwick (1994), Maugans, & Wadland (1991), Morgan, & Cohen (1994), Mickley, Soeken, & Belcher (1992), Ginsburg, Quirt, Ginsburg, & MacKillop (1995), Landis (1996), Rutledge, Levin, Larson, & Lyons (1995), Goldbourt, Yaari, & Medalie (1993), Harris, Dew, Lee, Amaya, Buches, Reetz, & Coleman (1995)

Mental Health- Bradley (1995), Levin, Chatters, & Taylor (1995), Ellison (1995), Krause (1995), Burgener (1994), Carson (1993), Carson, & Green, (1992), Pargament, Ishler, DuBow, Stanik, & Rouiller (1994), Pollner (1989), Valentine, & Feinauer (1993), Westgate (1996)

Hospice and Emotions Surrounding Death- Millison (1995), Millison, & Dudley (1990), Alvarado, Templer, Bresler, & Thomas-Dobson (1995)

Evaluation of Suicidal Potential- Kehoe, & Gutheil (1994)

Mortality- Bryant, & Rakowski (1992), Janoff-Bulman, & Marshall (1982)

Youth Substance Use- Burkett, & Warren (1987), Lorch, & Hughes (1985), Turner, Ramirez, Higginbotham, Markides, Wygant, & Black (1994), Cochran, Wood, & Arneklev (1994)

Delinquency- Chadwick, & Top (1993), Evans, Cullen, Dunaway, & Burton (1995), Foshee, & Hollinger (1996)

General- Witter, Stock, Okun, & Haring (1985)

Figure 1 (Continued)

MEASUREMENT OF SPIRITUALITY (5 ARTICLES)
Technology

Bufford, Paloutzian, & Ellison (1991), Butman (1990), Ellison, & Smith (1991), Hatch, Hellmich, Naberhaus, & Berg (1995), Wolf (1998).

Empirical Quantitative (9 Articles)

Alford, Koehler, & Leonard (1991), Byrd (1988), Carroll (1991), Janowiak, & Hackman (1994), Kutz, Leserman, Dorrington, Morrison, Borysendo, & Benson (1985), Miller, Fletcher, & Kabat-Zinn (1995), Pearl, & Carlozzi (1994), Smith, Compton, & West (1995), Stern, Canda, & Doershuk (1992)

Empirical Qualitative (4 Articles)

Kaye (1985), Nakhaima, & Dicks (1995), Sweet, & Johnson (1990), Urbanowski, & Miller (1996)

Literature Review (2 Articles)

Delmonte, M. M. (1983), Delmonte, & Kenny (1985)

General Relevance of Spirituality and Religiosity to the Helping Professions

These articles are presented as evidence for the importance of spirituality and religiosity, and as support for the pertinence of spiritually-based interventions to the helping professions. There are dozens of articles in this section, and as a whole they provide strong evidence that social workers, psychologists, counselors, psychiatrists, nurses, doctors, and other professionals will enhance their abilities to serve people by serious consideration of spiritual and religious factors. Detailed analysis of methodology is not provided, as it is for articles in the spiritual interventions category, because the mass of evidence is adequate to demonstrate the essential point of potential relevance of the topic to helping professionals, notwithstanding shortcomings in some of the studies. Before addressing the results of research articles, commentary articles will be presented to provide a framework for the empirical pieces.

Commentary Articles

Social Work

Canda (1988) appeals to social workers to consider spiritual and religious issues in their dealings with clients. Claiming that spirituality is common to all people, he asserts that it is relevant to all areas of social work practice, and calls for a spiritually aware social work profession. Human dignity and potential, according to Canda, is intricately entwined with spiritual needs, and a helping professional must recognize this facet of human existence in order to wholly benefit individuals and society. He suggests that social work theory, research, education and practice need to more fully explore the spiritual dimension. Further, he advises that social workers should develop self-understanding regarding spiritual growth, examining their beliefs, motivations, values and activities in relation to spirituality, and should consider the impact of these factors on clients' spirituality. He goes on to overview Christian, Jewish, Shamanist, and Zen perspectives on social work, and concludes that professional helping may be significantly enhanced by the introduction of prayer, meditation, contemplation, ritual, and study of scripture, as appropriate to client orientation. Additionally, he maintains that there are numerous meditative techniques, from Eastern and Western traditions, that have not yet been discussed and applied in social work.

Keefe (1996) presents Eastern-style meditative techniques as potentially important in social work practice and treatment, describing specific applications in treating depression, substance abuse, excessive anxiety, and development of social work skills in professional training. Many social workers have adopted a bio-psycho-social model in their practice, and Keefe's article provides a framework for progression to a bio-psycho-social-spiritual model, as is being developed in nursing and medicine (Mckee & Chappel, 1992). Keefe asserts that the potential of meditation in social work treatment and psychotherapy has already been recognized by some researchers and practitioners, and that meditative methods are natural adjuncts to social work interventions. He concludes that meditation "has the potential to be valuable in work with clients from diverse cultures. Yet meditation as a method continues to demand much from, and occasionally challenges, some theories underlying social work treatment for its full description and explanation. (p. 451)"

Medicine

Levin, Larson, and Puchalski (1997) argue that more attention needs to be given by helping professionals to the religious and spiritual beliefs of the people whom they serve. They cite statistically significant associations between religious belief and health measures and measures pointing to differences in morbidity and mortality rates. Further, they state that systematic reviews and meta analyses quantitatively confirm that religious involvement is an epidemiologically protective factor. Additionally, they suggest that physicians should be more inquisitive about patients's spiritual beliefs and practices, citing that 80% of Americans believe in the power of God or prayer to improve the course of illness, while only 10% of physicians ever inquire about spiritual and religious beliefs. Empirical research articles, which will be discussed in the next section, provide further evidence that clients and patients want professionals to inquire about spirituality more than they do at present.

In medicine, a bio-psycho-social-spiritual model is being developed and practiced, as the spiritual dimension is gradually being recognized as essential (Mckee & Chappel, 1992). Mckee and Chappel claim that there is ample evidence to support the inclusion of spiritual issues in medical education and practice. They write:

> There is growing evidence that spiritual practices can complement medical treatments in cases of both acute and chronic disease....It is evident that there is a growing body of medical literature suggesting that spirituality is of interest and beneficial to the practice of primary care medicine. (p. 204)

Hudson (1996) stresses the importance of faith in a higher power as a fundamental ingredient in guiding many patients to health. In relation to caring for AIDS patients, Peri (1995) claims that the spiritual dimension is routinely overlooked, and that development of spiritual well-being is crucial in helping persons with AIDS find meaning in life and death.

Mental Health

Lukoff, Lu, and Turner (1995) point to the importance of recognition and understanding of client spirituality and religiosity in the mental health professions. Generally, they assert, spiritual and religious issues that clients bring to treatment are ignored or pathologized. This unfavorable view is not warranted, however, as a meta-analysis of religiosity and mental health determined that they are significantly and positively related. In addition, church affiliation and perceived relationships with divine others, such as God, show a significant, positive correlation with several measures of well-being. For most people, religion and spirituality are viewed as sources of strength and well-being, rather than evidence of psychopathology. This article examines the roots of these attitudes, which, statistically, are not representative of the general population or persons who enter therapy, amongst mental health professionals. They conclude that this tendency towards a negative view of religion/spirituality can be traced to the roots of behaviorism, cognitive therapy and psychoanalysis. Freud regarded religion as a universal obsessional neurosis, Skinner largely ignored religious experience, and Ellis viewed religion as equivalent to irrational thinking and emotional disturbance. Similarly, spiritual experiences have been considered to be evidence of psychopathology. Surveys of therapists have revealed that distinct references to religion appear in about one-third of all psychoanalytic sessions. Carl Jung wrote (Templeton, 1994):

> During the past thirty years...among all my patients in the second half of life-i.e. over thirty-five- there has not been one whose problem in the last resort was not that of finding a religious outlook on life. It is safe to say that every one of them fell ill because he had lost that which the living religions of every age has given their followers, and none of them has been really healed who did not regain his religious outlook. (pgs. 142-143)

To ignore or to adversely evaluate this dimension may be perceived as a sign of cultural insensitivity, a trait which social workers must strive to avoid.

Empirical Research

Social Work

Joseph (1988) explored whether social workers consider religious and spiritual issues to be a significant parameter of the client's internal and external environment. In addition, he inquired whether social workers explore spiritual and religious issues and assess them in relation to other psychosocial factors. Also, he evaluated the extent to which social workers actively deal with spiritual and religious issues in the treatment process. This mail survey randomly selected 90 field instructors affiliated with a Master of Social Work program in Washington, D.C.. Sixty-one instructors responded to the survey, which included four sections. One section examined personal background, the second section addressed spiritual and religious issues in social work, the third section explored practitioner experience in using religious/church related resources in practice, and the fourth section dealt with religious issues that surfaced in practice. Joseph concluded "Data clearly show that practitioners consider religious issues important despite the lack of emphasis on them in graduate education" (p. 448). Further, the data "clearly reflect the prominence of God and religion in times of illness and crises and suggest that such phenomena can hardly be overlooked in social work practice" (p. 450). He concludes that the religious dimension of the person, particularly as it interacts with life-cycle and ecological concerns, has been muted in social work practice, especially in dealing with populations such as the frail elderly.

Medicine

King and Bushwick (1994), in a cross-sectional survey of hospital inpatients found that many patients believe that physicians should consider patients' spiritual needs, and that 21% of patients believe it is the physician's responsibility to inquire about religious issues. This research included a pre-survey power analysis to determine sample size. Maugans and Wadland (1991) cite many studies indicating the pervasiveness of religion and spirituality in the United States, and several studies pointing to the benefit of religious/spiritual association on various aspects of health. Their study, a cross-sectional survey of physicians and patients, found that patients tended to be more religious than physicians, though more doctors than patients reported that religion should affect the choice of a physician. Maugans and Wadland suggest, based on results of the survey, that doctors became more aware of spiritual and religious factors. Other notable findings were that physicians felt more strongly than patients that they had a right and responsibility to inquire about religion in their medical practice, though patients and doctors acknowledged that such inquiry occurs very infrequently. In this study, seven factors were found significant at the .01 level. These factors are that patients believe in the existence of God more than doctors, patients engage in prayer more often than doctors, patients feel closer to God than doctors, doctors believe more than patients that religion should be an important factor in choosing a physician, doctors believe more than patients that religion should be an important factor in the maintenance of the doctor-patient relationship, doctors believe more than patients that doctors have the right to inquire about religious matters, and doctors believe more than patients that physicians have the responsibility to inquire about such matters. Morgan and Cohen (1994) obtained results indicating that psychiatrists are increasingly recognizing the importance of spirituality and religion to their clients.

In an investigation of the relationship between spiritual well-being, religiousness, and hope amongst women with breast cancer, Mickley, Soeken, and Belcher (1992), using a cross-sectional survey design with a sample of 175 women with breast cancer, determined that intrinsic religiosity, defined as considering relationship with God more important to overall well-being than an existential sense of well-being, is positively associated with spiritual well-being. However, they did not assess whether spiritual well-being is correlated with survival rates among oncology patients. The authors did provide useful suggestions on how

26

results from this study could be applied to hospital practice. For example, they outline a program for encouraging health-promoting spiritual expression among inpatients. Ginsburg, Quirt, Ginsburg, and MacKillop (1995), in a study of lung cancer patients, found that religion is commonly cited as an important means of symptom alleviation. Landis (1996) and Rutledge, Levin, Larson, and Lyons (1995), utilizing cross-sectional survey designs, found similar results in studies of chronic illness and coping of parents who have a chronically ill child, respectively. These assessments represent measurement at a single-point in time, and a longitudinal design with multiple points of data collection would be useful in future studies on these topics.

In research sponsored by the Israeli Ministry of Health, the Hadassah Medical Organization, and the United States National Institute of Health, Goldbourt, Yaari, and Medalie (1993) studied 10,059 Israeli adult males, using a prospective, longitudinal cohort with a stratified sample. They found that highly orthodox religious groups experienced significantly reduced coronary heart disease death rates and all-cause mortality rates, as compared with the other participants. These effects were maintained even after controlling for conventional risk factors of heart disease, such as smoking, diabetes, and high cholesterol. Also, controlling for area of birth did not eliminate the differences between groups. With such a large sample size, there is naturally concern about the magnitude of the effect of religious orthodoxy on the diagnoses. After multivariate analysis, performed with Cox's life table proportional hazards model with estimations derived from Breslow's modification for tied observations, the authors concluded that:

> fatal coronary heart disease events according to religiosity indicated a small 'independent' advantage, in terms of the probability of dying from coronary heart disease and all causes, enjoyed by 20% of the sample who reported themselves as orthodox. In another study in Israel, albeit of a case-controlled nature, myocardial infarction odds ratios as high as 4.2 and 7.3 for men, after adjustment for 'conventional' risk factors, have been estimated for secular persons relative to religious ones among Jewish residents of Jerusalem... Since the results of our study suggest that differences in the distribution of blood pressure, serum cholesterol, cigarette smoking, prevalence of diabetes and prior coronary heart disease do not eliminate the advantage of the highly

orthodox group, additional research is suggested to examine other associated life habits and other possible environmental sources of variability. (p. 119)

Harris, Dew, Lee, Amaya, Buches, Reetz, and Coleman (1995) conducted a prospective cohort study and found that, among heart-transplant patients, religious beliefs and practices predict improved physical functioning, enhanced adherence to medical regimens, higher self-esteem, and diminished anxiety.

Mental Health

Bradley (1995), in a prospective cohort study with a sample of 3,597 adults, found that religious attendance was strongly associated with support network size and perceived quality of relationships ($p<.001$), though he found no significant relationship between worship attendance and neuroticism or introversion. Levin, Chatters and Taylor (1995), in a cross-sectional survey of Black Americans using a national sample of 2,107 subjects, found, using maximum-likelihood structural modeling, that organizational religiosity is significantly associated ($p<.01$) with health and life satisfaction, non-organizational religiosity is inversely associated ($p<.05$) with health, and subjective religiosity and health are associated with life satisfaction ($p<.05$). Even controlling for health and several demographic factors, religiosity was shown to have a favorable effect on life satisfaction. This counters the assertion that religiosity serves as a proxy for functional health, which argues that those who are physically and emotionally healthier are more likely to attend church.

Ellison (1995), in a cross-sectional survey study of 2,956 adults in North Carolina, found that public religious participation is inversely associated with depressive symptoms, particularly among African-Americans. Krause (1995), in a cross-sectional survey using a national sample of 1,103 elderly persons, found that use of religious coping mechanisms is associated with increased self-esteem. This survey used ordinary least squares multiple regression procedures, though the relationship between religious coping mechanisms and self-esteem appears to be U-shaped, casting doubt on the analytic procedure. Specifically, those who make most use of religious coping mechanisms, and those who make no use of them, appear to have the highest levels of self-esteem. The article did not attempt to explain why those not using religious coping had high self-esteem. Burgener (1994) found that, for caregivers of Alzheimer's patients, general well-being was positively associated with religious worship attendance. In this study, however, only 30% of the questionnaires sent to caregivers were returned, indicating the possibility that self-selection bias influenced the results.

In studies of persons with AIDS, Carson (1993) and Carson and Green (1992), using cross-sectional survey designs, found that spiritual well-being is positively correlated with hardiness, as measured by a questionnaire consisting of 50 items divided into three subscales (challenge, commitment and control). Results of these studies indicated that spiritual well-being is an important factor in coping with HIV/AIDS, though the research did not investigate a relationship between spirituality and long-term survival.

Pargament, Ishler, Stanik, and Rouiller (1994), in a prospective cohort study of 215 undergraduate students, examined the effects of religious coping on levels of distress among college students, and determined that use of religious coping mechanisms makes a significant and positive contribution to individuals' ability to cope with stressful events like the Gulf War. Pollner (1989) found that perceived relationships with divine others, such as God, has a significantly positive effect on several measures of well-being. Valentine and Feinauer (1993) concluded that religiosity and spirituality were positively correlated with successful coping in female survivors of childhood sexual abuse. In a review of counseling and medical literature, Westgate (1996) found a consistent inverse relationship between spiritual wellness and depression.

Hospice and Emotions Surrounding Death

Millison (1995) and Millison and Dudley (1990) found that spirituality was an important component in the lives of hospice workers. More specifically, their research indicated that job satisfaction for hospice workers, 12.5% of whom were educated as social workers, was positively correlated with spirituality.

Alvarado, Templer, Bresler, and Thomas-Dobson (1995) found that belief in life after death was inversely correlated with death depression and death distress (p<.01). Strength of religious conviction was inversely proportional to death anxiety, death depression and death distress (p<.05). This study is especially significant because it indicates that, with regard to tempering death depression and death anxiety, religious beliefs are actually more important than religious practices, whereas many other studies in the field of religiosity/spirituality find that practices, such as church attendance, are more important than beliefs. This study, however, is limited by its heterogeneous and non-clinical sample. A study of death depression and death distress that samples persons who are seriously ill or who are actually dying would be interesting and productive.

Evaluation of Suicide Potential

Kehoe and Gutheil (1994) examined measurement tools for suicidal patients with regard to spiritual and religious issues. This study is included here, rather than in the measurement of spirituality section, because it evaluates instruments for assessing suicidal characteristics, not spirituality. The measurement of spirituality section analyzes scales that directly attempt to measure spirituality, whereas this study simply adds to an understanding of the importance of spiritual factors, and therefore belongs in the general relevance section. Kehoe and Gutheil cited psychiatric literature that suggests that religion and spirituality are significant and meaningful forces in the lives of patients with mental disorders, particularly when these persons consider suicide. Yet scales assessing suicidal risk almost entirely fail to consider religion and spirituality. Durkheim, in 1897, found an inverse relationship between suicide and religious affiliation. Though Durkheim concluded that social integration was the active factor in this relationship, Kehoe and Gutheil cite other studies, that controlled for social factors, and determined that religious affiliation is directly connected to decreased suicides. Kehoe and Gutheil assess 12 scales commonly used for assessing suicidal risk. They write:

> Designers of the scales appear to seek factors that may construct a profile of the suicidal person. Yet they seem to ignore the possible impact of what a person, on the brink of life itself,   believes about life and about life after death....Possibly clinicians simply ignore this aspect of a person's life

in their ordinary practice and therefore continue to do so in a suicidal crisis. If this   hypothesis is true, then the designers of suicide scales simply reflect clinicians at large. .. This result may point to neglect in training as well as a possible prohibition against such exploration created during clinicians' role socialization....Comparison of the literature on religion and suicide and the literature on suicide assessment scales reveals a remarkable and paradoxical inconsistency. Although religion is noted as a highly relevant factor in the suicide literature, the number of religious items included on suicide scales approaches zero. (pgs. 367-368)

Mortality

In a prospective cohort design, Bryant and Rakowski (1992), studying mortality rates among elderly (at least 70 years old) African-Americans in the United States, found that less frequent church attendance is related to higher mortality. This finding was maintained even after controlling for variables such as age, gender, health status, and extent of social networks. Conducting research on mortality rates amongst elderly nursing home residents, Janoff-Bulman and Marshall (1982), in a prospective cohort study with a sample size of 30, found that increased religious beliefs are predictive of increased mortality among elderly nursing home patients. The researchers suggest that patients who report enhanced well-being and greater religiosity are more accepting of the inevitability of death, and perhaps those who are already approaching death may turn to religion in old age. The findings of this study differ from other studies that have produced evidence that, among institutionalized patients, increased longevity correlates positively with religiosity. In this study, sample size is small, and 17% of the 30 persons sampled were lost to follow-up, two and a half years after the initial survey.

Youth Substance Use

Examining the relationship between religion and adolescent marijuana use among high school youth, Burkett and Warren (1987), in a prospective cohort study of 264 high schoolers in a medium-sized city in the Pacific Northwest, found that religion has an indirect inhibitory effect on adolescent marijuana use by encouraging associations with peers who do not use drugs. Lorch and Hughes (1985), in a cross-sectional survey of 13,878 junior and senior high school students in a Colorado metropolitan area, determined that church members have a lower percentage of substance users than non-church members, and that the more important religion is to a young person, the less likely he/she is to use alcohol or drugs. Further, findings suggest that the controls operating in the youths' choice not to use drugs exist as internalized values and norms rather than external pressures associated with church ideology or peer pressure. Turner, Ramirez, Higginbotham, Markides, Wygant, and Black (1994), using a convenience sample of 247 9th-graders in Austin, Texas, found similar results. Cochran, Wood, and Arneklev (1994), in a study of 1600 high school students, found that, even after controlling for the variables of arousal, parental control and institutional control, religious participation remained significantly and inversely correlated with substance use.

Delinquency

Studying juvenile delinquency, Chadwick and Top (1993), in a survey of 2,143 Latter-Day Saints adolescents, found that religious factors are inversely related to delinquent activities. This study focused on a highly religious group and may therefore be limited in its application to less religious youths. Cochran, Wood, and Arneklev (1994) concluded, in their survey of 1,600 high school students in Oklahoma, that the effects of religious participation and intensity of religious involvement upon interpersonal delinquency, property theft, and property damage were no longer statistically significant after controlling for arousal (e.g., impulsivity and thrill-seeking) and social control (e.g., parental control and institutional control) variables. Foshee and Hollinger (1996), in a prospective cohort study using a probability sample of 2,102 adolescents and their mothers, determined that maternal religiosity is predictive of lower rates of adolescent alcohol use (p=.003) when controlling for demographic variables, social control variables, and baseline adolescent alcohol use. Maternal religiosity was also positively associated with adolescent academic commitment (p=.001). Studying the relationship between religion and delinquency amongst adult males, Evans, Cullen, Dunaway, and Burton (1995) found that religious activity, though not necessarily religious beliefs, inhibits criminal activity among adult males. This study used a sample of 550 men from a midwestern urban area.

Summary

In summary, commentators from many helping professions assert that spiritual and religious factors must be seriously considered by responsible practitioners in their professions, and that efforts to dovetail spiritual practices with current modes of treatment are necessary. Empirical findings demonstrate a clear and positive association between spirituality and religiosity and favorable outcomes in many helping fields. An understanding of spiritual and religious factors and their dynamics can be important for professionals to understand people and maximize service to clients. As a final empirical reference, Witter, Stock, Okun, and Haring (1985) conducted a meta-analysis on 556 empirical sources on subjective well-being and 17 correlates such as health, social activity, and religion. From the sources they extracted 56 religion/subjective well-being effect sizes. They found that, compared to the other 16 predictors of subjective well-being, religion was as strongly or more strongly associated with subjective well-being on half of the predictors. The authors made an appeal for researchers not to ignore religion when forming and testing causal models of subjective well-being.

Research on Related Interventions

Since this dissertation describes a study on the effects of mantra chanting, it is appropriate to briefly delineate aspects of behavior therapy that relate to the chanting of mantras, as well as other yogic techniques.

Behavior therapy is largely based on the principle of operant conditioning, which involves increasing or decreasing a person's behavior by systematically changing its consequences each time the behavior is performed. According to the behavioral model, behaviors are caused by present events that surround

33

the performance of behaviors. Antecedents are events that occur before the performance of the behavior, and they set the stage for the behavior to occur. Consequences are events that occur after the behavior has been performed and that influence future occurrences of the behavior. For example, feeling sleepy is an antecedent for going to sleep, and feeling refreshed is a consequence of that behavior (Spiegler & Guevremont, 1993).

Chanting the Hare Krsna *maha mantra*, according to Vedic theory, provides the internal gratification of pleasure for the self, the non-material entity that sits within the gross and subtle material bodies. This purported pleasure serves as a consequence and maintaining condition for chanting the Hare Krsna *maha mantra*. Also, according to Vedic philosophy, because the happiness of chanting Hare Krsna applies directly to the self, rather than to any outer covering of the self, the pleasure is more satisfying than gratification directed at components of the gross or subtle material bodies, such as the senses or mind. Therefore, this more satisfying enjoyment can hypothetically serve as a replacement for behaviors that produce a less satisfying type of gratification, and that also produce undesirable side effects. As Sri Krsna explains in the Bhagavad-gita (Prabhupada, 1972), "The embodied soul may be restricted from sense enjoyment, though the taste for sense objects remains. But, ceasing such engagements by experiencing a higher taste, he is fixed in consciousness" (p. 78). Chanting the *maha mantra* may provide a "higher taste" for the non-material entity situated in the modes of material nature.

In cognitive-behavioral therapy a common process is thought stopping, wherein a person interrupts disturbing thoughts by uttering the word "Stop!" After disrupting the distressing thought, the client is recommended to think about something that competes with the disturbing thought. However, it is often difficult for a person not to think about something (Spiegler and Guevremont, 1993). Chanting the Hare Krsna *maha mantra* can be an effective positive replacement thought in the thought stopping process, which is similar to aversion-relief therapy because it simultaneously reduces an undesirable target behavior and increases an alternative target behavior. For instance, persons who uncontrollably think depressing thoughts such as "I'm useless" may train themselves to replace such thoughts with thoughts of the syllables of the *maha mantra*. The undesirable target

34

behavior, which leads to a depressive state of mind, is supplanted by an alternative target behavior that, according to Vedic *guna* theory, increases *sattvic* qualities such as contentment and peacefulness.

In many areas of behavior therapy, such as medical applications, techniques such as emotive imagery and diversion of attention are included in treatment packages (Turk, Meichenbaum, & Genest, 1983). These techniques can utilize the *maha mantra, hare krsna hare krsna krsna krsna hare hare hare rama hare rama rama rama hare hare*, as a response to compete with anxiety and other unfavorable emotional responses. The *maha mantra* as a competing response might be used in treating conditions such as tic disorders and chronic pain, as well as in coping with painful medical procedures. Williams and Gentry (1977) describe the Shavasana yogic exercise, which was incorporated in the study of Janowiak and Hackman (1994), as a behavioral approach to medical treatment for conditions such as severe hypertension.

When a mantra is chanted privately on beads it is called *japa* chanting, and the beads are called *japa* beads. Though chanting the Hare Krsna *maha mantra* does not require *japa* beads, the beads, as will be described in the next chapter, provide a means to quantify the number of times that the mantra is chanted. Additionally, usage of beads while chanting engages the sense of touch. According to the Bhagavad-gita (Prabhupada, 1972), the senses are centered around the mind, and therefore, the more senses that are engaged in an activity, the easier it is for the mind to focus on that activity. Chanting the *maha mantra* involves the tongue and the sense of sound, and with *japa* beads, the sense of touch is also engaged. This facilitates focusing the mind on the *sattvic* vibration, and enhances the effect of the mantra. A practical application of this idea could be helping clients to stop smoking. Smoking involves the mouth and the fingers, as does the activity of chanting Hare Krsna on *japa* beads. By engaging the same senses and organs in the process of chanting Hare Krsna, the person may experience a higher taste that allows one to abandon a type of pleasure that is less satisfying.

Benson (1975) identified four common elements in relaxation techniques: 1) A mental device upon which to focus the mind; 2) A passive attitude regarding whether the relaxed response is achieved; 3) Decreased muscle tension- subjects should assume a comfortable position to reduce gross motor activity; 4) A quiet environment with minimal external distraction. Benson developed the "relaxation response" behavioral technique which utilizes a combination of body relaxation, attention to breathing, and repetition of the word "one" as a mental device to fix the concentration. One can note the similarity between "one" and the "Om" mantra used by Kaye (1985). This technique, as well as several other behaviorally-based approaches, such as autogenic training and biofeedback, have been effective in facilitating relaxation and treating ailments such as severe headache and essential hypertension (Williams & Gentry, 1977).

When chanting the *maha mantra*, a person focuses the mind on the syllables of the mantra. Although the chanter is not directed to think about relaxation, according to the Vedas relaxation is a natural effect of chanting the *maha mantra*. Further, the chanting is most efficacious when external distractions are minimized, which is achieved with a serene environment and comfortable body position. Thus, practice of *maha mantra* chanting is consistent with all elements of behavioral relaxation techniques as described by Benson (1975). In fact, Benson's relaxation response is a variant of meditation and yoga (Olton & Noonberg, 1980).

Mantra chanting is a yoga technique, and there are many similarities between biofeedback training and yoga. Biofeedback is defined as any technique that increases a person's ability to voluntarily control physiological activities by providing information about those activities. This technique, which utilizes machines to detect physiological states, has been effectively used to treat stress-related illnesses such as tension, ulcers, and asthma, as well as maladies such as incontinence and paralysis due to stroke.

Biofeedback is a fundamental component of behavioral medicine, which emphasizes the importance of patient participation in the treatment program through processes of self-regulation (Olton & Noonberg, 1980). Yoga techniques are also systems of self-regulation. Such self-regulatory techniques are inherently different from methods depending on external regulation, such as hypnosis and pharmacological approaches. Green and Green (1977) have developed a psychotherapeutic technique called "theta training", which is a combination of yoga practices and biofeedback that is designed to self-induce a state of integrative, relaxed introspection. Biofeedback evaluation of yoga practitioners has revealed that yogic meditative techniques are correlated with enhanced ability to control, recognize and regulate physiological conditions, such as metabolism rate and brain waves (Raskin, Johnson, & Roudestvedt, 1973; Green & Green, 1977). Just as mantra meditation engages several senses, biofeedback also regulates by engaging the senses of touch, sound, and sight.

Thus, in many ways the process and effects of mantra yoga can be understood in terms of behavioral therapy. Though the theoretical orientation of this paper is Vedic theory, with its accompanying explanatory concepts of gross, subtle and spiritual bodies, behavior theory provides an alternative way to view mantra and yogic meditation.

Measurement of Spirituality

During the 1960s and 1970s many tools for measuring social indicators, such as education, employment, health, and housing, were developed to assess quality of life. Many of these objective indicators reflected significant gains, though social unrest, substance abuse, family fragmentation, political alienation and several other negative indicators also increased during this period. This fostered the gradual recognition that quality of life was not solely dependent on objective factors, and thus efforts were increasingly directed toward measurement of subjective life experiences, such as life satisfaction and happiness (Bufford, Paloutzian, & Ellison, 1991).

Though religion has often been included as a factor in quality-of-life assessments, and several scales measuring aspects of religiosity have been developed (Butman, 1990), spirituality has largely been neglected in these evaluations. As evidenced by the general relevance section, religion, spirituality, and life satisfaction have generally been found to be positively related. However, scales that assess religiosity tend to overlook the purely spiritual component, such as an inner sense of the immediacy of a higher power and the sense of one's relationship with God, while focusing on aspects such as religious identification and lifestyle (Ellison & Smith, 1991).

Three attempts at measuring spirituality will be reviewed in this section: The Spiritual Well-Being Scale (SWBS), the Spiritual Involvement and Beliefs Scale (SIBS), and the Vedic Personality Inventory (VPI). The SWBS is based on Judeo-Christian, or Biblical, theory, the VPI is based on Vedic *guna* theory, and the SIBS is an attempt at measuring spirituality that is specifically designed to avoid the perceived sectarianism of the SWBS. This is not to imply that the SIBS is the most universally applicable of the three instruments. From the Judeo-Christian perspective, a Biblical approach to psychology and spirituality is considered universal, encompassing all ethnic and cultural variations in the human experience. Similarly, from the Vedic perspective the philosophy of the three *gunas* applies to all entities in this world. A researcher or practitioner seeking to use a scale for spirituality will need to assess each instrument according to the particular purpose of the research. Herein, for the benefit of such researchers and practitioners, the fundamental orientation of these three measures has been presented.

The following analyses are not intended to be detailed critiques of the instruments. Basic psychometric data are reported, though the essential reason for inclusion of this measurement of spirituality section is to illustrate that the construct of spirituality can be measured by empirical standards. Further, the existence of psychometric data for measures of spirituality strengthens the potential usefulness of the construct in clinical practice. For example, depression is a mental construct formulated in the minds of researchers. The development of reliable and valid self-report scales that measure the concept known as depression enhances the ability to utilize that construct when attempting to understand problems in human functioning and develop relevant interventions. Similarly, the development of spirituality scales with strong psychometric characteristics increases the practical utility of the concept of spirituality. Of course, nuanced questions about the nature and qualities of spirituality remain unresolved, but this is also true for most psychometric areas, such as self-esteem, anxiety, and depression. The instruments described below are technological pieces (Klein & Bloom, 1994) that facilitate the research of spirituality.

The Spiritual Well-Being Scale

This instrument attempts to measure the Biblical concept of *shalom*, whose root meaning includes ideas of completeness, wholeness, harmony and well-being. Also implicit in this notion is the experience of unimpaired relationships with others and being fulfilled in one's course of life. Additionally, *shalom* refers to physical health. According to Ellison and Smith (1991):

> *Shalom*, or well-being, may be viewed as the integral experience of a person who is functioning as God intended, in consonant relationship with Him, with others, and within one's self. *Shalom* describes the experience of being harmoniously at peace within and without. It presents a picture of the person functioning as an integrated system in proper equilibrium. (p. 36)

The SWBS is the most extensively researched measure of spiritual well-being. It has been used in hundreds of practice settings, including a wide variety of medical, nursing, and mental health environments. Also, research has been conducted on this instrument in numerous contexts, including universities, seminaries, hospitals, and prisons, and with various populations, including teenagers, Christians, hospital inpatients, housewives, professional women, non-Christians, and the elderly (Bufford, Paloutzian, & Ellison, 1991).

The scale consists of 20 items evenly divided to comprise two subscales. The Religious Well-Being (RWB) subscale contains 10 items that refer to God and assess the vertical dimension of spirituality. The Existential Well-Being (EWB) subscale contains 10 items that measure a horizontal dimension of well-being in relation to the world about us, including a sense of life purpose and life satisfaction. Each item is rated on a six-point modified Likert scale from Strongly Agree to Strongly Disagree, with no mid-point. Several items are worded in a reversed direction to minimize response sets (Ellison & Smith, 1991).

In seven samples (total n=994), alpha, a measure of internal consistency, ranged from .89 to .94 for the SWBS, from .82 to .94 for the RWB subscale, and from .78 to .86 for the EWB subscale. Research has shown test-retest reliability for the SWBS, at intervals ranging from 1 to 10 weeks, to vary from .82 to .99, and from .73 to .99 for the subscales. Overall, these data suggest that the SWBS has adequate reliability (Bufford, Paloutzian, & Ellison, 1991).

Factor analysis of the SWBS has revealed that it loads on two factors, corresponding to the two subscales, with the RWB subscale items loading stronger than the EWB items. Research has indicated that SWBS and its subscales correlate positively with several standard indicators of well-being, including a positive self-concept, strong meaning and purpose in life, high assertiveness, low aggressiveness, physical health, and emotional adjustment. Furthermore, SWBS is negatively correlated with ill health, dissatisfaction with life, and emotional maladjustment. In summary, this instrument appears to have strong factorial and construct validity (Bufford, Paloutzian, & Ellison, 1991).

Among spirituality scales, the SWBS is the only one that has norms. SWBS data are available on many samples, including clergy, seminarians, college students, counseling clients, prison inmates, caregivers for hospice patients, medical outpatients, and several religious groups. These data indicate good predictive validity with regard to differentiating between populations. For instance, persons in training for or currently in religious leadership positions scored higher than any other group sampled. Also, religious groups scored higher than non-religious groups (Bufford, Paloutzian, & Ellison, 1991).

A limitation of the SWBS is that many subjects among religious groups score at or near the ceiling score. For these groups, therefore, the scale is unable to differentiate. As a result, the scale's practical uses seem limited to groups of mid-range and low scorers. For example, the SWBS would not appear to be useful in identifying leadership potential amongst seminary students. In addition, this ceiling problem suggests that the distribution for the scale is not normal, and this casts doubt on assumptions for various statistical procedures used in analyzing the SWBS, such as parametric correlational techniques. Though there are norms for the SWBS for many populations, such norms are conspicuously lacking for genders and ages. Further scale development and analysis should address this matter. Another area for consideration is that research on the SWBS, although fairly extensive, has been conducted almost entirely in the Pacific Northwest region of the United States, which raises questions about its generalizability (Bufford, Paloutzian, & Ellison, 1991).

40

The Spiritual Involvement and Beliefs Scale

This instrument was specifically designed to create an assessment of spiritual status that is more comprehensive and widely applicable than the SWBS. It is meant to apply across religious traditions, and to assess actions as well as beliefs, whereas SWBS items focus on cognition. Formulation of items involved input from persons of varied spiritual and cultural traditions. Designers of the scale sought an instrument that could practically integrate spiritual assessment into client care and research (Hatch, Hellmich, Naberhaus, & Berg, 1995).

The scale contains 26 items in a 5-point Likert format, and was administered to 83 participants, 50 of whom were patients from a rural medical family practice setting, and 33 were medical professionals affiliated with a medical school in Northern Florida. To evaluate validity, participants completed the SIBS and SWBS consecutively. Retest data was gathered seven to nine months after initial administration of the SIBS. With this sample, Cronbach's alpha for the SIBS was .92, and test-retest reliability was .92. Correlation with SWBS scores was .80. Factor analysis revealed four factors- Faith/Ritual, Fluid/Reflective, Existential/Meditative, and Humility/Personal Hatch, Hellmich, Naberhaus, and Berg (1995).

Clearly, the SIBS has not been adequately tested to properly evaluate its psychometric strength. Still, initial reliability and validity data indicate a potentially useful instrument. Regarding factor structure, the sample size is too small to determine the validity of the current factor analysis.

Compared to the SWBS, the SIBS utilizes more generic wording, and appears, based on examination of item content, to be broader in scope than the SWBS. Authors of the SIBS acknowledge that it is not possible to design an instrument free from bias. However, their effort makes a deliberate attempt to avoid the biases of Western spiritual traditions, and the SIBS may therefore be useful with diverse cultural populations.

The Vedic Personality Inventory

The VPI is an attempt to measure the three *gunas*, or modes of material nature, as described in the Vedic literatures. According to the Vedas, all facets of material existence, including our mental processes, sound vibration, foods, disposition, and vocational choice, are permeated by the three *gunas- sattva, rajas* and *tamas*. Predominance of *sattva* indicates greater spirituality. In fact, according to Vedic philosophy, the state of complete spirituality is called *suddha sattva*, or pure *sattva*. In this way, the VPI serves as a spiritual assessment scale. Though there have been other attempts at *guna* inventories, such as Uma, Lakshmi, and Parameswaran (1971), Singh (1971), Rao and Harigopal (1979), and Das (1991), the VPI is the most extensively tested amongst the *guna* scales, incorporating larger sample sizes and more elaborate statistical analyses (Wolf, 1998).

This instrument contains 56 items, with the *sattva* subscale containing 15, the *rajas* subscale containing 19, and 22 items in the *tamas* subscale. There are seven Likert-type response choices for each item. The VPI has been tested on 494 subjects, most of whom were nurses or university students. For the *sattva* subscale internal consistency alpha is .93, for the *rajas* subscale alpha is .94, and for the *tamas* subscale alpha is .94. No test-retest reliability assessment has been conducted. Inter-subscale correlations are in the direction predicted by Vedic theory. That is, statistical analysis confirms that *rajas* is an intermediate mode between *sattva* and *tamas*. Research revealed evidence for construct validity in the form of correlations between verbal aggressiveness and *rajas*, hours of sleep per day and *tamas*, and life satisfaction and *sattva*. These correlations were substantially stronger than correlations of any mode with the discriminant validity variables of gender, height, and number of siblings. With regard to factor analysis, all items correlate positively and significantly with their intended subscale, though a few items have a higher correlation with another subscale, indicating that the subscales are not perfectly orthogonal.

Initial research on this instrument provides encouraging evidence for the existence of the *gunas*. Potential for its use includes mental health counseling and vocational guidance. In the field of mental health, a counselor could assess client progress with reference to changes in predominance of modes of nature. For instance, a person with anxiety disorder would be predicted to have a high *rajas* score. After intervention, *rajas* would be expected to decrease, and *sattva* would be predicted to increase. With regard to vocational guidance, the Vedas match occupational tendency with modal predominance. With this theoretical guide, vocational counselors could administer the VPI as an assessment tool. Much work remains to be done in establishing norms for the VPI for various populations, and in evaluating the practical capacity of the instrument for differentiation amongst various groups.

Spiritual Intervention Articles: Methodological Critique

Empirical Quantitative Studies

Appendix A presents a framework for a systematic synthesis of the research literature on spiritual interventions. For the quantitative studies, seven categories are included in this schema: purpose, theory, design, measurement, analysis, results and generalizability.

The purpose section is meant to clearly and succinctly present the aims of the researchers, as well as to state the tested hypotheses. In the theory section, the theoretical orientation underpinning the research is explained. Empirical research tends to assume a functionalist orientation to social science. This paradigm, typified by behaviorist theories, tends to focus on objectively verifiable results, often at the expense, sometimes deliberately, of theoretical formulations. As described previously, and as will be more substantially demonstrated later in this section, spirituality can lend itself to empirical verification and the scientific method, though such efforts are in their infancy. In this section on spiritual interventions the author considers it imperative to enunciate and examine the purpose and theory behind the research, as these components form the bridge and impetus for translating spiritual conceptualizations to the realm of empirical science.

In the design section, the intervention, sampling methods and type of design are described and critiqued. The measurement section includes description and critique of measurement instruments, focusing on psychometric characteristics. In the analysis section, statistical procedures used in the research are critiqued, and the results section presents the findings. Generalizability is the final section, and describes the applicability of the findings, based on the methodology of the sampling and design. Thyer (1991) delineates the importance of critiquing design, measurement, analysis, results, and generalizability for outcome studies.

Among these quantitative studies, only the article of Kutz, Leserman, Dorrington, Morrison, Borsendo, and Benson (1985) is more than 10 years old. This research is included due to its unique combination of clinical sample, quantitative methodology, and an interventive technique derived from the Buddhist tradition.

Empirical Qualitative Articles

For these research pieces, the purpose, theory, and design sections serve the same function as for the empirical quantitative studies. For the qualitative articles, the analysis and results sections are combined, as these reports did not contain numerical analysis, and analyses and results were presented in text form in the same paragraphs. Also, the generalizability section for the qualitative articles makes special note of the replicability of the study, as replicability is a key feature in assessing the reliability of qualitative research endeavors. The Sweet and Johnson (1990) article contains a measurement section, as the researchers utilized a tool for coding dyadic interpersonal behavior, though quantitative data is not provided. Otherwise, the articles in this section do not use psychometric instruments, and therefore they do not contain a measurement section. The Kaye (1985) article is included, although it is more than 10 years old, because of its innovative use of yoga techniques with an elderly population, as well as the interesting style in which the report is presented.

Literature Reviews

Among the spiritual intervention articles that are analyzed in Appendix A, there are two literature reviews (Delmonte, 1983; Delmonte & Kenny, 1985) (see Figure 1). The format for the analysis of the two literature reviews is the same as the basic format for the qualitative studies, including sections for purpose, theory, design, analysis/results, and generalizability. These literature reviews provide an overview of the research prior to 1985 on silent and mantra meditation techniques, with special attention given to the therapeutic effects of these interventions. These reviews describe results in a qualitative fashion, preferring narration to numerical analysis. Consequently, there is no measurement section for these articles, and the analysis and results sections are combined.

Methodological Considerations

Purpose

This research attempted to isolate the effects of an intervention that was postulated to be spiritual in nature and origin. This collection of studies dealing with spiritual interventions contains eight pieces focusing on Eastern-style meditation techniques, plus two literature reviews covering these meditative interventions. There is one study examining the effect of prayer to the Judeo-Christian God, two articles investigating 12-step interventions, one general study on non-medical interventions, and one qualitative study delineating a spiritual approach to social work practice. Regarding dependent variables, common targets in the meditation studies included stress, anxiety and empathy, and some studies also evaluated effects on self-actualization, happiness, compassion, self-esteem, friendliness, and trauma resolution. Coronary disease was the dependent variable in the prayer study, while substance abuse, with adolescents and adults, constituted the main dependent measure in the 12-step studies.

Theory

These articles contain a wide range of theoretical expositions. Some, such as Kaye (1985), do not address theoretical concerns, while others (e.g., Sweet & Johnson, 1990; Delmonte & Kenny, 1985) relate in some depth the theory behind the spiritual intervention. These more extensive attempts are sometimes integrated, relevant and informative, and occasionally disjointed (e.g., Janowiak, & Hackman, 1994).

Though ideas regarding effects are abundant (e.g., the effect of meditation on anxiety), there is a paucity of conceptualization related to mechanism. That is, rarely do authors attempt to explain how an intervention produces an effect. Interestingly, Byrd's (1988) article, though the theoretical section is surprisingly short, succinctly describes a mechanism for the improvement of coronary conditions. The process is prayer to the Judeo-Christian God, and this is effected by this personal God, who is omnipresent and omnipotent, taking personal action. When the Absolute is postulated to be personal, the implication is that this entity is sentient, meaning that the Absolute possesses desires, likes and dislikes. With such a personal philosophy, causal explanations are simplified. Such an explanation is of little empirical value, though it stands as a provocation for other theorists to explain the results of this experiment on intercessory prayer.

In the theoretical passages of the meditation and mantra articles, the question of how these interventions produce effects was not addressed. Of course, a research article is not the place for elaborate philosophical exposition. Still, with a basic understanding of the epistemology and ontology underpinning a practice, researchers will be enabled to formulate designs to isolate effects, and practitioners will increasingly be prepared to effectively apply techniques according to time and circumstance.

For example, mantra science, according to the Vedas, is based on sound vibration that is completely in the mode of material nature called *sattva*. Literally, a mantra is a sound vibration that can extricate the mind from the modes of material nature. Consciousness, from the Vedic viewpoint, is affected by all sounds that we encounter. If we associate with sounds in *rajas guna*, we develop *rajasic* qualities, and sound in *tamas* will cause us to cultivate *tamasic* attributes, such as depression and indolence. Attentive concentration on a mantra that is in the mode of *sattva* will, according to Vedic philosophy, help us to attain *sattvic* qualities, such as satisfaction, peacefulness, and compassion. A mantra can be tested by measuring effects, such as depression and life satisfaction, with respect to *guna* theory. Without an understanding of these *gunas*, it will be very difficult to effectively implement mantra therapy. In summary, these articles (e.g., Janowiak & Hackman, 1994; Kutz et. al., 1985; Miller, Fletcher, & Kabat-Zinn, 1995; Pearl & Carlozzi; Smith, Compton, & West, 1995; Kaye, 1985; and Sweet & Johnson, 1990) provide evidence indicating positive effects of mantras and meditation. Due to lack of understanding of the processes responsible for these effects, however, intervention techniques and research methodology, especially with regard to outcome variables, are often less than maximally efficient. For instance, with insight into *guna* theory, meditation techniques can be extensively tested with regard to the many qualities associated with each *guna* as described in the Vedas.

Design

Eleven of the studies are primarily quantitative, and 4 are mainly qualitative. Convenience sampling is the most common sampling strategy in spiritual intervention research, with the quantitative studies preferring random assignment to matching. Power analysis was not performed to determine sample size. College students were the most common subjects. Meditation and mantra research utilized group and qualitative designs, and a cross sectional survey design was used in 12-step research as well as in the general non-medical intervention investigation. Most of the group designs suffered from lack of follow-up assessment, and many did not contain adequate description of the interventive method. Duration of intervention ranged from 6 weeks to 2 years, with 8 weeks being the mode for meditation and mantra studies. Many studies lacked a control group as well as a true placebo group to adequately isolate the effects of the experimental intervention. In research on spiritual intervention it is common to mix group sessions, or sessions with a therapist, and private home practice of meditation or mantra chanting. Byrd's (1988) study on prayer involves a rigorous design and large sample size, with all parties blinded to group assignment of subjects.

Concerning outcome variables, they were generally appropriately selected with regards to theory and purpose of the research endeavor. For example, the study of Miller, Fletcher, and Kabat-Zinn (1995), using a clinical sample of persons with anxiety disorder or panic disorder, included measures of frequency and severity of panic attacks at pretest, posttest, and follow-up. Many studies could have included additional dependent measures, and presumably this was not done due to resource limitations and to minimize complexity of design. For instance, the study of

Janowiak and Hackman (1994), which investigated the influence of meditation on stress and personality, could have included relationship competency as an outcome variable, as personality is intimately connected with relationships.

With regard to Keefe's (1996) theoretical conceptualization of the link between social work and meditative interventions, the outcome variables of these studies are productive and useful. According to Keefe, social work and meditation intersect at the common human experience of stress. He theorizes that meditation has immense potential as a clinical adjunct technique in reduction of stress and anxiety. Moreover, he postulates that these techniques can facilitate other social work skills, and can be an antecedent to sober and productive action. Specifically, Keefe asserts that meditation can be an important component in the development of empathic skill, as well as in the development of the overall personality of therapists. He states that these endeavors "have generated interest among clinical social workers and social work educators. (p. 440)" Further, he cites the diverse origins of meditation as being compatible with social work's emphasis on oneness containing variety. To summarize this theory of social work intervention and meditative techniques, Keefe contends that meditation has the capacity to be relevant for the profession as a whole, and concludes that "The reciprocal influences between meditation and social work should be exciting" (p. 440). With this theoretical orientation in mind, the focus of the outcome studies included in this paper on dependent variables such as stress, anxiety, and development of empathy is commensurate with social work treatment.

The most glaring lacuna in outcome variables is spirituality. This may be due to the fact that measurement of spirituality is not a very developed field. Still, future studies of spiritual interventions can utilize the scales described in the measurement section, and researchers interested in this area can develop increasingly refined instruments, especially with regard to operationally defined indicators of spirituality.

Though a few studies discuss experience and training of intervention providers, many articles neglect this important point, which isn't to say that the practitioners were necessarily unskilled in the particular technique. Considering that empirical application of spiritual science is a new field, this issue is particularly poignant. In academe, spirituality is generally considered to be unscientific, primarily based on belief and faith. Therefore, those attempting to advance this field must be especially assiduous in assuring high standards in conducting scientific experiments on spiritual topics. As mentioned in the Introduction, Levin, Larson, and Puchalski (1997), referring to the field of medicine, concluded that research on spiritual and religious factors has been subject to greater scrutiny than most research. Thus, practitioners in this area must be well-trained in the interventions they utilize, just as a practitioner using behavioral, cognitive or psychodynamic techniques is expected to be expert in their theory and implementation. Otherwise, spiritual interventions will be considered to be a whimsical practice.

Measurement

Research on spiritual interventions utilizes self- and therapist-rated standardized tests as well as compliance logs, daily self-report inventories, and open- and closed-ended questionnaires developed by the researcher. Many articles failed to report psychometric data, though references were provided to locate this information. The 12-step studies did not use standardized instruments, instead relying on tools developed by the authors. In the study on adolescents and substance abuse, parents and subjects were interviewed for validity. A few meditation studies also sought validity by administering surveys to therapists and subjects. Interestingly, all of the research on Eastern-style interventions used instruments based in Western theory. Of course, this is largely due to lack of development of measuring devices that are rooted in Buddhist or Vedic conceptualizations. Moreover, as described above, direct measurement of spirituality is lacking in these studies, though this is approximated with measurement of constructs such as self-actualization and capacity for empathy.

Analysis

Quantitative studies consistently and appropriately utilize t tests and analysis of variance, reporting p levels. The most common alpha level, when it was set prior to analysis, was .05. Power analysis was conspicuously lacking in these analyses, both before and after design implementation. Prior to experimentation, such analysis could have helped to determine efficient sample size, and following intervention power analysis would have added to the understanding of effect magnitude of various factors, especially the element of spiritual intervention. Additionally, researchers regularly neglected to analyze gender differences. This may be significant, considering that there tends to be a difference between genders regarding spiritual and religious participation and issues. The two literature reviews included in this paper could have benefited by some form of numerical analysis, to assist understanding of effect sizes across research endeavors. Additionally, many of the reports would have been enhanced by multivariate analysis. This would assist in identifying interactive effects between predictor variables and isolating effects on outcome variables. For example, in the study of Janowiak and Hackman (1994), a multivariate analysis including age and gender, with respect to the three groups included in the experiment, would have been interesting and informative.

Results

Research has consistently found that meditation and mantra chanting are related to decreased stress and anxiety levels and improved capacity for restful sleep. Compliance with these interventions is positively correlated with psychological health, though there appears to be a ceiling effect. These practices also improve physiological outcomes, such as blood pressure and heart rate. However, due to design limitations and varying outcomes, it is not clear from the research whether these psychological and physiological effects are due to the intervention or some other factor, such as contact with therapist or a placebo effect. Moreover, it is not certain that mantra and meditation techniques are more effective than other methods, such as established relaxation procedures. Response to Eastern-style interventions does not appear to be related to gender. Also, research indicates that benefits of these practices are limited to those who are reasonably well-adjusted. Severely disturbed persons may incur harm from these practices. Further, the literature suggests that meditation can be a useful adjunct to psychotherapy, with the caveat that the therapist should be experienced in the meditative technique and expert in applying a combination of the Eastern and Western approaches to each client.

Regarding mantras, research indicates that any device upon which the mind can concentrate is as effective as mantras which are routinely prescribed by schools of meditation, with regards to stress, anxiety and physiological symptoms. These results should be considered in light of the fact that the research does not adequately differentiate, at least in the reports, between various techniques. Especially with regard to mantras, the mantra itself is almost never included in the article. This is significant, considering that many of the mantras popular in the West are not found in original sources, such as the Vedas. Thus, the possibility that the mantras being investigated are actually placebo interventions must be considered. At least, the mantra should be included in the research report, and the source of that mantra should be provided.

Eastern-style intervention studies that contained follow-up assessment found that benefits maintained over time. Also, a few researchers examined cost effectiveness and concluded that meditation and mantra interventions have potential value in this regard. Other results reported from these interventions include resolution of childhood trauma, decreases in anger, confusion and tension, and an increase in friendliness, sensitivity, and ability to work productively and socialize.

In the 12-step studies, the most significant result, with regard to spirituality, is that prayer and meditation positively correlate with alcohol use for recovering alcoholics. These activities also correlate positively and strongly with a sense of purpose in life.

In the study with cystic fibrosis patients, it was clear that prayer was used as a treatment method by many persons, and that most (92%) who used prayer believed it to be effective. Authors of that study conclude that physicians should at least be understanding of alternative, and especially religiously-based, treatment methods (Stern, Canda, & Doershuk, 1992). Byrd (1988) conducted a more rigorous study on the effects of prayer, and found that prayer to the Judeo-Christian God improves the health of coronary patients.

Generalizability

Since most of the Eastern-style intervention studies do not use random sampling, external validity of the designs are weak. However, most of the quantitative research incorporates random assignment, and therefore the results can be applied to the sample. Examining the studies together, a general impression of results and applicability can be gleaned. For example, though the results of Miller, Fletcher, and Kabat-Zinn (1995) can only be generalized to a clinical population of persons diagnosed with anxiety or panic disorder, combined with studies such as Delmonte and Kenny (1985) and Kutz, Dorrington, Morrison, Borysendo, and Benson (1985), we can understand that meditative and mantra techniques have good potential for effectiveness as an adjunct to psychotherapy, provided the client's disturbance is not too severe and the therapist is sufficiently competent and experienced with the intervention practices. In the qualitative studies (Sweet & Johnson, 1990; Kaye, 1985; Urbanowski & Miller, 1996; Nakhaima & Dicks, 1995), procedures are adequately described for replicability, and practitioners in the particular fields can judiciously apply the techniques. For instance, social workers in all fields can probably find some aspects of the model presented by Nakhaima and Dicks applicable in their work, since a large percentage of social work service recipients value spirituality and religiosity. Therapists who have experience with meditation and who work with persons who have suffered childhood trauma can probably benefit from the report of Urbanowski and Miller. Similarly, professionals working with a geriatric population should consider the results obtained by Kaye in relieving depression in elderly persons.

Byrd's (1988) study contains a large sample and rigorous design, providing an impressive combination of internal and external validity. Considering the import of the results, replications should be performed to confirm or negate the conclusions.

The 12-step studies are limited by somewhat homogeneous samples. Still, results can be cautiously generalized in the adult study (Carroll, 1991) to rural, White, Christian alcoholics.

Equivalent effects of mock mantras and experimental mantras, as reviewed by Delmonte (1983), can be generalized, though only to the mantras actually examined in the studies included in the literature review.

Conclusions

Byrd's (1988) study on the effects of prayer to the Judeo-Christian God provides the most startling results in the spiritual intervention literature. In this investigation, where all parties were blinded to the group identity of patients, prayer was found to have a significantly beneficial effect on many factors involved in the course of coronary disease. Perhaps more astounding than the results is the fact that this study has not been replicated. To illustrate, if a study, possessing the rigor, sophistication and sample size of this one, revealed that a new drug produced the same results as prayer apparently generated in this research endeavor, it is likely that millions would be spent to confirm the findings and then to publicize the results, and the treatment would then be advertised and made available on the market. That this process did not succeed Byrd's findings indicates that there may be bias at work. That is, there may be factors other than maximizing treatment outcomes that drive decisions concerning research projects. In any case, considering the outcomes of this study, replication studies with various samples should be conducted.

Several research endeavors have examined Eastern-style interventions, including Buddhist and Vedic techniques for silent meditation, mantra chanting, social interaction and relaxation. There is sufficient evidence that these practices have potential for enhancing several aspects of mental and physical health. Still, there is a gap in the research concerning differential effects of these processes. For example, analyses that control for variables such as gender and socio-economic class would be a valuable addition to the literature, and would assist practitioners in applying these interventions. Also, there is a need for more studies that compare Eastern-style interventions with each other, and with conventional counseling treatments, as well as with placebo groups.

Concerning mantra interventions, only in Kaye's (1985) article was the mantra itself printed (OM). This may be due to the fact that mantra meditation has become popularized in the West by a group that offers "secret mantras", though the author of this specialization paper is not aware of any justification, based on Vedic authority, for those mantras to be kept confidential. Delmonte's (1983) literature review indicates that the purported mantra-person fit suggested by many teachers and practitioners of mantra meditation is not validated.

Summary and Integration

According to the Vedas, we are currently in the Kali-yuga, an age that will continue for hundreds of years. In this particular age, the most recommended spiritual intervention for countering mental disturbances such as depression and anxiety is chanting of the *maha mantra*. Fortunately, this mantra is not secret, as the Vedas widely broadcast the *maha mantra*. The Kali-santarana Upanisada states (Prabhupada, 1975):

> *hare krsna hare krsna*
> *krsna krsna hare hare*
> *hare rama hare rama*
> *rama rama hare hare*
> *iti sodasakam namnam*
> *kali-kalmasa-nasanam*
> *nata parataropayah*
> *sarva-vedesu drsyate*

"Hare Krsna, Hare Krsna, Krsna Krsna, Hare Hare/ Hare Rama, Hare Rama, Rama Rama, Hare Hare. These sixteen names composed of thirty-two syllables comprise the only mantra that can completely eradicate the pernicious influences that afflict the mind in this Kali-yuga" (p. 274).

Similarly, the Brhad-naradiya Purana (Prabhupada, 1976) declares:

> *harer nama harer nama*
> *harer namaiva kevalam*
> *kalau nasty eva nasty eva*
> *nasty eva gatir anyatha*

"In the Kali-yuga, the mantra containing the name of *hari* is the most effective process to enhance one's spirituality" (p. 1463).

In this verse, the name of *hari*, and the word "only", are repeated three times for emphasis.Many similar references can be found in Vedic literatures, such as the *Srimad-Bhagavatam* (Prabhupada, 1976), *Bhakti-rasamrta-sindhu* (1971), and *Sri-Caitanya-Caritamrta* (Prabhupada, 1975).

Therefore, research on the *maha mantra* needs to be done. The *maha mantra* is customarily chanted congregationally (*kirtana*) or privately (*japa*). Both of these methods should be investigated, though a *japa* study may be more conducive for control of variables. Many studies lacked follow-up testing, which the *japa* study described in this dissertation included. Another helpful device, included in a few of the above investigations, is a compliance log, to assess the effects of chanting frequency.

As mentioned above, the studies on Eastern-style interventions did not utilize scales derived from Vedic knowledge. The study on the *maha mantra* described in this dissertation, in addition to using standardized Western-style measures of factors such as stress and depression, also incorporated a Vedic-based measure that assesses *guna* propensities. This study utilized a control group and a placebo treatment group that chanted a pseudo-mantra. There are many potentially effective meditative practices that have not been applied in social work (Canda, 1988). *Japa* chanting of the *maha mantra* may be one of these techniques.

Pilot Research

The author conducted a single-system design pilot study on the *maha mantra*. In this study, five subjects chanted the *maha mantra* for about 25 minutes per day for four weeks. These subjects were measured on well-being, *sattva*, *rajas*, *tamas*, spirituality, depression, stress, verbal aggressiveness, and life satisfaction. Measuring instruments for all of these variables are found in Appendix D. The hypotheses of this study were that chanting the Hare Krsna *maha mantra*, which was the independent variable, would reduce the dependent variables of stress, depression, verbal aggressiveness, *tamas guna*, and *rajas guna*, and would increase the dependent variables of *sattva guna*, spirituality, satisfaction with life, and a sense of well-being.

Although the design of this pilot study had many limitations related to external and internal validity, such as lack of random sampling, small sample size, and lack of a control group, the results were encouraging and suggested that further research on the *maha mantra* would be valuable. More specifically, examining baseline phase to intervention phase scores for each subject, 80% of the dependent measures responded according to the research hypothesis. A detailed analysis of this pilot study is provided in Appendix B. Overall, the results warranted that a more rigorous examination of the *maha mantra* be conducted.

The next chapter of this dissertation, entitled methodology of the *japa* experiment, will describe in detail the methodology of a group experimental study on the effects of the *maha mantra* chanted privately with *japa* beads. This study incorporated many of the features described above, such as a compliance log, follow-up testing, a placebo treatment group, and use of a Vedic-based scale to measure the three *gunas*.

CHAPTER 3

METHODOLOGY OF THE JAPA EXPERIMENT

Introduction

Below are the hypotheses for this experiment. Since these hypotheses were statistically evaluated, they should, strictly speaking, be stated in terms of null hypotheses, because statistical techniques actually test null hypotheses by analyzing the strength of the sample evidence against the null hypotheses. That is, statistical methods assess whether a null hypothesis can be shown to be inconsistent with the observed data, and the null hypothesis is rejected or not rejected based on statistical tests. The practical purpose of this research, however, is to gauge the amount of support that the data provide for directional research hypotheses. Therefore, the hypotheses are stated in such terms. For instance, the first hypothesis of this study is that, at the .05 level the *maha mantra* group will show significantly decreased stress from pretest to posttest compared with the alternate mantra and control groups. If this hypothesis were stated in terms of a null hypothesis, it would state that there will be no difference between the change in stress scores from pretest to posttest between the *maha mantra* group and the other groups. Agresti and Finlay (1986) confirm that it is acceptable to state research hypotheses in terms of alternate hypotheses, instead of in terms of null hypotheses, when performing statistical tests.

The primary hypotheses of this study were that, at alpha = .05:

1) The intervention group will show significantly decreased stress from pretest to posttest compared with both the alternate mantra and control groups.

2) The intervention group will show significantly decreased depression from pretest to

posttest compared with both the alternate mantra and control groups.

3) The intervention group will show significantly increased *sattva* from pretest to posttest compared with both the alternate mantra and control groups.

4) The intervention group will show significantly decreased rajas from pretest to posttest compared with both the alternate mantra and control groups.

5) The intervention group will show significantly decreased tamas from pretest to posttest compared with both the alternate mantra and control groups.
Secondary hypotheses of this study were that, at alpha = .05:

6) The intervention group will show significantly decreased stress from pretest to follow-up compared with the alternate mantra and control groups, though some decrement in the amount of decrease for the *maha mantra* group, compared with the other two groups, is expected in pretest-follow-up scores compared with pretest-posttest scores.

7) The intervention group will show significantly decreased depression from pretest to follow-up compared with the alternate mantra and control groups, though some decrement in the amount of decrease for the *maha mantra* group, compared with the other two groups, is expected in pretest-follow-up scores compared with pretest-posttest scores.

8) The intervention group will show significantly increased *sattva* from pretest to follow-up compared with the alternate mantra and control groups, though some decrement in the amount of increase for the *maha mantra* group, compared with the other two groups, is expected in pretest-follow-up scores compared with pretest-posttest scores.

9) The intervention group will show significantly decreased rajas from pretest to follow-up compared with the alternate mantra and control groups, though some decrement in the amount of decrease for the *maha mantra* group, compared with the other two groups, is expected in pretest-follow-up scores compared with pretest-posttest scores.

10) The intervention group will show significantly decreased tamas from pretest to follow-up compared with the alternate mantra and control groups, though some decrement in the amount of decrease for the *maha mantra* group, compared with the other two groups, is expected in pretest-follow-up scores compared with

pretest-posttest scores.

11) Gender will have no effect on stress, depression, *sattva*, *rajas*, or *tamas*, from pretest to posttest or from pretest to follow-up.

12) Age will have no effect on stress, depression, *sattva*, *rajas*, or *tamas*, from pretest to posttest or from pretest to follow-up..

13) Chanting frequency for the *maha mantra* group will be positively correlated with increase in *sattva*, and decrease in stress, depression, rajas and tamas, from pretest to posttest, and from posttest to follow-up.

The main hypotheses of this experiment were that chanting the Hare Krsna *maha mantra* will increase the effects of *sattva*, and will decrease stress, depression, and the effects of *rajas* and *tamas*. Secondary hypotheses were that gender and age will not effect the variables mentioned above. More specifically, it was hypothesized that, when controlled for the effects of gender and age, chanting Hare Krsna will continue to effect the five dependent variables in the manner described above. A related research hypothesis was that the frequency with which one chants the Hare Krsna *maha mantra* will be positively associated with the strength of the effects on the dependent variables.

Group status was the primary independent variable being tested. Other independent variables for which effects were statistically calculated were gender, compliance with required chanting frequency, and age. Gender and age were control variables. Dependent variables for this experiment included stress, depression, *sattva*, *rajas*, and *tamas*.

Chanting was a categorical variable, with three categories corresponding to the three groups- *maha mantra*, alternate mantra, and control. These groups will be described in greater detail in the procedures section. Gender was a categorical variable, and chanting frequency and age were treated as interval variables, with age measured as an integer and chanting frequency calculated as a fraction of complete compliance with the instructions of the experiment. Measurement of age and chanting frequency are described in more detail in the measurement section. Instruments for measurement of the dependent variables are mentioned later in this introduction, and described more extensively in the measurement section of the chapter.

There are three *gunas* described in the Vedas- *sattva, rajas*, and *tamas*. Descriptions of each *guna* were compiled from the *Bhagavad-gita As It Is*, Chapters 14, 17 and 18 (Prabhupada, 1972). *Sattva guna* is characterized by qualities such as cleanliness, truthfulness, gravity, dutifulness, detachment, discipline, mental equilibrium, respect for superiors, sharp intelligence, sense control, and staunch determination. Attributes of *rajas guna* include intense activity, desire for sense gratification, little interest in spiritual elevation, dissatisfaction with one's position, envy of others, and a materialistic mentality. Qualities associated with *tamas guna* include mental imbalance, anger, arrogance, depression, laziness, procrastination, and a feeling of helplessness. The *gunas* were measured with the Vedic Personality Inventory (Wolf, 1998) (see Table 1).

Personal stress was measured with the Index of Clinical Stress (ICS) (Abell, 1991) (see Table 1), which assesses a person's subjective response to external demands, as opposed to measuring one's life events as an indicator of stress level. Depression was measured with the Generalized Contentment Scale (GCS) (Hudson, & Proctor, 1977) (see Table 1). This is a short-form measure of nonpsychotic depression specifically developed for repeated administrations (Hudson, & Proctor, 1977). Table 1 shows the dependent variables and the instruments proposed to measure them.

Table 1

Dependent Variables and Their Measuring Instruments

Dependent Variable	Instrument
Sattva	Vedic Personality Inventory
Rajas	Vedic Personality Inventory
Tamas	Vedic Personality Inventory
Personal Stress	Index of Clinical Stress
Depression	Generalized Contentment Scale

In summary it was predicted that the chanting treatment group, compared with the alternate mantra and control groups, will increase in *sattva*, and will decrease in stress, depression, *rajas* and *tamas*. Chanting frequency was expected to be positively associated with the strength of effects of chanting Hare Krsna. To specify, increased chanting of the Hare Krsna *maha mantra* was predicted to increase *sattva*, and to decrease stress, depression, *rajas* and *tamas*. Further, as support for the main hypotheses, it was hypothesized that gender and age will have no effect on the dependent variables.

Design

This study incorporated an experimental design, utilizing an experimental, control and placebo group. Each group was pre- and post-tested with a package of surveys, including a scale on depression, personal stress, *sattva*, *rajas*, and *tamas*. Random assignment was used to place subjects in groups. There was also follow-up testing for all groups.

Two research assistants were employed for this study. Before contacting any subjects, each research assistant was trained in the basic principles and techniques of scientific experimentation, and specifically in the methods of this study. Specifically, the research assistants received instruction in confidentiality, preserving the integrity of data, and maintaining neutrality, as well as in the paperwork and timeframe for this study, and the method for teaching subjects how to chant.

For pretest, posttest and follow-up there was a 5-day window for all members of all groups to be tested. Ideally, to minimize history effects, all subjects should have been tested at precisely the same time. This was not practically achievable, however, and therefore a 5-day period of testing was used. This will be further explained in the procedures section of this chapter. In addition to the 5-day window for evaluation of all participants, each participant had an individual 3-day window for completion of each testing phase. For instance, if a subject was pretested on November 17, then posttest should occur, based on a scheduled 28-day intervention, on December 15. Due to scheduling difficulties, it was not always possible to schedule posttest after exactly 28 days. Therefore, the participant was allowed to be tested within the 3-day window December 14-16. A similar 3-day window was used for follow-up scheduling. Though this windowing method increased the chance that history will adversely affect internal validity, it was used to minimize diffusion effects. That is, it was desirable for study participants to not know the identity of other participants, for this might lead to discussion of intervention effects during the study. Therefore, the design did not arrange for all subjects to congregate together during any phase of the study.

After pretesting, members of the control group were informed that they were the control group, and they were requested to return in 28 days for the posttest. A member of the research team phoned control group members one or two days prior to posttest, to remind them of the appointment. Members of the treatment group were taught the intervention after pretest, and members of the placebo group were taught the placebo intervention. These two groups were instructed how to chant, and directed to do so for the next 28 days. Within three days after pretest for a member of a chanting group, a member of the research team phoned the chanter to check if there were any difficulties with following the procedures.Seven or eight days after a subject initially learned the chanting, the research team member met in-person with the subject to ensure that he/she was properly following the procedures. After this meeting, a member of the research team phoned the chanters approximately every seven days till the end of the chanting phase of the study, to ensure that procedures were properly followed. For these mid-intervention meetings and phone calls there was also a 5-day window, as well as a 3-day window for checking each individual participant, as described above with regards to posttest and follow-up. Each member of the study was phoned one or two days before follow-up, to remind them of the appointment.

Intervention

The subject was given a string of 109 beads (*japa* beads), with one bead markedly larger than the others. The research team member had his/her own set of *japa* beads, and demonstrated the chanting method for the subject. With the thumb and middle finger of the right hand, the chanter holds the bead on either side of the large bead. Then the subject chanted the mantra. After the mantra is completed, the subject moves one bead through the fingers so that s/he is holding the second bead from the large bead. Again the chanter should chant the *maha mantra*. In this way, the participant should chant one mantra for each bead, until 108 mantras have been chanted. This constitutes one "round" of *japa* meditation. *Japa* can be performed in any circumstance. For instance, one may be sitting or walking. The essential factor is that one is fully attentive to the chanting. The treatment group was taught to chant the *maha mantra- hare krsna hare krsna krsna krsna hare hare/ hare rama hare rama rama rama hare hare*, and the alternate mantra group was taught to chant s*arva dasa sarva dasa dasa dasa sarva sarva/ sarva jana sarva jana jana jana sarva sarva*. The *sarva dasa* pseudo-mantra is a meaningless combination of Sanskrit syllables made up by the author. The alternate mantra was composed of the same syllabic pattern as the *maha mantra*. This controlled for the effects of syllabic pattern, and helped to isolate the effects of the mantras themselves.

Members of both groups were instructed that this was an experiment on the efficacy of chanting the particular combination of words that they learned to chant. After the first day, subjects chanted on their own, though the research team member informed subjects that they could contact him/her if there were questions or concerns. Also, as described above, a research team member checked on the chanters approximately every seven days for the course of the intervention period. After 28 days of chanting, all three groups were posttested, and 28 days after posttest, all three groups were follow-up tested. Researchers kept a log of client contacts.

Internal Validity of Design

Internal validity of a design refers to the design's ability to allow inference about causality regarding the relationship between measured dependent and independent variables. Threats to internal validity of a design include history, maturation, testing, instrumentation, statistical regression, selection, mortality, diffusion, compensatory effects, resentful demoralization of subjects, and various interactive threats, such as the interaction between selection and maturation, selection and history, and selection and instrumentation (Cook and Campbell, 1979).

Random assignment, as used in the experiment described in this dissertation, reduces threats to internal validity. Of course, randomization is probabilistic, and does not ensure equivalence of groups.

The threat of diffusion was not eliminated with random assignment, and could be a factor in this study. However, each subject was dealt with privately, not in a group, except for a few instances when roommates or friends knew of each other's involvement in the experiment. Still, most of the dozens of participants resided in the same mid-sized town, and therefore it is possible that subjects discovered the identity of each other, and they may have discussed their experiences of the intervention. Thus diffusion of treatments may be an issue. Research team members cautioned participants about discussing the study with other subjects, in case the identity of other subjects become known to them. Another threat to internal validity that may be active in this study is resentful demoralization of subjects placed in a group perceived to be less desirable. For instance, members of the control group may have become discouraged because they didn't participate in the intervention. Posttest scores may reflect this discouragement, and this compromises the internal validity of the design. Further, while random assignment may effectively deal with the selection-mortality threat, mortality in this study did differ by group. The placebo mantra group experienced greater attrition than the *maha mantra* group, and this may be considered a threat to validity. However, such a mortality effect can also be viewed as a predicted consequence of the group design, especially when randomization is present (Cook & Campbell, 1979).

Cook and Campbell (1979) differentiate between internal validity and construct validity, with threats to construct validity conceived as effects that can lead to invalid conclusions about the construct labels that should be attached to manipulations and measures. Construct validity threats include the effects of the experimenter as an independent variable, and the Hawthorne effect. Random assignment with a placebo intervention group should control for a Hawthorne

64

effect, though differential effects of contact between research team members and the members of various groups may be a threat to internal validity. To reduce this risk, each team member was instructed in the importance of uniformity when they present study instructions and techniques to participants in the study.

Sampling

Participants in the study were self-selected, and then screened by the researcher. The researcher placed advertisements in the college and city newspapers of a major state university in a mid-sized town in the Southeastern United States, requesting volunteers for this experiment. The researcher chose the first 93 acceptably screened respondents to the newspaper advertisements. Respondents were screened by phone interview by the researcher for traits such as debilitating mental disorders, availability to participate in the entire duration of the study, willingness to devote approximately half an hour a day for involvement in the study for four weeks, and prior experience with chanting, biofeedback, meditation, and other yoga techniques. Information on prior experience of subjects with yoga, biofeedback, meditation, and chanting was used to create two blocks, "past experience" and "no past experience", for the random assignment to groups. With this method, the factor of prior experience was controlled. At the pretest meeting each subject signed a consent form for participating in research.

On the morning following the final day of newspaper advertisements, names of participants were assigned numbers, and participants were assigned into groups with a random number table. Specifically, the participant whose number corresponded with the first number chosen from the random number table was placed in the *maha mantra* group, the participant whose number corresponded with the second number chosen was placed in the control group, the participant whose number corresponded with the third number chosen was placed in the placebo group, the participant whose name corresponded with the fourth number chosen was placed in the *maha mantra* group, and so on. As described above, two blocks of participants, those having experience with mantras, meditation, yoga, or biofeedback, and those without experience, were randomly assigned to groups.

All participants were at least 18 years of age and signed a form of voluntary consent before participating. Thirty-three subjects per group began the study. To facilitate recruitment a $40 financial incentive was offered to participants who completed the study. Though such monetary encouragement may have affected the type and motivation of subjects, the strategy of random assignment was used to equally distribute such effects in all three groups.

External Validity of Design

According to Vedic theory, the effects of chanting *hare krsna* on the chosen dependent variables should apply to all people. Since the sampling method of this experiment was not random, results of the study cannot be inferred to apply to any population or sampling frame. Thus, the lack of random sampling greatly diminishes the generalizability, or external validity, of this study.

Bracht and Glass (1968) distinguish between population and ecological validity, both of which are forms of external validity. Ecological validity refers to the conditions, including settings and experimenters, under which the same results of an experiment can be expected, and population validity refers to the persons to whom the results can be applied. Ecological validity assumes that the experimental effect is independent of the environment. With the sampling strategy of this experiment, it is not possible to assume that the effects will apply in different environments. For example, this study was conducted in a Southeastern university town, and therefore the results may not apply to a setting such as a Northeastern industrial city, or a rural area of a third world country.

For population validity, the experimenter must make two inferential leaps-from the sample to the experimentally accessible population, and from the accessible population to the target population. Since the sample was self-selected, rather than randomly selected, even the leap to the population of the county where the study occurred is not possible.

Other factors affecting external validity in this study include novelty effects, experimenter effects, and pretest sensitization. Novelty effects refer to the effects caused by the newness of an intervention, which will fade after some time. These effects reduce the generalizability of the findings, as do effects caused by interaction between the experimenter and subjects. Pretest sensitization refers to the possibility that response to the treatment may be affected by the pretest, and therefore results are not generalizable to persons who did not take the pretest.

Though the external validity of this design is not strong, the procedures of the experiment are specified, and replication of the study is possible. With replication in various settings and with diverse populations, generalizability of the results of this study can be confirmed or disconfirmed.

Measurement

The instruments that were used in this study were the Vedic Personality Inventory (VPI) (Wolf, 1998), the Generalized Contentment Scale (GCS) (Hudson, & Proctor, 1977), and the Index of Clinical Stress (ICS) (Abell, 1991). A description of the VPI was given in the measurement of spirituality section of the previous chapter, and a summary of that description is provided below. All of the instruments used in this study are found in Appendix D.

The Vedic Personality Inventory

The VPI is an instrument that measures the three gunas- sattva, rajas, and *tamas*. The instrument contains 56 items, each of them with seven Likert-type response choices. Internal consistency alpha for the three subscales ranges from .93 to .94. Evidence for construct validity for the instrument has been obtained with relation to measures on verbal aggressiveness, hours of sleep per day, and life satisfaction. Regarding factor analysis, all items correlate positively and significantly with their intended subscale.

The Generalized Contentment Scale (GCS)

The GCS (Hudson & Proctor, 1977) measures the magnitude of nonpsychotic depression, and consists of 25 items. It is a summated category partition scale that is scored on a range from 0 to 100. Positively and negatively worded items are used to counter response bias. Psychometric testing of the GCS was done on a sample of 124 persons of diverse occupations, and income and education levels. Test-retest and split-half reliability scores for the GCS ranged from .887 to .963, with a mean of .930. Also, the instrument showed good ability to differentiate between groups who described themselves as depressed and not depressed. Construct validity for the GCS has also been established.

According to Hudson (1982), the GCS not only possesses strong reliability and validity, it is also suited for repeated measures with the same client. Specifically, the GCS is short, easy to complete and score, and does not suffer from response decay when used repeatedly over time. For these reasons, the GCS has been chosen as a measure for this pretest, posttest experimental design. Hudson (1982) provides scoring procedures for the instrument, including procedures to use when the subject does not complete all items. These procedures were used for scoring the GCS in this pilot study.

The Index of Clinical Stress (ICS)

This measure was designed to assess the subjective aspect of stress in a generalized, unidimensional form (Abell, 1991). The 25 items of the instrument were designed to reflect the range of perceptions involved with subjective stress. This approach to measuring stress is differentiated from stress measurement as a result of external life situation and life events. An internal approach to assessment of stress level is appropriate for *japa* intervention, since chanting is hypothesized to positively alter one's consciousness, or internal state.

Each ICS item has a five-point response range, with some items negatively worded to avoid response bias. Abell (1991) provides scoring procedures for the scale, including procedures to use when not all items are completed.

Psychometrics of the instrument were assessed using a sample of 265 persons, whose mean age was 33 years. Cronbach's alpha for the sample was .963. The ICS has also shown strong factorial validity, convergent construct validity, and discriminant construct validity. Based on these results, Abell (1991) suggests that the ICS can be used with confidence by social work practitioners and researchers when single or repeated measures of subjective stress are required.

Compliance Log

Subjects in the chanting groups were required to chant three rounds of *japa* per day. At pretest they were given a compliance log, in which they recorded the number of rounds they chanted each day for the duration of the intervention. A copy of this Compliance Log is in Appendix D. After the followup period a compliance percentage was calculated. The compliance percentage was calculated as:

$$\frac{\textbf{number of rounds chanted during intervention} \times \textbf{100}}{\text{number of days in intervention period} \times 3}$$

For example, if the subject chanted for 28 days, then 100% compliance would be 28 x 3 rounds = 84 rounds: (84 x 100)/(28 x 3) = 8400/84 = 100%

Other Data

During the initial phone conversation with each subject, information was gathered regarding prior experience with chanting, biofeedback, meditation, and other yoga practices. Also, each member of the research team noted comments after each contact with a subject, paying special attention to factors such as anxiety about receiving payment for study, enthusiasm for the chanting, and discouragement about participation in the study. Experiences with the subjects of the pilot study alerted the researcher to the possible importance of noting reactions of these types.

Procedures

From November 5-14, 1998 (see Table 2), the researcher placed newspaper advertisements in three community and student newspapers in a university town in North Florida. The advertisements read as follows:

Wanted: Participants in a study examining the effects of an Eastern-style intervention on stress and depression. $40 reimbursement. If interested, contact David Wolf at [phone number].

When people responded by telephoning the researcher, he explained to them that this is an experiment testing the efficacy of an Eastern-style intervention on factors such as stress, depression, and spirituality. One-hundred-eight calls in response to the ads were accepted. Of the 108 callers, 93 made it to the stage of being randomly assigned to an experimental group, and the others either didn't respond to return calls, or lost interest after hearing about the study. For the 93 participants, pretest meetings were scheduled from November 16-20, 1998 (see Table 2), at a place where the respondent felt comfortable, such as their home or a public place on campus. Also, during the phone call the researcher asked each subject "Do you have prior experience with chanting mantras, meditation, yoga, or biofeedback?" and noted the answer. Results from this question were used to create two blocks ("past experience" and "no past experience") for the random assignment. On November 15, 1998, the researcher, by use of a random number table, randomly assigned respondents from each block to the three groups- *maha mantra*, alternate mantra, and control.

From November 16-20 the researcher, or one of two research assistants, met with the study participants for a pretest meeting. At the beginning of each meeting the research team member explained the nature and purpose of the research, and the subject read and signed the Consent Form for Participating in Research. After signing this form each participant completed the package of surveys, including the VPI, ICS, and GCS. At the bottom of the VPI the participants filled in demographic items for gender and age. For control group members the research team member scheduled a posttest meeting between December 14-18, 1998 (see Table 2), making all efforts to schedule the posttest exactly 28 days after the pretest. For members of the two chanting groups, the research team member instructed the subjects to chant on *japa* beads, as described in the Design section of this Methodology chapter. At the end of the pretest session the research team member paid each subject $20. Upon receipt of this payment each subject completed a payment receipt (Appendix D). Also, at the end of the pretest session subjects in either of the chanting groups received a compliance log (Appendix D), and the research team member instructed them to record in this log the number of *japa* rounds they chanted each day. Control group members were informed at pretest that at the end of the study they would be introduced to the mantra.

Of the 93 subjects who were randomly assigned to the three groups, 81 completed the pre-test session. Regarding the other 12, they either didn't show up for the pre-test meeting and didn't respond to attempts to schedule another meeting within the 5-day window, or during the pre-test meeting they decided they didn't want to participate.

Each subject was phoned by a research team member one or two days after pretest, to ensure that they understood and were following the procedures of the experiment. A researcher visited each member of the two chanting groups between November 23-27. This visit occurred 6 to 8 days after pretest. The purpose of this visit was to ensure that the participants were chanting properly. During the visit the research team member chanted at least one round with the subject. Also, compliance logs were collected, and new compliance log sheets were distributed to subjects. From November 30-December 4, a research team member phoned each subject to check if there were any difficulties in participating in the study, to check if procedures were being properly followed, and to obtain any notable responses to the study by participants. A similar phone contact was made between December 7-11.

Between the dates of December 14-18 (see Table 2) there was an in-person posttest meeting. During this posttest meeting, subjects completed the packet of measuring instruments after completing their chanting for that day. This posttest day was the final day of chanting for the two chanting groups. Posttest meetings were scheduled within 27-29 days of the pretest. Members of the control group were phoned one or two days before posttest to remind them of the schedule.

Of the 81 participants who completed the pretest session, 64 remained after the posttest session. Of these 64, 20 were in the control group, 20 were in the alternate mantra group, and 24 were in the *maha mantra* group.

For the 64 participants remaining after posttest, two had their 1-week meeting one day after the closure of the 3-day window, and one had the 1-week meeting 2 days after the closure of the 3-day window. For two subjects the posttest meeting was held two days after the closure of the posttest window. After the followup meetings, when data was analyzed, it was decided to retain the five subjects described above because none of them had outlying scores on any of the dependent variables.

All participants were phoned on January 9 or January 10, 1999, to remind them of the follow-up appointment. A research team member personally met with each subject to administer the follow-up surveys and pay the remaining $20. In some cases, where a personal meeting was not possible, participants mailed the surveys to the researcher in a stamped envelope provided by the researcher at posttest, and the researcher mailed $20 to the participant upon receipt of the follow-up package. Follow-up measures were completed within 27-29 days of posttest. Participants signed a receipt for the $20 follow-up payment. Sixty-two subjects completed the entire study. After all subjects completed the follow-up session, surveys were scored and data was entered and analyzed using SPSS.

Table 2

Schedule for Hare Krsna Maha Mantra Japa Research Project

Newspaper Ads for Participants	November 5-14, 1998
5-day pretest window	November 16-20
5-day 1st week chanting check window	November 23-27
5-day 2nd week phone call chanting check window	Nov. 30- Dec. 4
5-day 3rd week phone call chanting check window	December 7-11
5-day posttest window	December 14-18
5-day follow-up window	January 11-15

Analysis

Data for all instruments were treated as interval. For each instrument, a mean for each group in the study was calculated at pretest, posttest, and follow-up. Mean compliance log percentages were calculated for the two chanting groups, and mean ages were calculated for all three groups. Thus, there were four independent variables. Two of the independent variables, gender and group status (*maha mantra*, alternate mantra, or control) were categorical, and two were interval (age and compliance log frequency). There were five dependent variables, which were measured at the interval level by the instruments assessing stress (ICS), depression (GCS), *sattva* (VPI), *rajas* (VPI), and *tamas* (VPI).

For each of the standardized instruments there were three means (pretest, posttest and follow-up) for each of the three groups. Therefore, there were 45 means for the standardized instruments. Also, each of the two chanting groups had a mean compliance log frequency, and all three groups had an average age.

The main effects examined in this study were the effects of the group (*maha mantra*, control, and alternate) independent variable on the five dependent variables. Analysis of data in this study utilized the hierarchical analysis approach described by Cohen and Cohen (1983). With this approach to data analysis, independent variables are entered cumulatively in a prespecified sequence, in accord with the purpose and logic of the research. This procedure permits extrication of as much causal inference as the data allow. This is accomplished by protecting the main effects from potentially weakening statistical influences produced by secondary variables (Cohen & Cohen, 1983). Applied specifically to this study, gender and age were analyzed at the first level, since they are not caused by the group independent variable or chanting frequency. Since gender and age could be spurious variables in the analysis of the chanting variables, it was best to remove their effects before analyzing the variables related to chanting. Chanting frequency was analyzed at the next level of the hierarchy, and then the group status variable was analyzed. ANCOVA, with gender, age, and chanting frequency as covariates, was used to determine similarity of group means. When ANCOVA resulted in a significant F test, t tests were performed to determine which groups significantly differed. Analytical procedures will be described in more detail in the following chapter.

Power Analysis

Power analysis for this 3-group design is explained in Cohen and Cohen (1983). Alpha level for each F test was .05. Orme and Combs-Orme (1986) offer three general strategies for determining effect sizes. These are estimations from previous research, effect sizes selected to indicate a population effect that would have either practical or theoretical significance, and effect sizes chosen from suggested conventional definitions of small, medium and large effect sizes. Based on the study of Janowiak and Hackman (1994), the *maha mantra* single system design pilot study, and Vedic theory, an effect size of at least $r2 = .3$ was expected. To be reasonably sure that effects would be detected, an $r2$ of .25 was used for calculation of power and sample size. According to Rosenthal (1997), an $r2$ of .25 indicates a strong association and large effect size. Multiple $R2$, the effect size of all the independent variables combined, was estimated to be .50, with chanting frequency expected to account for most of the explained model variance not explained by group status. From formula 4.5.1 on page 155 of Cohen and Cohen:

$$f2 = (R2Y.AB - R2Y.A)/(1-R2Y.AB)$$
$$= (.50 - .25) / (1 - .50) \quad = \quad .25/.50 \quad = \quad .50$$

Table E.2 on page 527 (Cohen & Cohen, 1983) provides power values for alpha = .05. Referring to that table, kB, which is the number of main effect independent variables, equals one. Therefore, from table E.2, to achieve power of .8, as recommended by Cohen and Cohen, the L value for kB = 1 is 7.85.

From page 155, formula 4.5.2, sample size (n) = L/f2 + kA + kB + 1. kB = 1, as described above, and kA = 3. kA represents the number of covariates.

Therefore, n = (7.85/.50) + 3 + 1 + 1 = 20.70

Thus, to achieve a power of .8 (Type II error rate of .2), with alpha (Type I error rate) = .05, a sample of at least 21 persons per group is necessary to detect an effect size for group status of $r2 = .25$.

Statistical Tests

An ANCOVA was performed for each of the five dependent variables, and the t-tests within the ANOVAs were protected t tests (Cohen & Cohen, 1983). Using the protected t-test combines strong power attributes of the individual t test with the protection against large experiment-wise Type I error, due to the condition that the F test must meet the alpha significance level in order for subsequent t tests to be performed. Thus, the t tests are protected from the accumulation of small alpha levels to large expermimentwise error rates. Cohen and Cohen conclude that the protected t test is effective in keeping Type I errors low while maintaining good power levels. The independent variables of gender and age underwent the same procedures for analysis as the chanting-related variables, although these two other independent variables were analyzed at the first level in the hierarchical analysis in order to remove their effects from the chanting-related variables.

CHAPTER 4

RESULTS AND DATA ANALYSIS

Loss of Participants and Missing Data

One-hundred-eight persons responded to the newspaper ads for this study. Of these 108, 93 made it to the stage of random assignment, with 31 designated for each of the three groups. Out of these 93 people, 81 completed the pretest surveys, and 62 completed the entire study. For the 81 who completed the pretest, 26 were in the *maha mantra* group, 27 were in the alternate mantra group, and 28 were in the control group, and for the 62 who completed the experiment, 24 were in the *maha mantra* group, 19 in the alternate mantra group, and 19 in the control group. Reasons for subjects leaving the study were described in the procedures section of the methodology chapter (chapter 3).

Cohen and Cohen (1983) write "Because Y represents the outcome or effect of the IVs, when the Y value for a subject is not known, there is little that can be done in MRC but drop that subject......because the research is focally concerned with Y, we find unattractive, in general, attempts to make up Y values so as to avoid the loss of information in the IVs and the reduction in n" (p. 276). Thus, they recommend that data from dropout subjects be dropped from the statistical analysis. Still, for the sake of completeness, means and standard deviations for subjects who did not complete the study were calculated, and t tests were performed to determine if dropout scores at pretest (n=19) were significantly different from non-dropout scores at pretest (n=62). Specifically, pretest scores for dropouts for each group for each of the five dependent variables, as well as for gender and age, were compared with pretest scores for non-dropouts. Altogether 21 t tests were conducted (3 groups x 7 variables), and none of them were significant at the .05 level. This indicates that dropouts from the survey were random with respect to the variables studied, rather than due to some systematic factor.

There were very few missing data points in the surveys that were completed. There were no missing data for any of the independent variables, and none of the dependent variables had more than 1.1% of its scores missing. Cohen and Cohen (1983) describe a process for creating a missing data variable in order to positively utilize missing data as valuable information. However, they explain that when missing values are very few, such a variable is unnecessary. Therefore, the pairwise deletion method was used for missing values in the surveys. Nunnally and Bernstein (1994) write that pairwise deletion is preferable to listwise deletion when there are only a small number of omissions.

Demographics

Tables 3 to 5 show demographic statistics for age, gender, and chanting frequency.

Demographic statistics for age are shown in Table 3. The average age of participants was 24.63 years, ranging from 18 to 49 years. For the *maha mantra* group the average age was 22.46 years, ranging from 18 to 48 years, for the alternate mantra group the average age was 24 years, ranging from 19 to 39 years, and for the control group the average age was 28 years, ranging from 19 to 49 years. An ANOVA comparing average age for each group resulted in a non-significant F statistic at the .05 level.

Table 3

Demographic Statistics for Age

Variable	Mean	Std Dev	Minimum	Maximum	N
AGE	24.63	7.71	18.00	49.00	62
AGEMAHA	22.46	5.90	18.00	48.00	24

Table 3 - continued

Variable	Mean	Std Dev	Minimum	Maximum	N
AGEALT	24.00	5.76	19.00	39.00	19
AGECON	28.00	10.24	19.00	49.00	19

Demographics for gender are shown in Table 4. Among subjects who completed the study, 31 were female and 31 were male. In the *maha mantra* group there were 9 males and 15 females, in the alternate mantra group there were 13 males and 6 females and in the control group there were 9 males and 10 females. A chi-square statistic comparing the gender distribution between groups resulted in a non-significant p value at the .05 level.

Table 4

Demographic Statistics for Gender

Variable	Females	Males	N
GENDER	31	31	62
GENMAHA	15	9	24
GENALT	6	13	19
GENCON	10	9	19

Table 5 shows average chanting frequency for the *maha mantra* group and alternate mantra group. A t test comparing the differences between these two groups resulted in a nonsignificant p value at the .05 level.

Table 5

Chanting Frequency Means and Standard Deviations
N = 24 for Maha Group; N = 19 for Alternate Group

	Mean	Std Dev	Minimum	Maximum
Maha Mantra Group	2.95	.12	2.46	3.00
Alternate Mantra Group	2.88	.22	2.34	3.04

Scores on Dependent Measures by Group

Stress

Table 6 shows stress scores, as measured by the ICS, for each group at pretest, posttest and followup. An ANOVA comparing mean ICS scores for each group at pretest resulted in a non-significant F statistic at the .05 level.

Table 6

Stress Scores by Group at Pretest, Posttest and Followup
N = 24 for Maha Group; N = 19 for Alternate Group; N = 19 for Control Group

Pretest	Mean ICS Score	Std Dev
Maha Group	33.43	11.13
Alternate Group	36.59	19.32
Control Group	27.11	13.97
Posttest		
Maha Group	22.11	6.80
Alternate Group	40.39	23.16
Control Group	28.06	16.52
Followup		
Maha Group	26.76	9.77
Alternate Group	35.87	22.11
Control Group	28.28	14.25

Depression

Table 7 shows depression scores, as measured by the GCS, for each group at pretest, posttest and followup. An ANOVA comparing mean GCS scores for each group found a significant difference at pretest (F= 5.56; p= .006).

Table 7

Depression Scores by Group at Pretest, Posttest and Followup
N = 24 for Maha Group; N = 19 for Alternate Group; N = 19 for Control Group

Pretest	Mean GCS Score	Std Dev
Maha Group	29.75	11.23
Alternate Group	32.02	12.25
Control Group	21.07	8.28
Posttest		
Maha Group	21.48	6.76
Alternate Group	30.41	15.59
Control Group	20.34	8.91
Followup		
Maha Group	25.18	11.27
Alternate Group	32.30	15.02
Control Group	21.49	9.10

Sattva

Table 8 shows *sattva* scores, as measured by the *sattva* subscale of the VPI, for each group at pretest, posttest and followup. An ANOVA comparing mean pretest *sattva* scores between groups found a significant difference at pretest (F= 3.30; p= .044).

Table 8

Sattva Scores by Group at Pretest, Posttest and Followup

N = 24 for Maha Group; N = 19 for Alternate Group; N = 19 for Control Group

Pretest	Mean Sattva Score	Std Dev
Maha Group	71.38	7.71
Alternate Group	67.30	8.28
Control Group	73.71	7.43
Posttest		
Maha Group	76.61	5.07
Alternate Group	66.45	9.08
Control Group	72.92	7.00
Followup		
Maha Group	71.95	6.78
Alternate Group	65.74	9.99
Control Group	73.83	6.87

Rajas

Table 9 shows *rajas* scores, as measured by the *rajas* subscale of the VPI, for each group at pretest, posttest and followup. An ANCOVA comparing mean *rajas* scores at pretest for each group found a significant difference at pretest (F= 8.75; p= .001).

Table 9

Rajas Scores by Group at Pretest, Posttest and Followup
N = 24 for Maha Group; N = 19 for Alternate Group; N = 19 for Control Group

Pretest	Mean Rajas Score	Std Dev
Maha Group	52.44	9.12
Alternate Group	56.21	7.67
Control Group	44.42	9.73
Posttest		
Maha Group	50.79	6.60
Alternate Group	51.40	9.27
Control Group	46.10	9.77
Followup		
Maha Group	53.75	10.56
Alternate Group	52.02	9.46
Control Group	44.96	9.88

Tamas

Table 10 shows *tamas* scores, as measured by the *tamas* subscale of the VPI, for each group at pretest, posttest and followup. An ANOVA comparing pretest *tamas* scores between groups found a significant difference at pretest (F= 5.70; p= .010).

Table 10

Tamas Scores by Group at Pretest, Posttest and Followup

N = 24 for Maha Group; N = 19 for Alternate Group; N = 19 for Control Group

Pretest	Mean Tamas Score	Std Dev
Maha Group	49.97	10.22
Alternate Group	52.31	10.62
Control Group	40.64	13.35
Posttest		
Maha Group	43.61	7.08
Alternate Group	49.12	10.68
Control Group	41.53	13.03
Followup		
Maha Group	46.19	7.51
Alternate Group	50.52	9.74
Control Group	40.27	13.08

Correlations of Covariates

A large correlation matrix was generated, with computations of all correlations between all variables in the study. This included correlations involving dependent and independent variables, as well as all possible combinations of test time (pre, post, and followup) and group (maha, alternate, and control). This section discusses correlations involving the covariates in this study, namely gender, age, and

84

chanting frequency, which were assessed as covariates of the primary independent variable, group status.

Gender

Correlations between gender and the other variables in the study were calculated using Pearson r. Specifically, correlations for gender in each group- maha, alternate and control- were calculated for each variable in that group. For instance, correlations for gender in the alternate group were calculated for pretest, posttest, and followup scores for the alternate group for each of the five dependent variables. Also, correlations between gender and age, and gender and chanting frequency, were computed.

For the *maha mantra* group there were 18 correlations computed (3 test times x 5 dependent variables + age + chanting frequency + gender). Of these 18 calculations, none were significant at the .05 level, except of course for gender with itself.

For the alternate mantra group there were also 18 calculations, and of these the only correlation significant at the .05 level, other than gender with itself, was gender alternate group with age alternate group (r=-.63; p=.004). This indicates that for the alternate mantra group the 13 males were significantly younger than the 6 females. For the gender variable females were coded as "1" and males were coded as "2".

For the control group there were 17 calculations, because the control group had no chanting frequency values. Of these 17 correlations, 6 were significant at the .05 level. Gender for the control group was significantly correlated with control group scores for Pretest *Sattva* (r=-.46; p=.048), Followup *Sattva* (r=-.50; p=.029), Pretest *Tamas* (r=.50; p=.028), Posttest *Tamas* (r=.46; p=.047), Followup *Tamas* (r=.50; p=.029), and Gender (r=1.00; p=.000).

These correlations indicate that for the control group males had higher *tamas* scores, at all three measurement times, than females, and that females had higher *sattva* scores, at pretest and followup, than males.

For gender, 6 out of 50 (12%) of the correlations with other variables were significant at the .05 level. Gender was hypothesized to not be significantly correlated with the other variables.

Age

Correlations between age and the other variables in the study were calculated using Pearson r. Specifically, correlations for age in each group- maha, alternate and control- were calculated for each variable in that group. For instance, correlations for age in the alternate group were calculated for pretest, posttest, and followup scores for the Alternate Group for each of the five dependent variables. Also, correlations between age and gender, and age and chanting frequency, were computed.

For the *maha mantra* group there were 18 correlations computed (3 test times x 5 dependent variables + gender + chanting frequency + age). Of these 18 calculations, none were significant at the .05 level, except for the correlation of age with itself.

For the alternate mantra group there were also 18 calculations, and of these three were significant at the .05 level. The correlation with Gender was significant, as described above, and the correlation between Age Alternate Group and Chanting Frequency Alternate Group was also significant (r--.47; p=.041), as was the correlation of age with itself (r=1.00; p=.000). This shows that for the Alternate Group younger subjects had a higher chanting frequency.

For the control group there were 17 calculations, since the control group had no chanting frequency values. None of these were significant at the .05 level, except for the correlation of age with itself.

For age, 2 out of 50 correlations (4%) with other variables were significant at the .05 level. Age was hypothesized to not be correlated with the other variables.

Chanting Frequency

Chanting frequency was hypothesized for the *maha mantra* group to correlate positively with *sattva*, and negatively with stress, depression, *rajas* and *tamas*.

For the alternate mantra group chanting frequency was hypothesized to have no correlation with the other variables.

For the *maha mantra* and alternate groups correlations between chanting frequency and all other variables in that group were computed using Pearson r. For each of these groups there were 18 correlations calculated, as described above for the gender and age variables.

For the *maha mantra* group none of the correlations were significant, except for chanting frequency with itself.

For the alternate mantra group 11 of 17 correlations were significant at the .05 level. These correlations are presented in Table 11.

Table 11

Significant Chanting Frequency Correlations

	Pearson r	p value
Pretest Stress Alternate Group	-.54	.017
Pretest Sattva Alternate Group	-.60	.007
Pretest Rajas Alternate Group	-.65	.003
Posttest Stress Alternate Group	-.55	.015
Posttest Rajas Alternate Group	-.56	.013
Posttest Depression Alternate Group	-.47	.043
Followup Stress Alternate Group	-.64	.003
Followup Rajas Alternate Group	-.55	.016
Followup Depression Alt. Group	-.48	.038
Chanting Frequency	1.00	.000

Also, as explained in the above section on Age, the correlation between age alternate group and chanting frequency alternate group was significant (r=-.47; p=.041). These data indicate that those who chanted more, compared with those who chanted less, scored lower on stress at all three measurement periods. For depression, increased chanting was associated with lower depression scores at posttest and followup. Also, increased chanting correlated with lower *rajas* scores at all measurement periods.

Contrary to the secondary hypotheses, chanting frequency had no correlation with the *maha mantra* group variables, and it did significantly correlate with several of the alternate mantra group variables. This will be discussed in the next chapter.

General Covariate Correlations with Other Covariates

Without specifying group status, age and chanting frequency were significantly correlated (r=-.31; p=.015). That is, chanting frequency is significantly correlated with age, without regard for whether subjects were in the *maha mantra* group or the alternate mantra group. Other intercovariate correlations, without specifying group status, were not significant. This information is useful in assessing the effects of multicollinearity on the ANCOVA models that will be presented later in this chapter. Specifically, age and chanting frequency were significantly correlated at the .05 level, and therefore it is possible that their effects on dependent variables were somewhat overlapping. Concerning multicollinearity, Cohen and Cohen (1983) explain that a hierarchical approach to ANCOVA serves to separate effects of the different independent variables. This hierarchical approach was used in this study.

Pretest Group Comparisons

In order to evaluate the effectiveness of random assignment in this experimental design, pretest scores for each group were compared using ANOVA tests. At the .05 level there were significant differences between at least two groups at pretest for depression (p=.006), *sattva* (p=.044), *rajas* (p=.001), and *tamas* (p=.010). Therefore, for these four variables random assignment was apparently not successful.

For depression, the control group differed significantly at pretest from both the *maha mantra* and alternate mantra groups. For *sattva*, the difference in pretest scores between the alternate and control groups was significant. For *rajas* and *tamas*, the control group differed significantly at pretest from both the *maha mantra* and alternate mantra groups.

Reliability Analyses for Dependent Variable Measures

For all five measures, observed Cronbach's alpha was less than that reported in the literature, and as described in the methodology chapter of this dissertation. Still, all of the scores were in the acceptable range, as Nunnally and Bernstein (1994) explain that, for group comparisons, an alpha of .70 is satisfactory (see Table 12). Therefore, each of the scale or subscale scores was retained for subsequent analyses.

Table 12

Alpha for Dependent Measures

	Alpha
Sattva (VPI):	.86
Rajas (VPI):	.82
Tamas (VPI):	.87
Stress (ICS):	.94
Depression (GCS):	.90

Analysis of Effects of Group Status and Covariates on the Dependent Variables

ANCOVA was used to assess the effects of group status on the dependent variables. Gender, age and chanting frequency served as covariates in the

ANCOVA analyses. These analyses were performed hierarchically, with age and gender assessed first, then chanting frequency, and then group status. This order of variable analysis was selected in accord with the principles of causal priority and removal of confounding variables, as described in Cohen and Cohen (1983). According to the principle of causal priority, variables that are temporally prior and unlikely to be affected by other variables should be analyzed first. Since age and gender fit this description, they were the first variables analyzed in the hierarchical ANCOVAs. The principle of removal of confounding variables dictates that variables other than the primary variable(s) being studied should be assessed prior to the main independent variables, in order to remove the effects of secondary variables when evaluating the effects of the main variables (Cohen & Cohen, 1983). Therefore, chanting frequency was analyzed prior to group status in the hierarchical analysis, so that the effects of all covariates were removed when assessing group status.

ANCOVA is a combination of analysis of variance with a categorical level independent variable, and standard regression analysis with an interval level independent variable. This is an effective method for modeling an interval dependent variable in terms of both interval and categorical independent variables (Agresti and Finlay, 1986). This type of analysis is relevant to this study, because all the dependent variables are interval level, and the independent variables are both categorical, such as group status and gender, and interval, such as chanting frequency and age.

The main hypotheses of this experiment, stated in the hypotheses section of the methodology chapter (chapter 3), were that chanting the *maha mantra* will decrease stress, depression, *rajas* and *tamas*, and will increase *sattva*, from pretest to posttest. These changes were additionally predicted to be significantly greater, at the alpha = .05 level, than any similar changes in the dependent variables occurring in the alternate mantra or control groups. Secondary hypotheses are that chanting frequency will effect the dependent variables in the same direction as the *maha mantra* group. That is, the greater the chanting frequency of the *maha mantra*, the greater was the expected decrease in stress, depression, *rajas* and *tamas*, and the greater was the expected increase in *sattva*. Chanting frequency of the alternate

90

mantra was predicted to not have an effect on the dependent variables. Also, gender and age were predicted to not have an effect on the dependent variables. Changes in pretest-followup scores were expected to be in the same direction as for pretest-posttest for each variable, though the changes for pretest-followup were predicted to be smaller than the changes from pretest-posttest.

Since the hypotheses described above involve comparisons of means while controlling for covariates, the ANCOVA statistic was chosen for the purpose. Although MANCOVA could have also been used in this analysis, with difference scores of pretest-posttest and pretest-followup serving as the simultaneous dependent variables, the sample size of the study did not provide sufficient power for efficacious use of the MANCOVA (Montgomery, 1997). Also, although repeated measures ANCOVA could be used for this experimental design, repeated measures ANCOVA is more typically used for time series analysis and trend studies with many more than three data points per subject. Therefore, ANCOVA was selected for this analysis (McNeil, Newman, & Kelly, 1996).

Since group equivalence of means was not achieved for some of the dependent variables, it was especially important that the statistical procedure incorporated the difference in pretest scores. Calculating difference scores (e.g., from pretest to posttest) and then analyzing these difference scores with ANCOVA is one method of doing this. However, Cohen and Cohen (1983) note that the reliability of a difference score is likely to be lower than the variables being differenced, and that change scores tend to be correlated with pretest scores. Therefore, they are not an objective measure because the difference scores contain some variance that is due to the pretest score, and thus change scores do not actually remove the effect of the pretest. Cohen and Cohen recommend partialling the pretest score from the observed difference score, thus creating a regressed change score. Nunnally and Bernstein (1994), however, write "...the observed difference score...is the simplest and most direct definition of change, despite its problems. Also, remember that standardizing the elements of a difference score may produce spurious results" (p. 245). Nunnally and Bernstein critique the partiallizing method, pointing out shortcomings such as treating the pretest score as if it were an error-free true score. They conclude, "Consequently, observed differences need not be as fatally flawed as was once thought" (p. 246).

To compensate for pretest inequalities, ANCOVA was first performed using the partialling method. To check for substantial differences in the results of the two statistical approaches, ANCOVA using observed difference scores was also performed for each dependent variable. Regressed change scores, as described in Cohen and Cohen (1983, p. 416), were calculated according to the following formula:

$$a-b(rab^*sda / sdb)$$

a: posttest score

b: pretest score

rab: correlation of pretest scores with posttest scores

sda: standard deviation of posttest scores

sdb: standard deviation of posttest scores

Before running ANCOVA, the data for each dependent variable was evaluated for adherence to assumptions for the ANCOVA statistic. Bartlett's Box statistic was used to assess homoscedasticity, with a .05 significance level chosen to determine whether there is adequate homoscedasticity for a distribution. Dowdy and Wearden (1991) compare the homoscedasticity tests of Cochran, Hartley and Bartlett, and conclude that Bartlett's test is the most powerful of the three. Also, they explain that the F test is robust with respect to departures from homogeneity, and that a significance level of p = .05 in the Bartlett statistic is an adequate measure of homoscedasticity for evaluating the homoscedasticity assumption for using the F distribution. The method of weighted least squares is a viable option for using regression techniques when there is severe violation of the homoscedasticity assumption. Sen and Srivastava (1990) explain that the weighted least squares approach ascribes smaller weights to larger errors, and that the method is a special case of generalized least squares. They caution that weighted least squares should not be utilized unless deviation from homoscedasticity is extreme.

For each ANCOVA a test comparing a linear explanation for the data with a nonlinear relationship was performed. In some cases neither a linear nor a nonlinear model produced a significant p value (at p = .05). This indicates that the

92

relationship between the dependent variable and the independent variable being tested for linearity was so weak that no model explained a statistically significant portion of the variance. In the case of dependent variables regressed on the age variable, a non-significant p value was predicted by the hypotheses of this study, namely that age will not have a significant effect on the dependent variables. Still, when neither the p value for a linear or nonlinear explanation was significant, the lower p value indicated which type of model best explained the relationship between the two variables (Ryan, 1997). That is, the type of model with the lower p value explained more variance than the other type of model. Besides age, chanting frequency was the other interval-level independent variable, and therefore chanting frequency was also tested for a linear relationship with the dependent variables. According to the hypotheses of this study chanting frequency was predicted to have a relationship with the dependent variables, and therefore the p values for chanting frequency in the linearity tests are expected to be lower than the p values for age, indicating that a linear model explains more of the variance for chanting frequency than for age.

Slopes for the dependent variables for each group of the age variable were calculated to estimate similarity of slopes and effects of interactions. Rigdon, Shumacker, and Wothke (1996) explain that markedly different slopes across groups between two variables indicate that an interaction term is necessary to explain the relationship between the three variables. According to Rigdon et al., similarity of slopes is also support for the fulfillment of the linearity assumption. Specific to *japa* studies, if the slope of age regressed on the dependent variable is the same for the *maha mantra* group, the alternate group, and the control group, then it means that there is no significant interaction between age and group status in relation to the dependent variable. Sheskin (1997) suggests that a difference in slopes between groups of more than .50 may be considered large, and this standard was used in the following analyses.

If the total explained variance for an ANCOVA was significant at the .05 level, then t tests were performed to determine which of the three group comparisons had significant differences at the .05 level. Also, 95% confidence intervals (CI) were calculated for each t test. For each ANCOVA a model with a group status-gender interaction term was computed. In no case did this term have a statistically significant effect on the dependent variable, and therefore the term was dropped from the model in all cases.

After the ANCOVA, t tests for the main effects of the different groups on the dependent variable were performed if the F test for the explained variance of the entire model was significant at the .05 level. In addition, effect sizes are presented with the eta squared statistic. Nunnally and Bernstein (1994) describe eta as a universal measure of relationship that can be used regardless of the form of the relationship. Eta is a correlation ratio that is calculated by computing the variance in the dependent variable about any curve of the relationship. Further, they state that eta applies equally well to categorical or continuous variables, which is relevant to this study because there are independent variables that are categorical and continuous. They write "Although F is basic to statistical inferences about group mean differences in the population, eta indicates how strong the relationship is, thus describing the independent variable's explanatory power." (p. 138).

Difference Scores

The ANCOVAs in the following analyses used difference scores. Therefore, difference scores for the dependent variables, which can also be calculated from Tables 6-10, are presented below in Table 13.

Table 13

Difference Scores for Dependent Variables by Group from Pretest to Posttest and from Pretest to Followup

	Mean Difference
Stress Scores	
Maha Group From Pretest To Posttest	-11.32
Alternate Group From Pretest To Posttest	3.80
Control Group From Pretest To Posttest	.95

Table 13 - continued   Mean Difference

Stress Scores

    Maha Group From Pretest To Followup   -6.67

    Alternate Group From Pretest To Followup   -.72

    Control Group From Pretest To Followup   1.17

Depression Scores

    Maha Group From Pretest To Posttest   -8.27

    Alternate Group From Pretest To Posttest   -1.61

    Control Group From Pretest To Posttest   -.73

    Maha Group From Pretest To Followup   -4.57

    Alternate Group From Pretest To Followup   .28

    Control Group From Pretest To Followup   .42

Sattva Scores

    Maha Group From Pretest To Posttest   5.23

    Alternate Group From Pretest To Posttest   -.85

    Control Group From Pretest To Posttest   -.79

    Maha Group From Pretest To Followup   .57

    Alternate Group From Pretest To Followup   -1.56

    Control Group From Pretest To Followup   .12

Rajas Scores

    Maha Group From Pretest To Posttest   -1.65

    Alternate Group From Pretest To Posttest   -4.81

    Control Group From Pretest To Posttest   1.68

    Maha Group From Pretest To Followup   1.31

    Alternate Group From Pretest To Followup   -4.19

    Control Group From Pretest To Followup   .54

Table 13 - continued	Mean Difference
Tamas Scores	
Maha Group From Pretest To Posttest	-6.36
Alternate Group From Pretest To Posttest	-3.19
Control Group From Pretest To Posttest	.89
Maha Group From Pretest To Followup	-3.78
Alternate Group From Pretest To Followup	-1.79
Control Group From Pretest To Followup	-.37

The difference scores shown in Table 13 reflect the change in average group scores from pretest to posttest and pretest to followup for each dependent variable. ANCOVAs tested the difference in these change scores between groups, controlling for age, gender, and chanting frequency. Table 14 shows the difference in change scores between groups, which are the values that were actually evaluated for statistical significance. The values in Table 14 can be calculated from Table 13. For calculation of partiallized change scores, the formula in Cohen and Cohen (1983, p. 46), which was described in the preceding section, was applied to the mean difference scores in Table 14.

Table 14

Difference in Change Scores for Dependent Variables by Group from Pretest to Posttest and from Pretest to Followup

	Mean Difference
Stress Scores	
Maha/Alternate From Pretest to Posttest	-15.12*
Maha/Control From Pretest to Posttest	-12.27*
Alternate/Control From Pretest to Posttest	2.85

Table 14 - continued   Mean Difference

Stress Scores

    Maha/Alternate From Pretest to Followup   -5.95

    Maha/Control From Pretest to Followup   -7.84

    Alternate/Control From Pretest to Followup   -1.89

Depression Scores

    Maha/Alternate From Pretest to Posttest   -6.66*

    Maha/Control From Pretest to Posttest   -7.54*

    Alternate/Control From Pretest to Posttest   -.88

    Maha/Alternate From Pretest to Followup   -4.85

    Maha/Control From Pretest to Followup   -4.99*

    Alternate/Control From Pretest to Followup   -.14

Sattva Scores

    Maha/Alternate From Pretest to Posttest   6.08*

    Maha/Control From Pretest to Posttest   6.02*

    Alternate/Control From Pretest to Posttest   -.06

    Maha/Alternate From Pretest to Followup   2.13

    Maha/Control From Pretest to Followup   .45

    Alternate/Control From Pretest to Followup   -1.68

Rajas Scores

    Maha/Alternate From Pretest to Posttest   3.16

    Maha/Control From Pretest to Posttest   -3.33

    Alternate/Control From Pretest to Posttest   -6.49

    Maha/Alternate From Pretest to Followup   5.50

    Maha/Control From Pretest to Followup   .77

    Alternate/Control From Pretest to Followup   -4.73

Table 14 - continued	Mean Difference
Tamas Scores	
Maha/Alternate From Pretest to Posttest	-3.17
Maha/Control From Pretest to Posttest	-7.25*
Alternate/Control From Pretest to Posttest	-4.08
Maha/Alternate From Pretest to Followup	-1.99
Maha/Control From Pretest to Followup	-3.41*
Alternate/Control From Pretest to Followup	-1.42

*Indicates a statistically significant value at alpha = .05.

Statistical Analysis of the Stress Variable

Pretest-Posttest Analysis of Stress Variable

Tests of Assumptions, Interaction, and Outliers for Pretest-Posttest Analysis of the Stress Variable.

Analysis of residuals was performed for partiallized difference scores and observed difference scores for the pretest-posttest analysis of the stress variable. For partiallized scores, Bartlett's Box statistic for homogeneity, F (2, 7601), had a p value of .166, and for observed scores, Bartlett's Box statistic for homogeneity, F (2, 7601), had a p value of .125. These non-significant p values indicate that the data possess adequate homogeneity of variance for the ANCOVA.

According to Nunnally and Bernstein (1994), about 5% of standardized residuals can be expected to have a value greater than 2. Cohen and Cohen (1983) state "When residuals are standardized by dividing them by their standard deviation, a residual that is as much as three (or, certainly, four) of these units in absolute size is reasonably considered an outlier" (p. 48). They further state that outliers are particularly bothersome when they are predominantly of the same sign.

For partiallized scores, 4 of 62 standardized residual scores had values greater than 2. These four values were -3.64, -3.29, 2.97, and 2.04. The raw data for these scores were examined for correct entry, and no mistakes were found. Since posttest roughly coincided with finals week, the end of the semester, and the start of the December holiday season, the author conjectured that these factors combined to produce substantially increased or decreased amounts of stress on the outliers. These influences are expected, especially with a student population. For this reason, as well as the fact that two outliers were positive and two were negative, thus reducing their negative impact on the statistical calculation, these outlying scores were retained for the analysis. Also, 4 outliers out of 62 scores is only slightly above 5% (6.45%), and Cohen and Cohen (1983) caution that the decision to discard data from outliers "should not be taken lightly" (p. 128).

For observed difference scores, only 3 (4.84%) of the data points had a standardized residual greater than 2, and one of these outlying scores was of a different sign than the other two. The same analysis as provided for the partiallized residuals applies, and therefore the data for the outliers was retained for the ANCOVA analysis.

To test for adherence of the data to the linearity assumption of the ANCOVA, F tests were conducted to determine whether a linear or non-linear model best explained the relationship between pretest-posttest stress scores and chanting frequency scores. The p value of the F statistic for a linear explanation was .087, and the p value of the F statistic for a non-linear explanation was .477. This indicates that a linear model is a better fit for the data. The same statistical procedure was used to assess the form of the relationship between pretest-posttest stress scores and age values. The p value of the F statistic for a linear explanation was .037, and for a non-linear explanation the p value was .320. This indicates that a linear explanation for the relationship between age and pretest-posttest difference scores for stress explained more variance than a non-linear explanation, and was therefore a better fit for the data.

As an additional test for linearity, observed difference scores for each group for pretest-posttest were regressed on the age variable. For the alternate mantra group the slope was -.03, for the *maha mantra* group the slope was .03, and for the control group the slope was .04. These similar slopes across groups suggest a linear relationship.

ANCOVA Using Partiallized Pretest-Posttest Stress Difference Scores.

Hypothesis 1 in the methodology chapter stated that the *maha mantra* group will show significantly decreased stress, at the .05 level, from pretest to posttest compared with the alternate group and the control group. Table 15 shows the results of a hierarchical ANCOVA, using partiallized difference scores, assessing the effects of group status on stress, with gender, age and chanting frequency as covariates. Effects of gender and age were calculated first, then chanting frequency was assessed, and then the effects of group status were analyzed:

Table 15

Results of ANCOVA Using Partiallized Pretest-Posttest Stress Difference Scores

Source of Variation	F	Sig. of F (p value)	Effect Size (Part Eta2)
Group Status	13.92	.000	.33
Age	7.52	.008	.06
Gender	.092	.763	.00
Chanting Frequency	.308	.581	.08
Total Var. Explained	7.15	.000	

Pearson R for this ANCOVA was .62 (Multiple R2= .39). Three t tests were performed to identify significant comparisons. Significant p values were found for the maha and alternate comparison (p= .000; CI for difference= [8.26, 24.19]) and the maha and control comparison (p= .001; CI for difference= [-15.84, -4.30]).

The result of the F test of the ANCOVA for group status (p= .000) indicates that group status had an effect on stress. The t tests and confidence intervals for maha-control and maha-alternate comparisons show that the decrease in the maha group's stress score was significant at the .05 level, compared to the change in score of either of the other groups. This was shown by the significance levels as well as the confidence intervals, both of which indicate that such results can be expected by chance less than 1 % of the time. The Multiple R2 value of .39 means that 39% of the variance in stress difference scores was accounted for by the complete model. The partial eta squared values for the four variables show the proportion of variance explained by each variable, controlling for all of the other variables in the model. From the F tests, age was the only covariate with a significant effect on stress, though the effect size for age was only 6.0%.

ANCOVA Using Observed Pretest-Posttest Stress Difference Scores.

Table 16 shows the results of a hierarchical ANCOVA, using observed difference scores, assessing the effects of group status on stress, with gender, age and chanting frequency as covariates. Effects of gender and age were calculated first, then chanting frequency was assessed, and then the effects of group status were analyzed.

Table 16

Results of ANCOVA Using Observed Pretest-Posttest Stress Difference Scores

Source of Variation	F	Sig. of F (p value)	Effect Size (Part Eta2)
Group Status	9.06 .	000	.25
Age	5.62	.021	.03
Gender	.11	.740	.00
Chanting Frequency	1.83	.182	.02
Total Var. Explained	5.14	.001	

Pearson R for this ANCOVA was .56 (Multiple R2= .31). Three t tests were performed to identify significant comparisons. Significant p values were found for the maha and alternate comparison (p= .001; CI for difference= [-23.14, -7.11]) and the maha and control comparison (p= .000; CI for difference= [6.23, 18.32]).

Using observed difference scores instead of partialled difference scores, the results were essentially unchanged. The lower value for Multiple R2 indicates that the model explained less of the variance using observed scores, and the lower partial eta squared score for group status shows that group status explained less of the variance in the stress variable, compared with the partialled score calculation. However, the effects of group status were still statistically significant for maha-alternate and maha-control comparisons. Effect size measures and significance tests reveal that age was less of an influence on stress using observed difference scores. Chanting frequency and gender remained non-significant factors.

Pretest-Followup Analysis of the Stress Variable

Tests of Assumptions for Pretest-Followup Analysis of the Stress Variable.

Analysis of residuals was performed for partiallized difference scores and observed difference scores for the pretest-followup analysis of the stress variable. For partiallized scores, Bartlett's Box statistic for homogeneity, $F(2, 7601)$, had a p value of .108, and for observed scores, Bartlett's Box statistic for homogeneity, $F(2, 7601)$, had a p value of .104. These non-significant p values indicate that the data possess adequate homogeneity of variance for the ANCOVA.

For partiallized scores, only 1 of 62 (1.61%) standardized residual values were greater than 2. This outlying score, after confirming that data entry for the score is correct, was retained for the statistical analysis. For observed difference scores, only 2 of 62 (3.23%) scores had a standardized residual value greater than 2. Because they represent less than 5% of the scores, and because the two outliers are of opposite sign, they were retained for the analysis.

To test for adherence of the data to the linearity assumption of the ANCOVA, F tests were conducted to determine whether a linear or non-linear model best explains the relationship between pretest-followup stress scores and chanting frequency scores. The p value of the F statistic for a linear explanation was

102

.0056, and the p value of the F statistic for a non-linear explanation was .130. This indicates that a linear model is a better fit for the data. The same statistical procedure was used to assess the form of the relationship between pretest-posttest stress scores and age values. The p value of the F statistic for a linear explanation was .078, and for a non-linear explanation the p value was .303. This indicates that a linear explanation for the relationship between age and pretest-followup difference scores for stress explains more variance than a non-linear explanation, and is therefore a better fit for the data.

As an additional test for linearity, observed difference scores for each group for pretest-followup were regressed on the age variable. For the *maha mantra* group the slope was -.155, for the alternate mantra group the slope was .199, and for the control group the slope was .069. These similar slopes across groups suggest a linear relationship, and thus the linearity assumption for the ANCOVA was adequately satisfied.

ANCOVA Using Partiallized Pretest-Followup Stress Difference Scores.

Hypothesis 6 in the Methodology Chapter stated that the *maha mantra* group will show significantly decreased stress, at the .05 level, from pretest to followup compared with the alternate group and the control group, though this decrease was hypothesized to be less than the decrease from pretest to posttest. Using a hierarchical ANCOVA with partiallized difference scores, assessing the effects of group status on stress from pretest to followup, with gender, age and chanting frequency as covariates, the p value for the F statistic for the variance explained for the entire model was .096, which is not significant at the .05 level, and the p value for the effects of group status was .724. Partial eta2 for group status was .011, and none of the covariates had an eta squared greater than .02, nor did any of the covariates have a significant t value at the .05 level. These results show that the model as a whole does not explain variance in the dependent variable at a significant level. Group status t tests were not performed because the F test was not significant.

ANCOVA Using Observed Difference Scores for Pretest-Followup Stress Scores.

Using a hierarchical ANCOVA with observed difference scores, assessing the effects of group status on stress from pretest to followup, with gender, age and chanting frequency as covariates, the p value for the F statistic for the variance explained for the entire model was .056, and the p value for the effects of group status was .082. Eta squared for group status using observed differences was .12. Chanting frequency had a significant p value for the F test (.004), indicating that, controlling for the other variables in the model, chanting frequency had a significant effect on stress from pretest to followup. Chanting frequency had an eta2 of .155. Group comparison t tests for group status were not conducted because the F test for total explained variance was not significant at the .05 level.

Statistical Analysis of the Depression Variable

Pretest-Posttest Analysis of Depression

Tests of Assumptions, Interaction and Outliers for Pretest-Posttest Depression Scores.

Residual analysis for partiallized difference pretest-posttest depression scores revealed five standardized residual values greater than 2. These values were 2.31, 2.01, -2.18, -2.201, and -2.26. Since these values contain two positive numbers and three negative numbers, and because none of them exceed 2 by more than .308 in absolute value, all these scores were retained for the ANCOVA analysis. Cohen and Cohen (1983) explain that "a residual that is as much as three (or, certainly, four) of these units in absolute size is reasonably considered an outlier" (p. 48). Bartlett's Box statistic for homoscedasticity was .130, indicating that the data was adequately homoscedastistic for the ANCOVA. Residual analysis for observed difference pretest-posttest depression scores also showed five standardized residual values greater than 2. These values were 2.09, 2.067, 2.13, -2.09, and -2.37. For the same reasons applied in the case of partiallized pretest-posttest depression scores, all five outlying scores were retained for the ANCOVA. Bartlett's Box statistic for observed scores was .240, and thus the distribution was adequately homoscedastistic for the ANCOVA.

To test for linearity, F tests were run to compare the appropriateness of a linear explanation for the depression scores charted against chanting frequency values with a non-linear explanation. The p value for the F statistic for a linear explanation was .004, and the p value for a non-linear explanation was .011, indicating that a linear model is a better fit. For depression scores charted against age, the p value for the F statistic for a linear explanation was .052, and the p value for a non-linear explanation was .557, again providing statistical evidence for the linear model.

Observed difference scores for each group for pretest-posttest were regressed on the age variable. For the *maha mantra* group the slope was -.191, for the alternate mantra group the slope was -.250, and for the control group the slope was -.034. These similar slopes across groups suggest a linear relationship and lack of interaction.

ANCOVA for Pretest-Posttest Depression Scores Using Partiallized Differences.

Hypothesis 2 in the Methodology Chapter stated that the *maha mantra* group will show significantly decreased depression, at the .05 level, from pretest to posttest compared with the alternate group and the control group. Table 17 shows the results of a hierarchical ANCOVA, using partiallized difference scores, analyzing the effects of group status on depression, with gender, age and chanting frequency as covariates. Effects of gender and age were calculated first, then chanting frequency was evaluated, and then the effects of group status were assessed.

Table 17

Results of ANCOVA Using Partiallized Pretest-Posttest Depression Difference Scores

Source of Variation	F	Sig. of F (p value)	Effect Size (Part Eta2)
Group Status	7.54	.001	.21
Age	4.71	.034	.01
Gender	.54	.467	.01
Frequency	6.85	.011	.15
Total Var. Explained	5.43	.000	

Pearson R for this ANCOVA was .57 (Multiple R2= .33). Three t tests were performed to identify significant comparisons. Significant p values were found for the maha and alternate comparison (p= .002; CI for difference= [1.03, 11.88]) and the maha and control comparison (p= .010; CI for difference= [-12.58, -4.06]).

The result of the F test of the ANCOVA (p = .001) for group status indicates that group status had an effect on depression, and the p value for overall explained variance (p= .000) shows that the model as a whole had a significant effect on pretest-posttest depression scores. Significance levels of t tests and t test confidence intervals for maha-alternate and maha-control show that the decrease in the maha group's depression score was significant at the .05 level, compared to the change in score of either of the other groups, controlling for the covariates. This was demonstrated by the p values as well as the confidence intervals, both of which indicate that such results can be expected by chance less than 1% of the time. The Multiple R2 value of .33 means that 33% of the variance in depression difference scores is accounted for by the complete model. The partial eta2 values for the four variables show the proportion of variance explained by each variable, controlling for the other variables in the model. Although the p value for the F test for age was significant at the .05 level, age explained less than 1% of the variance, while chanting frequency, which also had a significant p value for the F statistic, explained 15% of the variance.

ANCOVA Using Observed Difference Scores for Depression Pretest-Posttest.

Table 18 shows the results of a hierarchical ANCOVA, using observed difference scores, evaluating the effects of group status on pretest-posttest depression scores, with gender, age and chanting frequency as covariates. Effects of gender and age were computed first, then chanting frequency was assessed, and then the effects of group status were analyzed:

Table 18

Results of ANCOVA Using Observed Pretest-Posttest Depression Difference Scores

Source of Variation	F	Sig. of F (p value)	Effect Size (Part Eta2)
Group Status	9.26	.000	.25
Age	5.34	.025	.01
Gender	.65	.422	.01
Chanting Frequency	5.41	.024	.17
Total Var. Explained	5.98	.000	

Pearson R for this ANCOVA was .59 (Multiple R2= .35). Three t tests were performed to identify significant comparisons. Significant p values were found for the maha and alternate comparison (p= .013; CI for difference= [-11.85, -1.47]) and the maha and control comparison (p= .000; CI for difference= [3.62, 11.46]).

Using observed difference scores instead of partiallized difference scores, the results were basically the same. Effects of group status were significant, as are effects of chanting frequency and age. However, age explained only a very small percentage of the variance (1%). Significance levels of t tests illustrate that maha-alternate and maha-control differences were significant.

Pretest-Followup Analysis of the Depression Variable

Tests of Assumptions, Interaction and Outliers for Pretest-Followup Depression Scores.

Analysis of residuals was performed for partiallized difference scores and observed difference scores for the pretest-followup analysis of the Depression variable. Partiallized and observed scores each had 3 values with a standardized residual greater than 2. Also, for each method two of the outliers were of one sign, and the third was of the opposite sign. Therefore all outlying scores were retained for the ANCOVAs.

The p value for Bartlett's Box statistic for homogeneity, $F(2, 7601)$, for partiallized scores was .109, and for observed scores the p value was .103, indicating that the data possess sufficient homogeneity of variance for the ANCOVA.

F tests were performed to determine whether a linear or non-linear model best explained the relationship between pretest-followup depression scores and chanting frequency scores. For a linear explanation the p value was .004, and for a non-linear explanation the p value was .054. Comparing the dependent variable with age, the linearity p value was .025, and the non-linear value was .3480. Therefore, these relationships adequately satisfied the linearity assumption of the ANCOVA.

Observed difference scores for each group for pretest-followup were regressed on the age variable. For the *maha mantra* group the slope was -.191, for the alternate mantra group the slope was -.1433, and for the control group the slope was -.0245. These similar slopes indicate that the linearity assumption was satisfied for the pretest-followup depression data.

ANCOVA Using Partiallized Pretest-Followup Depression Difference Scores.

Hypothesis 7 in the Methodology Chapter stated that the *maha mantra* group will show significantly decreased depression, at the .05 level, from pretest to followup compared with the alternate group and the control group, though this

108

decrease was hypothesized to be less than the decrease from pretest to posttest. Table 19 shows the results of a hierarchical ANCOVA, using partiallized difference scores, evaluating the effects of group status on pretest-followup depression scores, with gender, age and chanting frequency as covariates. Effects of gender and age were computed first, then chanting frequency was assessed, and then the effects of group status were analyzed.

Table 19

Results of ANCOVA Using Partiallized Pretest-Followup Depression Difference Scores

Source of Variation	F	Sig. of F (p value)	Effect Size (Part Eta2)
Group Status	3.97	.024	.12
Age	.64	.429	.06
Gender	.06	.815	.01
Chanting Frequency	6.67	.012	.11
Total Var. Explained	3.06	.016	

Pearson R for this ANCOVA was .46 (Multiple R2= .22). Three t tests were performed to identify significant comparisons. Significant p values were found for the maha and control comparison (p= .004; CI for difference= [-12.23, -2.54]).

The p value for group status (.024) was statistically significant at the .05 level, and shows that group status had an effect on depression from pretest to followup. Although the overall effect of the three covariates was not statistically significantly at the .05 level, chanting frequency did have a significant effect (p = .012), controlling for other variables. Group status and chanting frequency explained 12% and 11%, respectively, of the variance. Gender and age did not have significant p values. Results of the t tests show that the maha-control comparison was the only significant difference at the .05 level for pretest-followup depression data.

ANCOVA Using Observed Difference Scores for Pretest-Followup Depression Values.

Table 20 shows the results of a hierarchical ANCOVA, using observed difference scores, evaluating the effects of group status on pretest-followup depression scores, with gender, age and chanting frequency as covariates. Effects of gender and age were computed first, then chanting frequency was assessed, and then the effects of group status were analyzed.

Table 20

Results of ANCOVA Using Observed Pretest-Followup Depression Difference Scores

Source of Variation	F	Sig. of F (p value)	Effect Size (Part Eta2)
Group Status	6.94	.002	.20
Age	.81	.372	.03
Gender	.12	.729	.01
Chanting Frequency	2.70	.106	.16
Total Var. Explained	3.50	.008	

Pearson R for this ANCOVA was .49 (Multiple R2= .24). Three t tests were performed to identify significant comparisons. Significant p values were found for the maha and control comparison (p= .016; CI for difference= [.88, 9.10]).

Using observed difference scores instead of partiallized difference scores for pretest-followup depression, there were minor differences in the results. Most notably, chanting frequency had a significant effect (.012) on depression difference scores using partiallized differences, and the effect of chanting frequency was non-significant using observed differences.

110

Pretest-Posttest Analysis of the Sattva Variable

Tests of Assumptions, Interaction and Outliers for Pretest-Posttest Analysis of the Sattva Variable.

Analysis of residuals was performed for partiallized difference scores and observed difference scores for the pretest-posttest analysis of the *sattva* variable. For partiallized scores there were 2 outliers, with values of -2.02 and -2.25. Since these two scores represented only 3.23% of the values, and 5% of the values can be expected by chance to have standardized residuals greater than 2, these scores were retained for the ANCOVA. For standardized scores there were 3 outliers (4.84%), none of which had an absolute value greater than 2.152, and therefore these scores were also retained for the ANCOVA.

The p value for Bartlett's Box statistic for the partiallized distribution was .065, and for the observed distribution the p value was .169. These values, which were not significant at the .05 level, indicate that the distributions are adequately homosecedastistic for the ANCOVA.

To test for the linearity assumption, F tests were performed to determine whether a linear or non-linear model best explains the relationship between pretest-posttest *sattva* scores and chanting frequency scores. The p value of the F statistic for a linear explanation was .040, and for a non-linear explanation the p value was .169, indicating that a linear approximation is a better fit for the relationship than a non-linear approximation. The same procedure was applied to the relationship between pretest-posttest *sattva* scores and age scores. For this relationship, the p value of the F statistic for a linear explanation was .088, and for a non-linear explanation the p value was .234, suggesting that a linear approximation is a better fit for the data.

As an additional test for linearity, observed difference scores for each group for pretest-posttest were regressed on the age variable. For the *maha mantra* group the slope was -.189, for the alternate mantra group the slope was .033, and for the control group the slope was .057. These similar slopes across groups suggest a linear relationship and lack of interaction.

ANCOVA Using Partiallized Pretest-Posttest Sattva Difference Scores.

Hypothesis 3 in the Methodology Chapter stated that the *maha mantra* group will show significantly increased *sattva*, at the .05 level, from pretest to posttest compared with the alternate group and the control group. Table 21 shows the results of a hierarchical ANCOVA, using partiallized difference scores, assessing the effects of group status on *sattva*, with gender, age and chanting frequency as covariates. Effects of gender and age were calculated first, then chanting frequency was assessed, and then the effects of group status were analyzed.

Table 21

Results of ANCOVA Using Partiallized Pretest-Posttest Sattva Difference Scores

Source of Variation	F	Sig. of F (p value)	Effect Size (Part Eta2)
Group Status	8.24	.001	.23
Age	.86	.357	.01
Gender	1.06	.308	.00
Chanting Frequency	2.22	.142	.03
Total Var. Explained	4.12	.003	

Pearson R for this ANCOVA was .52 (Multiple R2= .27). Three t tests were performed to identify significant comparisons. Significant p values were found for the maha and alternate comparison (p= .011; CI for difference= [1.47, 10.68]) and the maha and control comparison (p= .001; CI for difference= [-9.43, -2.60]).

These statistics show that group status had a statistically significant effect on *sattva* from pretest to posttest at the .05 level, accounting for 23% of the variance. As a whole (p = .259) and individually the covariates did not have a statistically significant effect on the dependent variable. Significance levels of the t tests provide evidence that the *maha mantra* group differed significantly from both the alternate mantra group (p = .011) and the control group (p = .001), and that the Alternate Mantra and control groups did not significantly differ from each other.

Results of ANCOVA Using Observed Pretest-Posttest Sattva Difference Scores.

Table 22 shows the results of a hierarchical ANCOVA, using observed difference scores, assessing the effects of group status on *sattva*, with gender, age and chanting frequency as covariates. Effects of gender and age were calculated first, then chanting frequency was assessed, and then the effects of group status were analyzed.

Table 22

Results of ANCOVA Using Observed Pretest-Posttest Sattva Difference Scores

Source of Variation	F	Sig. of F (p value)	Effect Size (Part Eta2)
Group Status	6.31	.003	.18
Age	1.46	.233	.00
Gender	.05	.822	.00
Chanting Frequency	3.64	.061	.07
Total Var. Explained	3.55	.007	

Pearson R for this ANCOVA was .49 (Multiple R2= .24). Three t tests were performed to identify significant comparisons. Significant p values were found for the maha and alternate comparison (p= .014; CI for difference= [1.49, 10.70]) and the maha and control comparison (p= .002; CI for difference= [-9.70, -2.32]).

Using observed difference scores instead of partiallized difference scores, the results were essentially unchanged. With observed scores group status explained more of the variance, and chanting frequency explained less of the variance, compared with partiallized scores. Still, covariates, as a whole and individually

113

were not significant at the .05 level, and group status was significant, with both the maha-alternate and maha-control comparisons showing statistically significant comparisons.

Pretest-Followup Analysis of the Sattva Variable

Tests of Assumptions, Interaction and Outliers for Pretest-Followup Sattva Scores.

Analysis of residuals was performed for partiallized difference scores and observed difference scores for the pretest-followup analysis of the *sattva* variable. For both observed and partiallized scores there were 3 outliers, representing 4.84% of the 62 scores in each data set. Since this was less than the 5% of scores that would be expected by chance to have a standardized residual greater than 2, these outlying scores were retained for the ANCOVAs.

The p value for Bartlett's Box statistic for partiallized scores was .129, and for observed scores the p value was .112. These non-significant p values indicate that there is adequate homogeneity for the ANCOVA.

Linearity tests for Chanting Frequency and pretest-followup *sattva* scores produced a p value for a linear explanation of .000, and a p value for a nonlinear explanation of .894. For age charted against pretest-followup *sattva* scores the linearity p value was .050, and the nonlinear explanation produced a p value of .215. These results indicate that a linear explanation is a better fit for the data than a nonlinear explanation.

When observed difference scores were regressed on Age, the slope for the *maha mantra* group was .156, for the alternate mantra group the slope was .056, and for the control group the slope was .147. These similar slopes indicate a linear relationship and absence of interaction, and thus the linearity assumption for the ANCOVA was adequately satisfied.

ANCOVA Using Partiallized Pretest-Followup Difference Scores for Sattva.

Hypothesis 8 in the Methodology Chapter stated that the *maha mantra* group will show significantly decreased *sattva*, at the .05 level, from pretest to followup compared with the alternate group and the control group, though this decrease was hypothesized to be less than the decrease from pretest to posttest.Table 23 shows the results of a hierarchical ANCOVA, using observed difference scores, assessing the effects of group status on *sattva* from pretest to followup, with gender, age and chanting frequency as covariates. Effects of gender and age were calculated first, then chanting frequency was assessed, and then the effects of group status were analyzed.

Table 23

Results of ANCOVA Using Partiallized Pretest-Followup Sattva Difference Scores

Source of Variation	F	Sig. of F (p value)	Effect Size (Part Eta2)
Group Status	5.00	.010	.15
Age	.83	.367	.01
Gender	.24	.625	.01
Chanting Frequency	.78	.380	.11
Total Var. Explained	2.37	.051	

Pearson R for this ANCOVA was .42 (Multiple R2= .18). Although the p value for the F test for group status was significant at the .05 level (p = .010), the overall explained variance did not have a significant p value (p = .051). Apparently, the extra degrees of freedom supplied by the covariates, as well as their added standard error, diminished the explanatory ability of the model, which otherwise accounts for 18% of the variance in pretest-followup *sattva* scores. None of the covariates had a significant p value for the F test.

ANCOVA Using Observed Pretest-Followup Difference Scores for Sattva.

Using a hierarchical ANCOVA with observed difference scores, assessing the effects of group status on *sattva* from pretest to followup, with gender, age and chanting frequency as covariates, the p value for the F statistic for the variance explained for the entire model was .058, and for group status the p value was .504, neither of which are significant at the .05 level. Eta2 for group status was .131, and for chanting frequency eta2 was .102. Multiple R2 for the model was .145. These results show that the model as a whole did not explain variance in the dependent variable at a significant level.

Statistical Analysis of the Rajas Variable

Pretest-Posttest Analysis of Rajas

Tests of Assumptions, Interaction and Outliers for Pretest-Posttest Rajas Scores.

Residual analysis for partiallized difference pretest-posttest *rajas* scores resulted in 3 standardized residual values greater than 2. Since this represents only 4.84% of the values, the three outlying scores were retained for the ANCOVA. For observed scores there were 4 residuals, whose values were -2.00, 2.37, 2.52, and 2.11. Since none of these outliers had an absolute value greater than 2.52, they were retained for the ANCOVA.

Bartlett's Box statistic, F (2, 7601), produced a p value of .118 for partiallized values, and .176 for observed values, indicating that the distributions were adequately homoscedastistic for the ANCOVA.

A test assessing the appropriateness of a linear model for pretest-posttest *rajas* scores charted against chanting frequency values produced a p value of .002 for a linear model and .169 for a nonlinear model. For *rajas* scores charted against age values, a linear model produced a p value of .404, and a nonlinear model had a p value of .415. These results indicate that a linear model was the best fit for the data.

116

Observed pretest-posttest difference scores were regressed on the age variable to assess similarity of slopes. For the maha group the slope was -.207, for the Alternate Group the slope was .390, and for the control group the slope was .0568. Sheskin (1997) suggests that a difference in slopes between groups of more than .5 may be considered large. Therefore F tests were performed to determine whether the relationship between age and pretest-posttest *rajas* scores is best described as linear or quadratic. The p value (.709) for the quadratic F test was larger than the p value for the linear F test, and the quadratic model explained only 4% more variance than the linear model. A quadratic approximation therefore does not significantly add to the explanatory ability of the model, and therefore a linear model was utilized in the statistical analysis of *rajas*.

ANCOVA for Pretest-Posttest Rajas Scores Using Partiallized Differences.

Hypothesis 4 in the Methodology Chapter stated that the *maha mantra* group will show significantly decreased *rajas*, at the .05 level, from pretest to posttest compared with the Alternate Group and the control group. Using a hierarchical ANCOVA with partiallized difference scores, evaluating the effects of group status on *rajas* from pretest to posttest, with gender, age, and chanting frequency as covariates, the p value for the F statistic for the variance explained for the entire model was .061, and the p value for the effects of group status was .103.

ANCOVA for Pretest-Posttest Rajas Scores Using Observed Differences.

A hierarchical ANCOVA using observed difference scores for pretest-posttest *rajas* values, with gender, age, and chanting frequency as covariates, resulted in a p value for the F statistic for variance explained for the entire model of .053, and a p value for group status of .180. The p value for covariates as a whole was .032, though none of the covariates explained more than 3% of the variance. R2 for the model was .089.

Pretest-Followup Analysis of Rajas

Tests of Assumptions, Interaction and Outliers for Pretest-Followup Rajas Scores.

For partiallized scores there were 3 outliers, with values of 3.06, -2.47, and -2.39. Since the largest score was of opposite sign to the other two outliers, and 3 of 62 scores represented less than 5% of the total scores, these outliers were retained for the ANCOVA. For partiallized scores the Bartlett's Box p value was .083, indicating that the distribution was adequately homoscedastistic for the ANCOVA.

For observed scores there were also three outliers, with the highest value being of opposite sign to the other two values, and therefore the outliers were retained for the ANCOVA. The p value for Bartlett's Box statistic for observed pretest-followup *rajas* scores was .065, and thus the homoscedasticity assumption was satisfied.

Linearity tests showed that a linear explanation for the relationship between pretest-followup and Age had a p value of .514 for a linear approximation, and a p value of .536 for a nonlinear explanation. For chanting frequency scores charted against the independent variable, a linear explanation produced a p value of .419, and a nonlinear explanation had a p value of .849. When observed difference scores for each group for pretest-followup were regressed against age, the *maha mantra* group had a slope of .275, the alternate mantra group had a slope of -.017, and the control group had a slope of -.008. All these statistics provide evidence for the appropriateness of a linear model without interaction between age and group status.

ANCOVA for Pretest-Followup Rajas Scores Using Partiallized Differences.

Hypothesis 9 in the Methodology Chapter stated that the *maha mantra* group will show significantly decreased *rajas*, at the .05 level, from pretest to followup compared with the alternate group and the control group, though this decrease was hypothesized to be less than the decrease from pretest to posttest. Effects of group status on pretest-followup *rajas* scores were assessed using partiallized difference scores, with gender, age and chanting frequency as covariates. The p value for the F statistic for the variance explained by the entire model was .067, and the p value for group status was .058. The covariates as a whole had a p value of .120, though chanting frequency had a significant p value of .048. Multiple R2 for the model was .12.

ANCOVA for Pretest-Followup Rajas Scores Using Observed Differences.

Effects of group status on pretest-followup *rajas* scores were evaluated using observed difference scores, with gender, age and chanting frequency as covariates. This ANCOVA resulted in a p value for group status of .051, though the p value for overall explained variance was .116, indicating that the additional degrees of freedom and error from the covariates decreased the effectiveness of the model to explain the difference scores. Using observed difference scores, chanting frequency had a significant p value (.048) using partiallized scores, and a non-significant p value (.289) using observed scores. Also, with the observed scores ANCOVA the Multiple R2 for the model was less than with ANCOVA using partiallized scores.

Statistical Analysis of the Tamas Variable

Pretest-Posttest Analysis of Tamas

Tests of Assumptions, Interaction and Outliers for Pretest-Posttest Tamas Scores.

There were four standardized residuals with absolute values greater than 2 for partiallized pretest-posttest *tamas* scores. Since none of these scores had an absolute value greater than 2.37, these outlying scores were retained for the ANCOVA. For observed difference standardized residuals for pretest-posttest *tamas* scores there were 3 outliers, none of which had an absolute value greater than 2.52, and one of which had a value of -2.00. Therefore these values were retained for the

ANCOVA.

For partiallized scores, Bartlett's Box statistic, $F_{(2, 7601)}$, was .294, and for observed scores Bartlett's Box statistic, $F_{(2, 7601)}$, was .160. Both of these scores provide evidence that the homogeneity assumption was adequately satisfied for ANCOVA.

A linearity test of the relationship between pretest-posttest *tamas* scores and chanting frequency produced a p value of .002 for a linear explanation, and a p value of .236 for a nonlinear explanation. For the linearity test of the relationship between pretest-posttest *tamas* scores and age, the p value for a linear explanation was .243, and for a nonlinear explanation the p value was .611. These statistics provided evidence for a linear model.

Observed difference scores for each group for pretest-posttest *tamas* were regressed on the age variable. For the alternate mantra group the slope was -.294, for the *maha mantra* group the slope was .187, and for the control group the slope was -.062. These similar slopes across groups indicate a linear relationship.

ANCOVA Using Partiallized Pretest-Posttest Tamas Difference Scores

Hypothesis 5 in the Methodology Chapter stated that the *maha mantra* group will show significantly decreased *tamas*, at the .05 level, from pretest to posttest compared with the alternate group and the control group. An ANCOVA was performed assessing partiallized pretest-posttest difference scores for *tamas*, with gender, age and chanting frequency as covariates. In a hierarchical analysis, effects of gender and age were calculated first, then chanting frequency was evaluated, and then the effects of group status were analyzed. Table 24 shows the results of this analysis.

Table 24

Results of ANCOVA Using Partiallized Pretest-Posttest Tamas Difference Scores

Source of Variation	F	Sig. of F (p value)	Effect Size (Part Eta2)
Group Status	2.37	.013	.21
Age	1.68	.201	.00
Gender	.04	.839	.00
Chanting Frequency	8.94	.004	.07
Total Var. Explained	3.08	.016	

Pearson R for this ANCOVA was .46 (Multiple R2= .22). Three t tests were performed to identify significant comparisons. A significant p value was found for the maha and control comparison (p= .000; CI for difference= [3.69, 10.00]).

The results of the F test of the ANCOVA show that group status, controlling for the covariates, had a statistically significant effect on pretest-posttest *tamas* scores. Significance levels of the t tests demonstrated that the maha-control comparison was the only significant comparison, meaning that the difference between the *maha mantra* group and the control group was statistically significant, though the difference between the *maha mantra* group and the alternate mantra group was not significant, nor was the difference between the alternate mantra group and the control group. Group status accounted for 21% of the variance, and chanting frequency, which also had a significant p value (.004) for its F test, explained 7% of the variance. Gender and age did not have a statistically significant effect on the dependent variable.

ANCOVA Using Observed Difference Pretest-Posttest Tamas Scores.

An ANCOVA was performed assessing observed pretest-posttest difference scores for *tamas*, with gender, age and chanting frequency as covariates. In a hierarchical analysis, effects of gender and age were calculated first, then chanting frequency was evaluated, and then the effects of group status were analyzed. Table

25 shows the results of this analysis.

Table 25

Results of ANCOVA Using Observed Pretest-Posttest Tamas Difference Scores

Source of Variation	F	Sig. of F (p value)	Effect Size (Part Eta2)
Group Status	2.47	.044	.18
Age	1.69	.199	.00
Gender	.00	.950	.00
Chanting Frequency	8.30	.006	.07
Total Var. Explained	2.98	.019	

Pearson R for this ANCOVA was .46 (Multiple R2= .21). Three t tests were performed to identify significant comparisons. A significant p value was found for the maha and control comparison (p= .000; CI for difference= [3.79, 10.70]). Using observed difference scores for the ANCOVA, results are essentially the same as using partiallized scores for pretest-posttest *tamas* values.

Pretest-Followup Analysis of the Tamas Variable

Tests of Assumptions, Interaction and Outliers for Pretest-Followup Tamas Scores.

Standardized residuals for both partiallized and observed difference scores for pretest-followup *tamas* values both had 3 outliers, representing 4.84% of all scores. Since this was less than the percentage of standardized residuals that would be expected by chance to have values greater than 2, these outlying scores were retained for the ANCOVAs.

Bartlett's Box statistic, F (2, 7601), for partiallized scores had a p value of .135, and for observed scores the p value was .371, indicating that the distributions were adequately homoscedastistic for ANCOVA.

Linearity tests between pretest-followup *tamas* scores and chanting frequency produced a p value for a linear explanation of .078, and for a nonlinear model the p value was .394. For linearity tests between the dependent variable and age, a linear explanation produced a p value of .597, and a nonlinear explanation produced a p value of .659. These values indicate that a linear model was a better fit for the data, and that the linear assumption was sufficiently satisfied.

Difference scores for each group for pretest-followup *tamas* values were regressed on the age variable. For the *maha mantra* group the slope was -.213, for the alternate mantra group the slope was -.282, and for the control group the slope was -.021. These similar slopes across groups indicate a linear relationship and lack of interaction between age and group status.

ANCOVA Using Partiallized Pretest-Followup Tamas Difference Scores.

Hypothesis 10 in the Methodology Chapter stated that the *maha mantra* group will show significantly decreased *tamas*, at the .05 level, from pretest to followup compared with the Alternate Group and the control group, though this decrease was hypothesized to be less than the decrease from pretest to posttest. Using a hierarchical ANCOVA with partiallized difference scores, assessing the effects of group status on *tamas* from pretest to followup, with gender, age and chanting frequency as covariates, the p value for the F test for variance explained by the complete model was .054, and the p value for variance explained by group status was .116. For chanting frequency F had a significance level of .023, and the other covariates had non-significant p values at the .05 level. For covariates as a whole the p value was .137. Multiple R2 for the model was .175. Partial Eta2, or effect size, for chanting frequency, was 9%. These results indicate that neither group status nor the covariates as a whole had a significant effect on pretest-followup *tamas* scores using partiallized differences, though the effect of chanting frequency was significant.

ANCOVA Using Observed Pretest-Followup Tamas Difference Scores.

An ANCOVA using observed scores for pretest-followup *tamas* values resulted in an explained variance for the model with a p value of .044. Results of this ANCOVA are shown in Table 26.

Table 26

Results of ANCOVA Using Observed Pretest-Followup Tamas Difference Scores

Source of Variation	F	Sig. of F (p value)	Effect Size (Part Eta2)
Group Status	3.56	.035	.11
Age	.32	.574	.00
Gender	.08	.773	.01
Chanting Frequency	2.44	.124	.12
Total Var. Explained	1.99	.044	

Pearson R for this ANCOVA was .44 (Multiple R2= .19). Three t tests were performed to identify significant comparisons. A significant p value was found for the maha and control comparison (p= .017; CI for difference= [.07, 6.30]).

ANCOVA with observed difference scores for pretest-followup *tamas* values produced a p value for explained variance of the complete model of .044, which is significant at the .05 level, as opposed to the p value using partiallized scores (.054). Also, the p value for group status (.035) was statistically significant, compared with the nonsignificant p value (.116) using partiallized scores. Though chanting frequency had a statistically significant p value using partiallized scores, with observed differences the p value for chanting frequency was nonsignificant. Group status explained 11.3% of the variance using observed scores, and the only comparison that is significantly different for observed scores is Maha-Control.

Data Analytic Summary
of Independent Variables

Group Status

The main hypotheses of this experiment were that subjects in the *maha mantra* group will decrease their stress, depression, *rajas* and *tamas* more than subjects in the alternate mantra group and control group from pretest to posttest, and that the *maha mantra* group will increase *sattva* from pretest to posttest more than the other two groups. Statistical analyses, summarized in Table 27, reveal that for four of the five variables the hypotheses are valid at the .05 significance level. Specifically, the *maha mantra* group showed statistically significant greater differences from pretest to posttest for the variables of stress, depression, *tamas* and *sattva*. For stress, depression, and *sattva*, the *maha mantra* group showed significantly greater change than both the other groups, and for *tamas* the *maha mantra* group changed significantly more than the control group, though not significantly more than the alternate mantra group. In no instance where the effects of group status on the dependent variable were statistically significant did the alternate and control groups significantly differ. For pretest-posttest ANCOVA that produced significant results for group status, effect sizes for group status on the dependent variable ranged from .18 to .33, correlating to 18% to 33% of the variance (see Tables 15, 16, 17, 18, 21, 22, 24, and 25) .

Secondary hypotheses for this study included predictions that pretest-followup scores for the dependent variables would be effected by group status in the same way as pretest-posttest scores, though it was expected that there would be some reduction in the effect. For depression the effects of group status from pretest to followup were significant at the .05 level, though only for the maha-control comparison. The effects of group status for *sattva* from pretest to followup were also significant, though the overall explained variance of the model for pretest-followup was not significant at the .05 level. *Tamas* scores from pretest to followup showed significant changes for the group status variable, with the t test for the maha-control comparison being the only significant t test of the three comparisons.

For ANCOVAs resulting in statistically significant results for group status, effect sizes for group status ranged from .11 to .20, corresponding with 11% to 20% of the variance (see Tables 19, 20, 23, and 26). These effect sizes were smaller than for pretest-posttest analyses, as predicted by the hypotheses.

Table 27

Summary of Group Status Effects on the Dependent Variables

Hypothesis #[a]	Sig. or Nonsig. p Value[b]	Group Effect Size[c, d]	
Primary Hypotheses			
1 (Stress pre-post)	Significant	.33	
2 (Depression pre-post)	Significant		.21
3 (Sattva pre-post)	Significant	.23	
4 (Rajas pre-post)	Nonsignificant		
5 (Tamas pre-post)	Significant	.21	
Secondary Hypotheses			
6 (Stress pre-followup)	Nonsignificant		
7 (Depression pre-followup)	Significant	.12	
8 (Sattva pre-followup)	Significant[e, f]		.15
9 (Rajas pre-followup)	Nonsignificant		
10 (Tamas pre-followup)	Nonsignificant[g]		

[a]Hypothesis # refers to the numbers of the hypotheses given at the end of the methodology chapter (chapter 3).
[b]Significance is determined at a .05 level for partiallized difference values. Unless otherwise noted, observed difference values had the same result with regards to significance or non-significance.
[c]Effect sizes for non-significant p values are not shown.
[d]Effect size values for partiallized difference scores are given.
[e]The overall explained variance of the model had a non-significant p value.
[f]The observed difference value had a non-significant p value.
[g]The observed difference value had a significant p value and an effect size of .11.

Chanting Frequency

It was hypothesized that chanting frequency for the *maha mantra* group would correlate positively with *sattva*, and negatively with stress, depression, *rajas* and *tamas*. For the alternate group, chanting frequency was hypothesized to have no correlation with the dependent variables. As shown in Table 11, chanting frequency did correlate significantly with several of the alternate group dependent variables, and with none of the *maha mantra* group dependent variables.

For ANCOVAs where group status and explained variance of the complete model had significant F statistics, chanting frequency had statistically significant p values only for pretest-posttest and pretest-followup depression scores, and for pretest-posttest *tamas* scores. Effect sizes for chanting frequency in these computations ranged from .07 to .17, corresponding with 7% to 17% (see Tables 17, 18, 19, 20, 24, and 25).

Age

Age was predicted to have no effect on the dependent variables. For ANCOVAs that resulted in significant effects of the group status variable, age had a significant p value only for pretest-posttest stress and depression scores. For these ANCOVAs, the effect sizes of age on the dependent variables ranged from .01 to .06, corresponding with 1% to 6% (see Tables 15, 16, 17, and 18).

Gender

Gender was hypothesized to have no effect on the dependent variables. As described in the correlations of covariates section, gender did have five statistically significant correlations with the control group, which contained 10 females and 9 males. These correlations indicate that for the control group males had a greater predominance of *tamas* and females had a greater predominance of *sattva*. In none of the ANCOVAs for which group status had a significant effect on the dependent variables did gender have an F test with a significant p value.

General Comparison of Partiallized
and Observed Difference Scores

In assessment of the main hypotheses of this study (hypotheses 1-5, as listed in chapter 3), there were not substantial differences between the results derived from partiallized differences and those obtained from observed differences. In all five cases the two methods produced the same results, with regards to significance or non-significance of group status and overall explained variance. For the secondary hypotheses of this study (hypotheses 6-10), the two methods produced the same results, with regards to significance or non-significance, for pretest-followup analysis of stress, depression, and *rajas*, though the results differed in the analysis of *sattva* and *tamas*. Specifically, partiallized difference scores resulted in a significant pretest-followup *sattva* p value, while observed difference scores resulted in a non-significant p value, and for pretest-followup *tamas* analyses, partiallized scores resulted in a non-significant p value, and observed scores resulted in a significant p value. For the ten hypotheses, therefore, eight resulted in the same basic result with the two methods. Further, the two instances culminating in different results did not show a pattern of difference, indicating that the methods did not systematically differ in their end results.

For the four dependent variables for which group status had a significant effect for pretest-posttest, partiallized scores resulted in a larger effect size for group status in three out of four cases, with depression being the only dependent variable for which observed scores resulted in a larger effect size for group status. Also, for two ANCOVAs, pretest-followup depression and pretest-followup *rajas*, chanting frequency had a significant effect with partiallized scores, though not for observed scores. Further, there is a slight trend in the data for the effect sizes for the covariates to be higher using partiallized scores than using observed scores. Overall, these statistics suggest that partiallized differences resulted in a slightly more favorable analysis of the data, with regard to confirmation of the hypotheses.

As described earlier in this section, Cohen and Cohen (1983) point out that a partiallized difference score will tend to be less correlated with pretest scores than a non-partiallized difference score, and therefore they assert that partiallized differences are a more objective measure. Nunnally and Bernstein (1994), however, claim that partiallizing scores tends to produce spurious results and to erroneously treat the pretest score as if it were an error-free true score. They conclude, therefore, that observed scores are the best measure of change. With relation to the results of this study, pretest scores between dependent variables tended to vary greatly (see Tables 7-10). Therefore, the partiallized method, which standardizes pretest scores, may be the better choice for data analysis. To clarify, it is typically found that subjects with a relatively low pretest score will have larger gains at posttest than subjects with a relatively high pretest score. This is a manifestation of the statistical phenomenon of regression to the mean (Cohen & Cohen, 1983). In instances where pretest scores vary greatly, partiallizing difference scores adjusts for the regression to the mean, and therefore in such cases this advantage may outweigh the potential disadvantages of partiallizing difference score

CHAPTER 5

DISCUSSION

Evaluation of Hypotheses and Discussion of Results

At the beginning of the methodology chapter it was explained that the hypotheses of this investigation will be stated in terms of research hypotheses instead of null hypotheses, as supported by Agresti and Finlay (1986). This convention will be followed in this discussion chapter, although it is understood that, technically speaking, the statistical tests used to analyze the data of this experiment can only provide evidence for rejecting or not rejecting the null hypotheses, and cannot directly evaluate the validity of the alternative, or research, hypotheses.

Hypothesis 1: The maha mantra group will show significantly decreased stress from pretest to posttest compared with the alternate mantra group and with the control group at the .05 level of significance.

This hypothesis was confirmed by the statistical analysis of the previous chapter. The maha mantra group decreased stress levels more than both of the other two groups, and effect sizes for group status on stress from pretest to posttest, 33% for partiallized values and 25% for observed values, are large according to Rosenthal (1997).

According to Vedic theory, chanting the maha mantra causes a person to decrease stress and anxiety (Dasa, 1994). Thus, the results of this study, in regards to hypothesis 1, support Vedic *guna* theory.

In behavioral terms, chanting the *hare krsna maha mantra* may have served as an effective positive replacement thought for stressful thoughts. According to Spiegler and Guevremont (1993), a common behavioral technique to reduce stress is to disrupt distressing thoughts and replace them with a competing, positive cognition. This stress-reduction technique has been successful in many environments, for diverse purposes and with several populations, including traumatology (Berk, 1998; Foa, 1997), rape victims (Foa, 1997), self-esteem development (Joiner & Sawyer, 1992), and post-traumatic stress disorder (Miller & Basoglu, 1991). According to the Vedas, the sound vibration of the *hare krsna maha mantra* can affect the mind to abandon stressful thoughts. Therefore, the results of this experiment with regard to hypothesis 1 are consistent with explanations based in behavioral and *guna* theory.

Hypothesis 2: The maha mantra group will show significantly decreased depression from pretest to posttest compared with the alternate mantra group and with the control group at the .05 level of significance.

This hypothesis is supported by the statistical analysis in the previous chapter. The maha mantra group decreased depression levels more than both of the other two groups, and effect sizes for group status on depression from pretest to posttest, 21% for partiallized values and 25% for observed values, are large according to Rosenthal (1997), and represent a strong association between the variables.

Srimad-Bhagavatam (Prabhupada, 1976) hypothesizes that the *hare krsna maha mantra* affects the mind to abandon depressing thoughts. Results of this study, therefore, support *guna* theory in relation to Hypothesis 2.

As described above in relation to stress, behavioral techniques such as thought stopping and thought replacement are also effectively used to treat depression (e.g., Albano and Morris, 1998; Freeston, Ladouceur, Provencher, and Blais, 1995). In such approaches, persons who habitually think depressing thoughts, such as "I'm worthless", train themselves to replace these thoughts with thoughts that are rewarding and supportive of self-esteem. From a Vedic viewpoint, the sound vibration of the *hare krsna maha mantra* provides fulfillment for the mind that takes the place of depressing thoughts. Therefore, the results of this study in regards to depression are consistent with *guna* and behavioral theory.

Hypothesis 3: The maha mantra group will show significantly increased *sattva* from pretest to posttest compared with the alternate mantra group and with the control group at the .05 level of significance.

This hypothesis is supported by the results of this study. The maha mantra group increased its *sattva* level significantly more than the alternate mantra group and more than the control group. Effect sizes for group status on *sattva* from pretest to posttest were .23 for partiallized scores and .18 for observed scores. According to Rosenthal (1997) this indicates a medium to large effect size and a moderate to strong association between the variables. The results of this experiment in connection with hypothesis 3 can be understood in relation to the Vedic assertion that the maha mantra is predominantly in *sattva guna*. The alternate mantra, according to the Vedas, is not in *sattva guna*.

Hypothesis 4: The maha mantra group will show significantly decreased *rajas* from pretest to posttest compared with the alternate mantra group and with the control group at the .05 level of significance.

This hypothesis is not supported by the statistical analysis of the previous chapter. No group showed a statistically significant change in *rajas* scores from pretest to posttest compared with either of the other groups.

From Vedic theory it can be understood that the formulation of hypothesis 4 may be faulty. As described above, the Vedas suggest that chanting the *hare krsna maha mantra* may transform *rajasic* and *tamasic* qualities into *sattvic* qualities. However, the Vedas also indicate that chanting the maha mantra will transform *tamasic* qualities into *rajasic* qualities. That is, Vedic teachings describe a progression from *tamas* to *sattva*, with *rajas* in the middle. Therefore, while some *rajasic* qualities are replaced by *sattvic* qualities, some *tamasic* qualities are transformed into *rajasic* attributes, and therefore the overall level of *rajas* is maintained. By continued chanting of the *hare krsna maha mantra*, according to the Srimad-Bhagavatam (Prabhupada, 1976), all *rajas* and *tamas* will be replaced by *sattva*. This study, however, entailed chanting the maha mantra for only one month, and thus a possible explanation could be that the full effects of the mantra were not allowed to take place, resulting in *tamasic* qualities transforming into *rajasic* qualities without *sattva* becoming prominent. For instance, the indolence of *tamas* may convert to the frenetic activity of *rajas*, before ultimately transforming into the calm determination of *sattva*.

Hypothesis 5: The maha mantra group will show significantly decreased *tamas* from pretest to posttest compared with the alternate mantra group and with the control group at the .05 level of significance.

This hypothesis is partially supported by the results of this experiment. The maha mantra group decreased pretest-posttest *tamas* scores significantly more than the control group, though not significantly more than the alternate mantra group. Effect sizes for group status on pretest-posttest *tamas* scores were 21% for partiallized scores and 18% for observed scores. Effects of this magnitude are medium to large, indicating a moderate to strong association between the variables (Rosenthal, 1997). Differences between the alternate and control groups for pretest-posttest *tamas* values were not statistically significant.

Tamas is characterized by a lack of determination, regulation and discipline. Persons predominated by *tamas guna* have difficulty fulfilling their responsibilities and gaining control over their life (Prabhupada, 1976). It may be conjectured that the regulated activity of chanting three *japa* rounds every day caused members of the alternate mantra group to reduce their level of *tamas*. That is, although the alternate mantra is not composed of *sattvic* vibrations, the disciplined act of chanting every day had the effect of increasing *sattva* sufficiently for the difference between the two chanting groups to not be statistically significant.

Secondary Hypotheses

Hypothesis 6: The maha mantra group will show significantly decreased stress from pretest to followup compared with the alternate mantra group and with the control group at the .05 level of significance, though some diminishing of effects compared with pretest-posttest is expected.

Hypothesis 7: The maha mantra group will show significantly decreased depression from pretest to followup compared with the alternate mantra group and with the control group at the .05 significance level, though some diminishing of effects compared with pretest-posttest is expected.

Hypothesis 8: The maha mantra group will show significantly increased *sattva* from pretest to followup compared with the alternate mantra group and with the control group at the .05 significance level, though some diminishing of effects compared with pretest-posttest is expected.

Hypothesis 9: The maha mantra group will show significantly decreased *rajas* from pretest to followup compared with the alternate mantra group and with the control group at the .05 level of significance, though some diminishing of effects compared with pretest-posttest is expected.

Hypothesis 10: The maha mantra group will show significantly decreased *tamas* from pretest to followup compared with the alternate mantra group and with the control group at the .05 significance level, though some diminishing of effects compared with pretest-posttest is expected.

None of these secondary hypotheses were fully confirmed by the results of this study, though hypothesis 7 and hypothesis 10 were partially confirmed. For pretest-followup depression and *tamas* scores the maha mantra group showed a statistically significant decrease in depression and *tamas* compared with the control group, though not compared with the alternate mantra group. In none of the pretest-followup comparisons did the alternate mantra group differ significantly from the control group. For *tamas* only the observed difference ANCOVA produced significant effects for group status, with group status accounting for 11% of the variance, which according to Rosenthal (1997) represents a moderate association between the variables and a medium effect size. For pretest-followup depression values effect sizes were 12% for partiallized scores and 20% for observed scores, representing a medium to large effect size (Rosenthal).

Vedic theory suggests that when one withdraws from the association of the *hare krsna maha mantra* or any *sattvic* influence, the effects of *sattva* will diminish, and effects of *rajas* and *tamas*, such as stress, lust, greed and depression, will reappear. Therefore the Vedas recommend that one remain constantly in *sattvic* association. Pretest-followup results of this experiment indicate that the effects of one month of chanting the maha mantra did diminish after a one month followup period in which no chanting was performed. However, as evidenced by depression and *tamas* scores, some effects did remain, though the effect sizes for these variables were less than the effects for the pretest-posttest period, as predicted by

Vedic theory. It should be noted that the Vedas claim that depression is a symptom of *tamas*, and therefore the two pretest-followup variables that retained significant effects are theorized to be related. Providing evidence for this relationship is the significant correlation (r= .51; p= .000) between pretest-followup depression scores and pretest-followup *tamas* scores.

From a behavioral perspective it can be understood that effects diminish when positive thoughts are discontinued. Thus, for example, it can be conjectured that stressful thoughts again became prominent for subjects when they ceased to chant the *hare krsna maha mantra* .

Hypothesis 11: Gender will have no effect on any of the dependent variables at a .05 significance level.

When ANCOVAs resulted in a significant group status effect, gender did not have a significant effect on the dependent variable. Therefore hypothesis 11 was supported. When group status had a significant effect on the dependent variable, the non-significant effect sizes associated with gender never had an effect size greater than 1%. Therefore it can be concluded that gender did not substantially effect the dependent variables, though including gender as a controlled variable in this study successfully removed the effects of gender as an unknown and uncontrolled source of variation, thus adding to the explanatory strength of the group status results. The correlations of covariates section of the results and data analysis chapter shows that for the control group gender did have 5 significant correlations, indicating that gender and the *gunas* may not be completely unrelated. In psychometric research on the VPI (Wolf, 1998) it was also found that gender was not completely neutral in relation to the *gunas*, with higher *sattva* scores for females and higher *tamas* scores for males.

Hypothesis 12: Age will have no effect on any of the dependent variables at a .05 significance level.

Age had a significant p value for pretest-posttest stress and depression scores, though the largest effect size for age among all the ANCOVA analyses was 6%, which was for pretest-posttest partiallized difference scores for stress. Pearson r for age correlated with pretest-posttest stress difference scores was -.26 (r2= .07), and r for age correlated with pretest-posttest depression difference scores was

136

-.25 (r2= .06). These correlations, along with the significant p values for the F tests mentioned above, demonstrate that older participants decreased their stress and depression from pretest to posttest more than younger participants. As described in the correlations of covariates section of the previous chapter, age did not significantly correlate with any of the pretest, posttest or followup scores for any of the three groups for any of the dependent variables. Overall, ANCOVAs indicate that age did have some effect on some of the variables, contrary to hypothesis 12, and controlling for age in the statistical analysis increases the explanatory strength of the group status analyses.

Hypothesis 13: Chanting frequency for the maha mantra group will be positively correlated, at the .05 significance level, with dependent variables in the same direction that the maha mantra group is related with the dependent variables. That is, increased chanting frequency for the maha mantra group will correlate with increased *sattva* and decreased stress, depression, *rajas* and *tamas*. Chanting frequency for the alternate mantra group will have no correlation at the .05 significance level with any of the dependent variables.

Out of the six analyses resulting in significant p values for group status effects, chanting frequency had significant p values for three of the analyses. These three were pretest-posttest depression, pretest-posttest *tamas*, and pretest-followup depression (for partiallized scores only). For the observed difference pretest-posttest depression ANCOVA, chanting frequency had an effect size of 17%, which was the highest of the effect sizes for chanting frequency. For some analyses chanting frequency had a medium or even large effect size, but the p value for the F test was not significant. For instance, for partiallized pretest-posttest stress scores chanting frequency had an effect size of 8%, and the p value was .581, for observed differences pretest-followup depression scores chanting frequency had an effect size of 16%, and the p value was .106, for observed differences pretest-posttest *sattva* difference scores chanting frequency had an effect size of 7%, with a p value of .061, for partiallized pretest-followup differences for *sattva* chanting frequency had an effect size of 11% and a p value of .380, and for observed differences pretest-followup *tamas* scores chanting frequency had an effect size of 12% and a p value of .124. These noteworthy effects with non-significant p values suggest that a study with a larger sample size, and thus greater power, might detect more significant differences with chanting frequency in relation to the dependent variables.

Also, in some cases chanting frequency had a significant p value, though the effects of group status were not significant. For example, the observed differences pretest-followup stress analysis resulted in an effect size of 16% for chanting frequency, with a p value of .004, and the p value for chanting frequency in the pretest-followup partiallized differences *rajas* scores was .048. When group status did not have a significant effect on the dependent variable, thorough analysis of effects of chanting frequency were not particularly relevant, even if chanting frequency had a significant p value, because it is not especially consequential to discuss effects of chanting frequency if the overall effects of chanting were found to be nonsignificant.

Table 11 shows that chanting frequency significantly correlated with several of the alternate group dependent variable scores, and with none of the maha mantra group dependent variables. This means that in the ANCOVAs with a significant chanting frequency p value, the effects were more prominent for the alternate group than for the maha mantra group, contrary to hypothesis 13. Apparently there was some placebo effect in this study, as dependent variables were effected by changes in chanting frequency of the alternate mantra group, although, as described in the section in this chapter entitled major hypotheses, in no case did the alternate and control groups significantly differ in pretest-posttest or pretest-followup differences in dependent variables.

According to Vedic theory, increased chanting of the *hare krsna maha mantra* will correspond to increased effects of the mantra (Prabhupada, 1976). In this experiment all subjects were instructed to chant three rounds of *japa* every day, and the actual range of chanting frequency for the maha mantra group was 2.46 to 3.00. It is suggested that this range is not adequate to obtain a true picture of the effects of chanting frequency. A range of 1 round per day to 30 rounds per day, with groups instructed to chant different numbers of rounds per day than other groups, would be more appropriate for a study of chanting frequency effects.

Also, it should be noted that although all of the groups began with equal numbers of subjects, the maha mantra group retained 24 members, while the other two groups each retained 19 members. Cook and Campbell (1979) note that when the treatment group keeps more members than other groups, it may be regarded as evidence of the hypothesis that the treatment is effective. That is, the comparative group dropout results of this study suggest that participants derived more value from the maha mantra, and therefore they were more likely to remain in the maha mantra group compared with the other two groups.

Limitations of the Study

Rosenthal (1997) explains that generalizability of a study is the degree to which similar findings will be observed in a different context or setting. As this study did not employ random sampling, the sampling method of the experiment does not allow statistical generalization to any population other than the 62 subjects who participated in the study. However, generalizability of a study also contains a qualitative component, requiring the researcher or practitioner to apply his/her expertise in an area to determine the degree of similarity of contexts. Therefore, a practitioner or researcher desiring to assess this study for applicability can evaluate the similarity of the participants and setting of this study to the context in which s/he wishes to apply the techniques and findings. Generalizability of course is enhanced or reduced by replication studies, none of which have yet been performed for the *hare krsna maha mantra* .

Another deficiency of this study in regards to generalizability is reactive effects of the pretest, which was not resolved with the experimental design utilized in this investigation. The effects of the pretest may have affected subjects in such a way that they were no longer representative of any larger population, and thus the effects of the interventions may only apply to those who completed such a pretest, and not to others (Royse, 1995).

Bracht and Glass (1968) explain that external validity, or generalizability, of a design can be divided into two categories- population validity and ecological validity. Population validity refers to the ability to make inferential leaps to a larger population, and the major threat in this experiment to population validity is lack of random sampling, and another threat is reactivity to pretests. Bracht and Glass describe novelty effects as an additional threat to population validity, and this may be a defect in the representativeness of this experiment. Specifically, the effects of chanting may have to some degree been caused by the novelty of the experience. If this is the case, then after the novelty effect wears off, the effects of the chanting process can be expected to diminish. Thus, the results may not apply to a general population, but only to the studied population in which the novelty effects were active.

Ecological validity refers to the degree to which the experimental effect is independent of the experimental environment. In this study, the Hawthorne effect, referring to the subjects' knowledge that they were participating in an experiment, may have been active, thus decreasing the generalizability of the findings (Bracht and Glass, 1968).

Bracht and Glass (1968) also describe experimenter effects as a threat to ecological validity. In this study the researchers were aware of the group status of each participant, and therefore experimenter effects must be considered. That is, the researchers were part of the setting of the experiment, and it is possible that different results would be achieved with different researchers, and this was a shortcoming in the ecological validity of the study. Specifically, the researchers may have behaved one way towards members of one group, and differently towards members of another group, thereby causing effects that are not directly attributable to any of the independent variables in the design. The design of this study attempted to control for experimenter effects by standardizing the training of each researcher to ensure consistent presentation to all members of each group of subjects.

While acknowledging the threat of experimenter effects to ecological validity, overemphasis on the effectiveness of double-blind studies must also be avoided. In the field of medical research, for instance, there is evidence that a physician's beliefs can alter the results of double-blind studies. For example, Dossey (1993) describes double-blind studies of the use of vitamin E in treating angina pectoris. In a double-blind study involving an enthusiastic doctor who believed in vitamin E the treatment was found to be more effective than a placebo, while two double-

140

blind studies conducted by skeptics showed no effect. Many analyses of drug research development show similar results, with enthusiasts arriving at opposite conclusions to skeptics, both using double-blind studies. Regarding the drug meprobamate, Dossey writes "Overall, therefore, three of the four meprobamate studies suggested strongly that the effectiveness of the drug over the placebo was correlated with the physician's attitudes and beliefs toward it, and that the beliefs of the prescribing physician can somehow penetrate the double-blind conditions of the experiment and shape the action of the drug" (p. 136). After reviewing many double-blind studies in the fields of medicine, neuropsychopharmacology, and psychiatry, Solfvin (1984) concluded "Studies with a wide variety of treatments have conclusively affirmed that the administering physician or researcher is not independent of the results in double-blind treatment effectiveness studies...As a general rule, the double-blind cannot any longer be assumed to guarantee the exclusion of the nonspecific effects of the treatment, especially when the actual treatment has a weak or variable effect." (p. 56). Still, double-blind replication studies conducted by researchers with a different world view than this author will surely add valuable information to the body of literature on the *hare krsna maha mantra* .

Another drawback to this investigation is that it did not involve a clinical sample. Therefore, practical significance of the statistically significant findings is difficult to determine. For instance, if the *hare krsna maha mantra* was tested with persons diagnosed with anxiety disorders or depressive disorders, then the results would indicate whether subjects improved sufficiently to tangibly enhance daily functioning, and whether the intervention effectively impacted the disorder. Lacking a clinical sample, interpretation of clinical or practical significance is limited to analysis of the reported effect sizes, and cannot be directly generalized to clinical settings.

When considering these shortcomings in the generalizability of the study, there should also be consideration of Mook's (1983) contention that generalizability is often overemphasized, and that it is important to realize that generalizability is sometimes not the prime intent of the experiment. Mook points out that important phenomena such as biofeedback could never have been discovered by sampling or mimicking natural settings, but only through laboratory experiments with a very controlled setting. Applying this idea to the current investigation, the fact that the study indicates that chanting the *hare krsna maha mantra* worked to some degree with the tested population has significance in itself, despite the lack of formal generalizability inherent in the design.

Royse (1995) explains that internal validity of a design assesses whether an intervention was truly responsible for the observed differences in the experimental group. Experimenter effects, described above in regards to ecological validity, were also an internal validity shortcoming of this study. That is, it is unclear to what extent the design detected the effects of the maha mantra on the dependent variables, or the effects of the researchers' influence on the subjects.

Though the random assignment of this study addressed some threats to internal validity, such as history and maturation, other threats, such as diffusion and resentful demoralization of respondents receiving less desirable treatments, were not resolved by random assignment. Though the study was designed so that researchers met individually with subjects, rather than in a large group, there were still a few roommate pairs, and they may have communicated with each other about effects they were experiencing, thus creating the shortcoming of diffusion. Also, it is possible that some subjects felt disappointed that they were not in a particular group, and the dependent measures may have assessed this disappointment, which compromises the validity of the study. Additionally, though the selection threat to internal validity is usually not a factor in studies utilizing random assignment, analysis of the pretest data of this study indicates that randomization may have been ineffective in creating group equality. Therefore it is possible that there were different kinds of people in the groups, which makes the design more like a quasi-experimental design rather than an experimental design, though the statistical procedures applied in the previous chapter are applicable to quasi-experimental designs. Related to selection, there may be other threats to the internal validity of this study, such as interactive effects of selection and history, and selection and maturation (Cook & Campbell, 1979).

With regards to procedures for random assignment, it should be noted that randomization was performed before pretest. Twelve subjects left the study after random assignment and before the pretest was administered. These 12 were not equally divided between the groups. Alternatively, randomization could have been performed after pretest, to ensure equal numbers of subjects in each group at the beginning of intervention. Logistical considerations did not allow randomization after pretest in this study. Specifically, time constraints related to schedules of the research team and of many of the subjects who were university students, prevented the scheduling of an additional meeting after pretest specifically for introduction of the intervention. Therefore, randomization had to be performed before pretest, and thus the pretest meeting also served as the first day of the intervention. This ordering of random assignment before pretest may be regarded as a procedural shortcoming and could be related to pretest group inequalities.

Though setting factors generally relate to external validity, there is a setting consideration of this study that is connected with internal validity. Meetings between researchers and subjects were sometimes held in a public place, such as the main plaza on the university campus, and sometimes in the home of the subject or the office of the researcher, depending on practicality and convenience of the research team member and subject. The salient point is that meeting place was not controlled in this study, and all three research team members noted that subjects seemed to respond best when the meeting was held in their home, and subjects seemed least comfortable when meetings were held in public. Thus, effects of meeting place may not be equally distributed across groups.

The factors of the timing of random assignment and uncontrolled settings may be related to pretest inequalities that were found in four of eight variables, including four of five of the dependent variables. Also, these pretest inequalities may indicate that unknown, uncontrolled variables affected pretest scores. This is a shortcoming of the study, though the ANCOVA statistical procedure, especially when pretest scores are partiallized, tends to neutralize the effects of pretest inequalities.

Concerning internal validity, it should be noted that the alternate mantra had the same syllabic pattern as the *maha mantra*. This controlled for the effects of syllabic pattern, and helped to isolate the effects of the mantras themselves.

Power of the statistical tests used in this study was sufficient to detect differences that supported four out of five of the major hypotheses, as well as some of the secondary hypotheses. However, analyses in this study that were found nonsignificant at the .05 level include p values such as .096, .061, .058, .056, .054, .053, and even .051. Therefore, it is reasonable to conclude that greater power, achieved by a larger sample size (Orme and Combs-Orme, 1986), may have detected a greater number of significant differences than were found in this experiment. For instance, the maha mantra group decreased pretest-posttest *tamas* scores significantly more than the control group, though not significantly more than the alternate mantra group, though the decrease in *tamas* scores for the maha mantra group was greater than the decrease for the alternate mantra group (see Table 25). This lack of a significant finding may be due to an inadequate sample size and consequent deficiency in statistical power. With regards to chanting frequency, the discussion of hypothesis 13 earlier in this chapter reports that for some analyses chanting frequency had a medium or even large effect size (Rosenthal, 1997), although the p value was not significant. This suggests that with a larger sample size there may have been a greater number of significant relationships discovered between chanting frequency and dependent variables.

Clinical Significance and Application of Techniques

Since this experiment did not involve a clinical sample, a main call to action of the findings is to research the *hare krsna mantra* in a clinical setting, such as with a sample of clients experiencing depressive, stress-related or anxiety-based disorders. Clinical studies have not yet been conducted with the maha mantra, though there are a few practitioners, such as the author, with some experience in using the maha mantra with clients.

If a practitioner wishes to try the technique of chanting the *hare krsna maha mantra* with a client, it is important that the client feels comfortable with the method and voluntarily agrees to practice the mantra. The practitioner can demonstrate how to chant the maha mantra according to the description provided in the procedures section of the methodology chapter. As many other interventions of Eastern origin have been incorporated into the mental health professions, the *hare krsna maha mantra* can also be presented as potentially effective therapy, without reference to sectarian conceptions.

Applications of the *hare krsna maha mantra* can include the same target problems that many other yoga, mantra and meditational techniques have been effective in treating. This *japa* study specifically dealt with stress and depression, both of which have been treated with various Eastern-style techniques. The spiritual intervention articles section of chapter two describes several studies reporting effective use of yoga, mantras and meditation in the treatment of stress and depression. Janowiak and Hackman (1994) found that meditation is effective in relieving stress, and Kaye (1985) successfully used mantra therapy to relieve depression and anxiety in an elderly population. Pearl and Carlozzi (1994) and Miller, Fletcher, and Kabat-Zinn (1995) found that Eastern-style interventions are effective in reducing stress, and Kutz et al. (1985) discovered that meditational techniques are effective as an adjunct to psychotherapy in relieving depression and anxiety. The literature reviews of Delmonte (1983) and Delmonte and Kenny (1985) concluded that mantras and meditation are effective in reducing anxiety and drug abuse, and also in improving physiological indicators. Though Delmonte found that a mock mantra is as effective as any other mantra, the results of this *japa* study indicate that the maha mantra produces desirable effects that an alternate, or mock mantra does not generate.

Many other studies also support the use of Eastern-style interventions in treating stress and depression, and, combined with the findings of this study, they support the experimental use of the *hare krsna maha mantra* for alleviating stress and depression. Wardlaw (1994) effectively used yoga techniques to treat stress-related symptoms such as bruxism. Khumar, Kaur, and Kaur (1993) successfully treated clinically depressed college students with yoga methods. Joseph (1998) asserts that throughout the mental health fields there is growing interest in yoga techniques as a stress reliever. The results of this study indicate that the maha mantra is a yogic method that should be tried with problems related to stress and depression.

Stress is often regarded as the underlying factor in substance abuse and addictions (Ellis and Corum, 1994), which points to other potential uses for the maha mantra. Many researchers and practitioners, such as Kremer, Malkin, and Benshoff (1995), Alexander, Robinson, and Rainforth (1995), Karel (1993, and Sands (1994), have been successful in using mantras and other yoga techniques in the prevention and treatment of substance abuse. According to Vedic theory, substance abuse is indicative of *tamas guna*, and this study indicates that the maha mantra decreased the level of *tamas guna*. A. C. Bhaktivedanta Swami Prabhupada (1976) suggests in the Srimad-Bhagavatam that chanting the *hare krsna maha mantra* is specifically effective for prevention and treatment of drug abuse. Eastern-style interventions have been efficacious in many other ways also, including development of empathy and prevention of stress and burnout in mental health professionals (e.g., Karel, 1993; Shapiro, Schwartz, and Bonner, 1998; Keefe, 1996), treatment of anxiety disorders with a clinical population diagnosed with panic disorder and generalized anxiety (Kabat-Zinn, Massion, Kristeller, & Peterson, 1992), treatment of phobias (Snaith, Owens, & Kennedy, 1992), trauma intervention (Urbanowski & Miller, 1996), treatment of asthma (Lane, 1994), and treatment of posttraumatic stress disorder (Canda & Phaobtong, 1992).

Vaisnavas, adherents of Vedic culture and philosophy, have been chanting the *hare krsna maha mantra* and utilizing other techniques described in the Vedas for many of the above purposes for centuries. Rangaswami (1996) explains that meditation, mantras and yoga are an integral part of the Indian system of psychotherapy. Canda and Phaobtong (1992) describe meditational techniques specifically implemented for treatment of posttraumatic stress disorder among Buddhist refugees. Similarly, a person experiencing a crisis or severe anxiety from any source can be guided to chant the *hare krsna maha mantra* for alleviation of stress and development of *sattvic* symptoms, such as serenity and contentment. Of course, as described above, the counselor must be confident that this technique is appropriate for the particular client, and that the client consents to practice the method.

Relevance to Social Work

Keefe (1996) describes social work applications of Eastern-style interventions in treating depression, substance abuse, and excessive anxiety. Further, he asserts that these techniques are potentially important in development of social work skills in professional training. Canda (1988) claims that there are many meditative practices that have not yet been applied in social work. Meditation on the *hare krsna maha mantra* is one of these techniques, and social workers with an inclination towards innovation and who feel comfortable with Eastern-style mantra meditation can apply this technique to help clients with stress, depression, and related problems.

Social workers are active in many fields, and yoga techniques are becoming increasingly popular in these fields. For example, medical social workers can note that Derr, Shaikh, Rosen, and Guadagnimo (1998) surveyed medical students and found that a majority of the students identified yoga as a beneficial complementary therapeutic technique. Cormier and Cormier (1997) describe yoga as an important and effective skill for mental health professionals utilizing behavioral interventions. Many hospice workers are trained and educated as social workers, and spirituality has been found to be an important component in hospice work (Millison, 1995). According to the Vedas, chanting the maha mantra is a spiritual activity, based in *sattva guna*, or *suddha sattva*. For centuries Vaisnavas have chanted the *hare krsna maha mantra* to deal with issues of death and dying. By becoming conversant in techniques such as chanting the *hare krsna maha mantra*, social workers can add a useful tool to their repertoire of skills that can be implemented in diverse settings with various populations.

Cultural diversity is a key element of the social work profession (National Association of Social Workers, 1990), and this entails respecting the world view and practices of cultures different from that of the social worker. In dealing with psychological issues, social workers should understand that Western paradigms may not be applicable for explicating and comprehending the psychology of indigenous peoples (Gergen, Gulerce, Lock, and Misra, 1996). Laungani (1993), in his examination of differences in cultural perspectives on stress, emphasized that in India people have been relying on yoga and mantra techniques to relieve stress long before the development of Western psychology. Familiarity with these techniques, such as chanting the *hare krsna maha mantra* will help social workers to appreciate and effectively work with persons from different backgrounds. Also, by incorporating methods from a different tradition, adherents of that tradition in the West will feel supported and validated, as individuals and as an ethnic group. Such multicultural upliftment is an important aspect of the mission of social work (National Association of Social Workers, 1990).

Though the maha mantra can be applied in a behavioral context, it is, according to the Vedas, a spiritual approach to psychological and social health. As described from the beginning of this dissertation, there is a need for social workers to explore spirituality and spiritually-based interventions more than they do at present (Canda, 1988). Lloyd (1997) urges social workers to broaden their perspective to incorporate the spiritual dimension of life, and he emphasizes that a spiritual perspective is especially important in social work surrounding issues of death and dying. Diagnostic and Statistical Manual of Mental Disorders-IV (American Psychiatric Association, 1994) includes spiritual problems as a focus of clinical attention, and this has raised the awareness of mental health professionals regarding the importance of considering a person's spiritual values in psychosocial development. Among helping professionals social workers are especially known for considering all dimensions of persons and problems. Jacobs (1997) concluded that attending to the spirituality of helping situations invites social workers to expand their personal and professional boundaries. Considering this, there is clearly benefit for social workers to learn and teach spiritual techniques such as chanting the *hare krsna maha mantra*, when it is compatible with the world view of the client.

Bullis (1996) asserts that, philosophically, both social workers and spirituality promote common interests and self-respect. Social work and spiritual professionals have similar goals, such as personal healing and alleviation of community strife, violence and ignorance. Bullis claims that spirituality offers social workers a way of transformation for their clients, and he offers several suggestions for spiritually-based assessment and interventions in social work practice. He recommends

148

that meditation and prayer be incorporated in social work interventions, and the *hare krsna maha mantra* is a type of meditation and prayer (Goswami, 1977). Bullis writes "...meditation or deep prayer is a safe, fun, and effective way to access the spiritual dimensions" (p. 62). Further, he states, "...social work should abandon the strictly physical cosmology in favor of a post-positive, spiritual cosmology...the great divorce between social work and spirituality is inauthentic and unsupportable. Clients who have a desire, articulated or not, to have their spiritual concerns addressed, deserve to be heard by a competent and thorough professional" (p. 145, 163).

Suggestions for Further Research

Bullis (1996) contends that the spiritual dimension is not well understood in the social work profession, and that much research needs to be conducted on spiritual assessment and intervention. Considering this, further research can be conducted on the VPI (Wolf, 1998) as a tool for assessment and evaluation in social work, and on the maha mantra as an intervention.

Path analysis is a statistical method for determining causal relationships (Agresti & Finlay, 1986), and this technique could be applied to research on the VPI (Wolf, 1998) and the maha mantra. Whereas the current study indicates several relationships of association between variables, path analysis could examine more deeply whether these relationships are causal. Even with the data of this maha mantra study path analysis could be applied in order to glean further information. For instance, each *guna* subscale of the VPI is composed of several attributes, with each attribute derived from the Bhagavad-gita (Prabhupada, 1972) and presented as an item or items on the subscale. The *sattva* subscale, for example, contains items on satisfaction, preferred foods, view towards violence, cleanliness, spirituality, intelligence, willpower, verbal gentleness, self-control, and dutifulness. Responses on each item could be averaged and causal relationships with dependent variables could be assessed through path analysis. This could potentially reveal much useful information about the detailed effects of the maha mantra, and also about the components of the VPI subscales. Path analysis involves explicitly defining the presumed causal relationships, and this will necessitate the researcher delving further into Vedic theory to ascertain hypothetical relationships. As an example, a fairly intricate theoretical relationship between the three *gunas* is described above in the discussion on hypothesis 4. This relationship can be tested with the VPI (Wolf) and path analysis.

Nugent (1996) describes the integration of single-system design and group-comparison methods using the Hierarchical Linear Models (HLM) analytical method. HLM allows the researcher to aggregate data from single-case and group designs, thereby minimizing, to some extent, the drawbacks of both approaches. With single-case experiments, for instance, it is generally difficult to analyze data for purposes of generalizability, due to lack of effective statistical methods that can be used with a small number of subjects. With group designs there are usually a very small number of data points for each subject, and therefore much information about each individual subject is lost. Thus, the dynamic nature of subject responses often goes unnoticed with group designs. In this dissertation both a single-system design and a group design examining the maha mantra are described. Consequently, the data from these experiments may be ideally suited for HLM.

Future *hare krsna maha mantra japa* studies can contain increased rigor, including elements such as a double-blind design, better control of location for meetings between researchers and subjects, a greater range for chanting frequency built into the design of the experiment, a clinical sample, and a larger sample size. Also, the alternate group can receive a treatment that has been proven effective, and then the researcher could assess whether the maha mantra is more effective in treating the target dependent variable than the other intervention. *Japa* studies can be performed in various settings, with various populations, and tested with different target variables. For instance, from *guna* theory many dependent variables, such as anger control and relationship satisfaction, can be incorporated into a maha mantra study. Future studies can also experiment with different time periods for the intervention, such as one week, eight weeks, or twelve weeks. In this way, the applicability and effectiveness of this technique can be evaluated across several dimensions.

150

Additionally, future studies can incorporate greater control for the factor of past experience of subjects with chanting and related techniques. As described in the sampling section of the methodology chapter, the initial phone conversation with each subject included a question concerning whether they had prior experience with chanting, biofeedback, meditation, or other yoga techniques. Answers to this question were used to create two blocks, "past experience" and "no past experience", for the process of random assignment. These blocks, however, controlled for the variable of past experienced based on a yes or no question, without differentiating between length or intensity of experience. Future studies on the maha mantra can include, for instance, a group with experience chanting the maha mantra, a group with experience chanting a different mantra, a group with silent meditation experience, and a group with biofeedback experience. In this way, differential effects of the maha mantra can be more precisely analyzed.

In the Vedas, chanting the *hare krsna maha mantra* is described more as a component of a spiritual lifestyle than as a therapeutic intervention. All aspects of this lifestyle are based on *guna* theory, and thus many aspects of the Vedic lifestyle can be assessed by the experimental method. With regards to further examination of the maha mantra, future studies can incorporate a group that continues to chant *japa*, without discontinuation at the end of an intervention period. As described earlier in this chapter with regards to hypotheses 6-10, effects of the maha mantra diminished during the followup period. In Vedic culture, many people daily chant a fixed number of *japa* rounds of the *hare krsna maha mantra*. Persons who have been regularly chanting in this way for years, as well as persons who have recently begun regular chanting, can be compared with chanters who cease chanting after a pre-determined time period, and with a control group, an alternate mantra group, as well as with alternate therapy groups. Alternate therapy groups would involve an intervention that has already been shown to be effective in addressing the dependent variable. For instance, the maha mantra could be compared with an established cognitive-behavioral therapy for relieving stress.

Many other aspects of a Vedic lifestyle could also be researched. For example, the Vedas explain that each time period of the day has predominant modes. The hour before sunrise, for instance, is called the *brahma-muhurta*, and is predominated by *sattva guna,* according to Vedic descriptions (Prabhupada, 1976). Therefore, one who chants the maha mantra at this time is predicted to achieve greater benefit, in terms of any of the dependent variables connected with increased *sattva,* such as reduction of stress and depression, compared with one who chants at a different time of the day. A study could be designed incorporating this aspect of Vedic *guna* theory.

As a final example, the Vedas assert that there is great benefit in eating *prasadam,* which is food that is prepared according to certain principles and is described in the Vedas to be completely in the mode of goodness, or *sattva.* Krsna indicates in the Bhagavad-gita (Prabhupada, 1972) that all foods are situated in the modes of nature, and to develop *sattvic* qualities one should eat *sattvic* foods, such as *prasadam. Prasadam* is vegetarian. Thus, a design could be formulated with a meat-eating group, a vegetarian *non-prasadam* group, a *prasadam* group, and a *prasadam* group that also chants a few rounds per day of the maha mantra. In this way *guna* theory and Vedic practices can be further tested.

APPENDIX A: Systematic Research Synthesis on Spiritual Interventions

Alford, G. S., Koehler, R. A., & Leonard, J. (1991). Alcoholics Anonymous-Narcotics Anonymous model inpatient treatment of chemically-dependent adolescents: a two-year outcome study. Journal of Studies on Alcohol, 52 (2), 118-126.

Purpose
To evaluate the efficacy of a 12-step inpatient program in treating chemically-dependent adolescents.

Theory
Chemical substance abuse is a major factor disrupting adolescent development in this country. Application of the principles of Alcoholics Anonymous (AA) and Narcotics Anonymous (NA) is a common method for addressing this problem, though evaluations of such adolescent treatment programs are rare, if not nonexistent. Steps 11 and 12 of the AA and NA program involve spiritually-based prayer and meditation, and therefore this study is included in this paper.

Design
This is a prospective cohort design, incorporating 2 groups and 6-month, 1-year and 2-year follow-up. Subjects consisted of 157 patients (98 male, 59 female) admitted to an inpatient adolescent chemical dependency unit. Those who completed the treatment program, which consisted of 45 days at an inpatient facility and 45 days at a halfway house, formed one group, and those who did not compete the protocol formed the second group. The treatment consisted of extensive individual and group therapeutic work, based on the principles of AA and NA, as well as many lectures and films, also founded on the same concepts. Approximately 3 weeks after admission, each subject was interviewed by a research staff member for initial evaluation of personal, family, social, academic, legal and chemical use factors. At least one family member was also interviewed, separately, for corroboration. All subjects, whether completing treatment or not, were strongly encouraged to attend AA/NA meetings after leaving the hospital.

Critique: This is outcome, as opposed to process, research.

(continued)

Alford, G. S., Koehler, R. A., & Leonard, J. (1991). Alcoholics Anonymous-Narcotics Anonymous model inpatient treatment of chemically-dependent adolescents: a two-year outcome study. Journal of Studies on Alcohol, 52 (2), 118-126.

Design (continued)

Since the intervention is complex, one naturally wonders which components of AA/NA produce which effects. Unfortunately, this design is not able to answer this question. Specifically, we cannot ascertain form this study what part the spiritual dimension plays in the recovery process. Also, there is not true control group, as even the non-completers received some of the same treatment as the completers. Moreover, there is no alternate treatment group.

Measurement

A structured interview format was used to assess patients' personal, family, social, academic, legal, and chemical use histories. Family members were separately interviewed in a similar structured interview format. For measurement of treatment outcomes, a 45-item questionnaire covering 5 domains-present living conditions, school and/or work behavior including problems and accomplishments, social-legal history, chemical use/abuse history, and involvement in AA/NA-was used to assess treatment outcomes at 6, 12, and 24 months following discharge. A similar questionnaire was given to family members at 6, 12, and 24 months. Patient self-report and family member reports were compared to substantiate patient report of progress. Outcomes were classified according to levels of a) chemical use/abuse (ordinal-level), b) familial-social level behavioral functioning (ordinal-level), c) general behavioral functioning (categorical-level), and d) attendance in AA/NA groups (ordinal-level).

Critique: The study would be strengthened by use of validated test instruments to measure risk factors, such as personal adjustment, achievement and religiosity, more accurately.

Analysis

Table 1 contains descriptive data regarding extent of use of 8 different substances upon entry into the program. Table 2 presents data for each group at 6 months, 1 year and 2 years, regarding degree of abstinence or substance use. p and z values are provided in the text. Table 3 contains data grouped by posttreatment usage and behavioral functioning at each follow-up period. Table 4 contains information related to familial/social/civil functioning at 2 year follow-up, and Table 5 presents substance use in relation to AA/NA attendance. p and z values for all data are provided in the text.

Critique: More details regarding statistical evaluation should have been noted, and p values could have been included in the tables. An analysis of variance would have been helpful to place the results in context.

(continued)

Alford, G. S., Koehler, R. A., & Leonard, J. (1991). Alcoholics Anonymous-Narcotics Anonymous model inpatient treatment of chemically-dependent adolescents: a two-year outcome study. Journal of Studies on Alcohol, 52 (2), 118-126.

Results

At 6 months, adolescents who completed the treatment program had a far higher abstinence rate than did non-completers (75% vs. 35%, p<.005). There was no significant difference between male completers and male non-completers one and two years after discharge, though 70% of female treatment completers were abstinent compared to 28% of female non-completers after 1 year discharge (p<.01), and 61% of female completers vs. 27% of non-completers were abstinent after 2 years. Noting the caveat of court-ordered, non-voluntary AA/NA participation of some patients, results revealed that 84% of high-frequency AA/NA attenders were abstinent or essentially abstinent, with only 13% of this group being high-frequency chronic users of drugs or alcohol. Of those who did not attend AA or NA, 31% were found to be abstinent or essentially abstinent, and 62% were high-frequency chronic users. Whether completers or non-completers of the treatment, subjects who attended AA/NA at relatively high frequencies were more likely to be abstinent than those in each of the other attendance categories. In summary, 12-step inpatient programs appear to be effective for treating chemically-dependent adolescents, though positive effects seem to wane with time. The authors stress the need for greater attention to relapse prevention strategies and for the development of out patient alternatives to lengthy residential treatment.

Generalizability

Based on the sampling, the results may be generalizable to the general population of adolescents who abuse a wide variety of substances. However, it is questionable whether the design allows, with regards to the practicality, sufficient precision in delineating the results. It can be said that the treatment program is helpful. Since many circumstances will only allow a portion of the program to be implemented, the generalized results form this study may not be very useful. Also, it should be understood that the comparison group was not a no-treatment control group, probably due to ethical considerations. Additionally, no non-AA/NA treatment was incorporated into the design. All subjects received the same treatment, though some terminated the treatment prematurely. In conclusion, the lack of control in the design precludes the results from being very meaningful, though the results that are obtained can, with caution, be generalized.

Byrd, R. C. (1988). Positive therapeutic effects of intercessory prayer in a conronary care unit population. South Med J, 81 (7), 826-829.

Purpose

To determine if intercessory prayer to the Judeo-Christian God effects a patient's medical condition and recovery while in the hospital, and, if so, how such effects are characterized.

Theory

Praying for help and healing during times of illness is one of the oldest forms of therapy, though it has had little attention in the medical literature. This particular study is based on the theory that prayer to the Judeo-Christian God is an effective means for helping coronary patients improve their heart condition and accelerate their recovery.

Design

Three-hundred-three patients from the coronary care unit at San Francisco General Hospital participated in this 2-group, pretest post-test design. All patients admitted to the unit during a 9-month period were eligible to participate in the study: 57 patients refused to participate. Before hospital entry, the nature of the project was explained to each patient and informed consent was obtained. Using a computer-generate list, patients were randomly assigned to either receive or not receive intercessory prayer. The patients, the staff and doctors in the unit, as well as the author, remained "blinded" throughout the study. Intercessors were "born again" Christians with an active life of daily devotional prayer and active membership with a local church. Several denominations were represented. Patients and intercessors were not matched by religion or denomination. After randomization, each intervention-group patient was assigned to 3 to 7 intercessors. The patients' first name, diagnosis, and general condition, along with pertinent updates in their condition, were given to the intercessors. The prayer was done outside of the hospital daily until the patient was discharged from the hospital. Under the direction of a coordinator, each intercessor was asked to pray daily for a rapid recovery and for prevention of complications and death.

Critique: A worthy aspect of the design is that religiosity, spirituality, and amount of prayer done by persons not in the study

Byrd, R. C. (1988). Positive therapeutic effects of intercessory prayer in a conronary care unit population. South Med J, 81 (7), 826-829.

Design (continued)
for the patient, are controlled by randomization.

Measurement
Upon entry, all subjects were assessed with regard to medical diagnoses, including 15 coronary diagnoses and 14 noncardiac diagnoses. After entry, new problems, new diagnoses, and new therapeutic interventions were measured as post-intervention data. This included 29 items, such as use of antibiotics, need for intubation, sepsis, and pneumonia. In addition, all subjects were rated, upon discharge, on the overall quality of the course of stay in the hospital. This rating was categorically determined, based on medical criteria, as *good, intermediate,* or *bad.*

Critique: Out come variables are clearly defined and measured, except for the score of the overall hospital course, as the category definitions appear to be somewhat vague and arbitrary.

Analysis
Data were entered into a PDP-11 computer for analysis, using the Biomedical Data Processing statistical package. analyses were performed using an unpaired t-test for interval data and a chi-square test for categorical data, utilizing Fisher's exact test when necessary. A stepwise logistic regression was used for the multivariant analyses.

Critique: A power analysis would have been very interesting in this study.

Byrd, R. C. (1988). Positive therapeutic effects of intercessory prayer in a conronary care unit population. South Med J. 81 (7). 826-829.

Results
On all entry criteria, including demographic variables, univariant and multivariant analysis showed no statistical differences between the two groups. On 6 of the 29 post-intervention measures, including congestive heart failure, cardiopulmonary arrest, pneumonia, diuretics, antibiotics, and intubation/ventilation, the intervention group scored significantly (p values from <.002 to <.005) lover than the experimental group, and on the hospital course rating, the experimental group scored significantly better (p<.01) than the control group. Multivariate analysis of outcome measures revealed a significant difference (p<.0001) between the two groups, in favor of the experimental group.

Critique: Statistically significant results on 6 of 29 outcome measures is somewhat suspect due to the large number of dependent variables. However, the researcher successfully overcomes this limitation by multivariate analysis, which revealed a significant result at a conservative p value (p<.0001) Also, the researcher attempts to overcome the limitation of a large number of outcome variables by summing them into a categorical severity score that assesses the general course of the hospital stay. Though the outcome on this score is significant (p<.01), the definitions of the categories are far less rigorous and definitive than ever other variable in the study, and therefore the validity of this measure is somewhat suspect. An important

Results (continued)
aspect of this study is the statistical similarity of the two groups at entry. However, the article does not mention at what p level this significance is determined.

Generalizability
The researcher concludes that intercessory prayer to the Judeo-Christian God has a beneficial therapeutic effect in patients admitted to a Coronary Care Unit. Given the sample size, which represents 87.3% of the sample frame, the results can be inferred to be at least generalizable to the Coronary Care Unit of San Francisco General Hospital. Arguably, the results can be generalized to apply to other coronary care units in the country, and perhaps in the world, also to hospital units other than coronary care. Arguments for or against a broader generalization would depend on one's explanation of the mechanism by which this prayer works, and whether this mechanism would be effective in different circumstances an for different diagnoses. In any case, this intervention deserves to be further studied with different populations to ascertain generalizability of these results.

Carroll, S. (1991). Spirituality and purpose in life in addiction recovery. J. Stud Alcohol, 54, 297-301.

Purpose

To examine the relationship between spirituality and recovery from alcoholism among Alcoholics Anonymous (AA) attenders. It is the thesis of this study that the extent to which the AA steps related to spirituality are practiced with be positively correlated with a sense of meaning and purpose in the lives of AA members. Also, the hypothesis that length of sobriety will be positively correlated with a sense of purpose in life was investigated.

Theory

The basis of recovery in AA is spiritual growth through the practice of certain spiritual principles. these principles include dependence upon a self-defined Higher Power, self-examination, prayer and meditation, and assistance of others. Though theorists have long postulated spirituality as an essential factor in alcoholism, research in this area has been neglected. A lowered sense of meaning in life has been seen as both the cause and effect of alcoholic drinking. A major aspect of growth in AA is to address the lack of purpose through assistance to others. This decreased sense of meaning is also related to unmet spiritual needs. Kurtz sees alcoholism as a misguided thirst for transcendence and believes it is the denial and misunderstanding of spiritual needs that is at the root of alcohol addiction.

AA emphasizes that it is not a religious organization. In AA literature, God is mentioned with the qualification "as you understand Him," and Higher Power is often the preferred term. Many AA members, through the course of treatment, find that they tap an unsuspected inner resource which they formerly identified with their conception of a Power greater than themselves. According to AA, the prime source of character defects is self-centered fear. These flaws are remedied by the 12-step program. Steps 11 and 12 specifically deal with spiritual development.

Design

This is a cross-sectional survey design. Subjects were 100 (51 male) members of AA, representing 20 different AA groups in northern California. The researcher attended these groups and members were asked to respond to 2 questionnaires, evaluating extent of perceived meaning in life and degree of practice of Steps 11 and 12. Length of sobriety of participants ranged from 7 days to 33 years, with a median of 3 years and mean education level of 3 years of college.

Critique: The study would be enhanced with probabilistic sampling covering a larger geographical area. The sampling method of this study may suffer from the limitation s of self-selection bias. Further, a broader study could have compared alternate treatments, such as Rational Recovery, to the AA program. This would have been especially useful in analysis of spiritual factors.

Carroll, S. (1991). Spirituality and purpose in life in addiction recovery. J. Stud Alcohol. 54, 297-301.

Measurement

Practice of Steps 11 and 12 was measured by a 38-item questionnaire developed by the researcher. Demographic data were collected on frequency of prayer, meditation, church attendance, and attendance of AA meetings. Also included were questions about the subject's record of service in various positions of AA. Purpose in life was measured by the Purpose in Life questionnaire (PIL). Length of sobriety and number of relapses were measured as additional outcome measures. Four questions on the PIL were slightly reworded "so that the subjects would, for example, be able to determine if the question concerned their lives before or after gaining sobriety." A reliability analysis of the modified PIL yielded an alpha coefficient of .89. The subscale of the 38-item questionnaire assessing Step 11 has an alpha of .78 and the Step 12 subscale has an alpha of .59. Construct validity of the inventory was ascertained by interjudge agreement on inclusion of items.

Critique: Future research in this area could use standardized measures that more directly relate to spirituality or religiosity. It is good that the authors included the 38-item inventory as an appendix.

Analysis

Pearson's r was calculated to determine correlations related to hypotheses of investigation. p levels and correlation scores are provided in 2 tables and explained in the text. Table 1 contains correlations between Steps 11 and 12, PIL scores, and length of sobriety. Table 2 presents Beta weights for Step 11, number of AA meetings, length of sobriety, age, Step 12, number of relapses, and years of education, along with their significance levels. A stepwise multiple regression was performed for explanation of variance.

Critique: Analytic procedures are thorough and appropriate for a cross-sectional study, except for the omission of analysis for gender correlations

Results

There was a significant correlation (p<.001) between self-reported Step 11 scores and PIL scores, though there was no significant correlation between Step 12 scores and PIL scores. Step 11 accounted for 32% of the variance of PIL scores. Analysis of beta weights showed that Step 11 and number of AA meetings attended were the only significant predictor variables of sobriety and PIL scores. Length of sobriety and PIL scores were significantly correlated (p<.001). Number of meetings attended, a partial measure of Step 12, was significantly correlated with length of sobriety, purpose in life, and a reduced number of relapses (p<.01).

Step 11 emphasizes prayer and meditation, and Step 12 is primarily concerned with sharing one's spiritual realization with others. The authors suggest that the finding that Step 12 was not significantly correlated with purpose in life or length of sobriety may be due to difficulty in operationalizing the practices of Step 12. In summary, the data support the idea that practice of prayer and meditation drive out the use of alcohol in the lives of recovering alcoholics.

(continued)

Carroll, S. (1991). Spirituality and purpose in life in addiction recovery. <u>J. Stud Alcohol, 54,</u> 297-301.

Generalizability
The article states "the majority
of the subjects were white," with
no specific data provided.
Further research could give more
attention to non-white ethnic
groups to enhance generalizability. Also, it is questionable
whether the results apply to various socioeconomic and education levels.

Janowiak, J. J., & Hackman, R. (1994). Meditation and college students' self-actualization and rated stress.. Psychological Reports, 75 (2), 1007-1010.

Purpose

To obtain objective measures of the ways in which Eastern-style meditation influence stress and personality, with special attention given to self-actualization.

Critique: No hypothesis is given, thought it appears from the article that the authors were testing the null hypothesis that there is no correlation between practice of meditation and yoga relaxation and level of stress and self-actualization.

Theory

Underlying this investigation is Maslow's concept of self-actualization. This idea is juxtaposed with theories of meditative states and stress experienced by college students. Meditation is described as a "technique to actualize and integrate the personality of humankind to those higher fulfilled states of personal integration." Regarding stress, the authors write "Many clinicians concur that individual responses to stress can be controlled when one begins to meditate."

Critique: In a very short introductory section, the authors describe theory and related to personality development of college students, stress, meditation, and self-actualization. It is vague how all these factors are supported to fit together. Also, the information regarding meditation is derived solely from Western sources, not from original literature. Additionally, there is only one sentence regarding the theory behind mantra meditation, and this statement is high speculative.

Design

This was a 3-group, pre-test post-test experimental design, using sample of convenience and a random assignment. There was a control group and two educational intervention groups. One intervention group practiced mantra meditation, and the other practiced Shavasana yoga relaxation.the meditation and control groups consisted of 21 college students enrolled in health education classes at a large university, and the relaxation group consisted of 20 students similarly enrolled. Intervention groups received 7 20-45 minute sessions, and were also asked to meditate or practice relaxation outside of class twice daily for 20 to 30 minutes for eight weeks. Both groups completed daily compliance logs and daily rated their stress.

Critique: There is no power analysis for determination of sample size. Otherwise, the basic design appears strong, though follow-up testing would have improved the design. However, there is practically no description of either interventive technique. The mantra utilized is not even provided in the article.

Janowiak, J. J., & Hackman, R. (1994). Meditation and college students' self-actualization and rated stress.. Psychological Reports, 75 (2), 1007-1010.

Measurement

All three groups were pre- and post-tested on the Personal Orientation Inventory and the Behavioral Relaxation Scale.

Critique: No reliability or validity data are provided for either instrument.

Analysis

Intra- and inter-group analysis of variance was calculated for the means of all groups at pre-test and post-test for scores on both instruments. Also, correlations with compliance scores were calculated.

Critique: for some calculations, only about half of the subjects were included in the analysis, "due to time constraints." This is a questionable procedure. Also, no analysis is performed between male and female subjects. In fact, the article does not provide demographic data on gender distribution of the sample.

Results

All groups showed significant (p=.01) increases in self-actualization and stress reduction. Differences between groups were not significant in self-actualization, and the only significant result between groups in the stress measure was between the meditation group and the other two groups. Compliance ratings significantly correlated with scores on both instruments for both interventive groups. This indicates that motivation to meditate or relax is an important factor.

Critique: Results regarding significance could have been presented ina table to clarify the findings. Also, the article would be enhanced by a discussion of the findings in relation to theory.

Janowiak, J. J., & Hackman, R. (1994). Meditation and college students' self-actualization and rated stress.. Psychological Reports, 75 (2), 1007-1010.

Generalizability

Since the sample was not randomly selected form any population or sampling frame, the results are not necessarily generalizable to a larger population. However, the findings regarding the effects of the interventive procedures, especially with regard to mantra meditation and stress, can be considered seriously, as the design was fairly rigorous.

Kutz, I., Leserman, J., Dorrington, C., Morrison, C. H., Borysendo, J. Z., Benson, H. (1985). Meditation as an adjunct to psychotherapy: An outcome study. Psychotherapy & Psychosomatics, 43 (4), 209-218.

Purpose

This study was conducted to examine the potential usefulness of meditation in psychotherapy.

Critique: In the introduction the authors refer to a recent article in which they explored the biological and psychological and psychological mechanisms by which emotional and cognitive changes that occur during meditation may facilitate the psychotherapeutic process. Further, they explain that their hypothesis was based in part on the clinical observations and research data that are reported in the study under discussion. However, the article does not clearly state the hypothesis, nor does it explain the inspiration for conducting this original study.

Theory

This intervention is based on the Buddhist practice of Vipassana meditation. The purpose of this type of mindfulness meditation is to increase insight by becoming a detached observer of the mind's activities. This is initially achieved by eliciting the relaxation response, after which the attention is allowed to scan an open focus shifting freely from one perception to the next. No thought or sensation is considered an intrusion. Mindfulness meditation has been successfully used in clinical settings to invoke attitudinal changes, pain alleviation, lowered blood pressure, anxiety relief, and alleviation of symptoms in other stress-related illnesses.

The authors also discuss the central place of anxiety in psychological symptoms, and cite the potential of meditation to alleviate this generalized symptom. They write "A reduction in anxiety is almost always expected to generalize to other areas in the patient's life."

Design

Twenty patients between 21 and 53 years of age (mean age=38) participated in this pre-test, post-test study. All were private psychotherapy patients involved in dynamic-explorative therapy. Length of therapy ranged from 1 to 10 years with a mean of 3.7. Diagnoses varied from severe narcissistic and borderline personality disorders to anxiety and obsessive neuroses. Seventeen patients were referred by their therapists, 3 were self-referred and therapist approval was subsequently obtained. Subjects were assigned to four different meditation groups at Boston's Beth Israel Hospital, with all groups undergoing the same intervention with different instructors. Nine therapists collaborated in the study. All are described as "highly experienced," and none had previous experience with meditation. The therapists were asked to rate their attitude to the proposed project.

The meditation intervention was 10 weeks long, and patients continued their weekly therapy sessions during the study. Patients and therapists were asked to complete questionnaires and rating scales during the week before the program began, during the week after the program ended, and 6 months after the program ended. The meditation program consisted of weekly 2-hour group meetings and daily home meditation. Group size ranged from 11 to 16.

Critique: There's no control, alternate treatment, or placebo treatment group, though

Kutz, I., Leserman, J., Dorrington, C., Morrison, C. H., Borysendo, J. Z., Benson, H. (1985). Meditation as an adjunct to psychotherapy: An outcome study. Psychotherapy & Psychosomatics, 43 (4), 209-218.

Design (continued)
including therapist and subject responses does provide some triangulation. It isn't mentioned whether assignment to the 4 groups was random, and this may be a source of bias. The term "highly experienced" is not defined. Due to lack of control groups, internal validity is a problem. Also, the method of participant selection compromises external validity.

Measurement
The following instruments were utilized: 1) the revised Hopkins Symptoms Checklist, 2) the Profile of Mood States inventory, 3) the Table of Level of Activity Interference, a 10-item checklist of activities, such as walking and social activity, rated on a 4-point scale on a continuum of difficulty, 4) a retrospective, open-ended questionnaire evaluating the impact of the meditation group program completed by the patients during the week after the program ended. For therapists, the following instruments were used: 1) the Clinical Rating Scale and 2) a retrospective, open-ended questionnaire, evaluating how the meditation experience influenced the process of psychotherapy. Also, before the experiment, therapists rated their attitude towards the project, as explained in the Design section.

Critique: Categories for therapist attitude towards the project don't appear to be mutually exclusive. Also, though references for the standardized instruments are provided, there is no information in the article itself regarding psychometric data.

Analysis
Data are presented in 3 tables, as well as in the text. Table 1 contains means and standard deviations on psychologic symptoms, such as somatization, depression, and anxiety, before and after the meditation group program, and also includes correlation coefficients between measures across time (pretest and post-test) and t tests for dependent samples. Table 2 presents means and standard deviations on mood states, such as vigor, tension, and confusion, before and after the meditation program, with correlation coefficients between measures across time and t tests for dependent samples. Table 3 displays means and standard deviations on therapist's ratings, on areas such as enjoyment of life, guilt, and optimism, before and after the meditation program with correlation coefficients between measures across time and t tests for dependent samples. Only 10 subjects were available for 6-month follow-up, and this data was described in the text. Analysis of variance with the Newman-Keuls test was computed to test for differences between means at the 3 time points. Significance levels are reported for all tests.

Critique: This study would benefit from an analysis comparing the meditation groups, to determine if meditation teachers significantly differed in their impact. Also, comparisons could have been made between therapy groups, for a similar determination. Additionally, gender and other demographic data could

Kutz, I., Leserman, J., Dorrington, C., Morrison, C. H., Borysendo, J. Z., Benson, H. (1985). Meditation as an adjunct to psychotherapy: An outcome study. Psychotherapy & Psychosomatics, 43 (4), 209-218.

Analysis (continued) have been included in the analyses.

Results

Patients' self-reported changes in psychologic symptoms demonstrated a consistent pattern of significant (p<.05) decreases on all symptoms from pre- to post-intervention, with the exception of paranoid ideation and psychoticism. Subjects experienced the largest decrease in depression and anxiety. Self-reported changes on mood states showed similar results, with subjects reporting significantly (p<.05) less mood disturbances over time on all measures, with decreases in tension, depression, fatigue, anger, confusion and in the total mood disturbance score. Also, activities such as work, socializing, house chores, and driving were reported as easier to perform after the intervention. No change in difficulty was evidenced in eating, sleeping or sexual activity. Consistent with patients' self-reports, therapists indicated significant improvement from pre- to post-test in anxiety, enjoyment of life, self-assertion, self-esteem, insight, and optimism. Six-month follow-up means on all measures continued to change in the direction of improvement, although most post-test and follow-up means were not significantly different. In no case did the follow-up measure indicate less improvement than post-test. In summary, the meditation program produced significant improvements in the well-being of psychotherapy patients as rated by themselves and their therapists. The authors acknowledge that results must be

Results (continued) considered within the context of the 1 -group design. That is, a placebo effect could account for much of the variance. Many other factors, such as a group effect, could have also contributed to the improvements. Upon termination of the program, participants were asked to rate the relative importance of meditation, group experience, body awareness skills, instructor contact, and other factors. Eighty percent of patients rated daily meditation as the most valuable factor responsible for change. The authors conclude that meditation may be an important adjunct to the process of psychotherapy.

Critique: The results and discussion section provide a helpful analysis of the data within the framework of the limitations of the design. Also, this discussion is presented with regard to the interface of psychotherapeutic and meditation theory.

(continued)

Kutz, I., Leserman, J., Dorrington, C., Morrison, C. H., Borysendo, J. Z., Benson, H. (1985). Meditation as an adjunct to psychotherapy: An outcome study. Psychotherapy & Psychosomatics, 43 (4), 209-218.

Generalizability

Caution must be applied in generalizing these results. Sampling involved a combination of self-selection, therapist selection, and researcher screening. Therefore, the biases of many persons were involved in forming the sample. Also, the results themselves are suspect, since the design does not allow much isolation of the effects of meditation. Still, since the results are basically consistent with other research, this study adds to the literature on meditation research. It appears, from this and other studies, that mindfulness meditation can enhance psychotherapeutic interventions, though benefits may not be achieved for those with severe symptoms, such as paranoid ideation, or psychoticism, or diagnoses, such as psychoses. Thus, these results should reinforce wariness in applying meditation techniques to those with extreme mental conditions, and should also support the prudent utilization of such techniques with reasonably well-adjusted persons.

Miller, J. J., Fletcher, K., & Kabat-Zinn, J. (1995). Three-year follow-up and clinical implcations of a mindfulness meditation-based stress reduction intervention in the treatment of anxiety disorders. Gen Hosp Psychiatry, 17 (3), 192-200.

Purpose

This was a 3-year follow-up study on the effects of an 8-week outpatient physician-referred group stress reduction intervention based on mindfulness meditation. The purpose was to ascertain long-term benefits of the intervention on a clinical population.

Critique: No specific hypotheses are stated.

Theory

The theory behind this outcome research is that mindfulness is a universal human attribute, though the prescribed exercises derive from the Buddhist and Upanisadic traditions. The authors relate that Freud's characterization of the ideal mind state of the psychoanalyst during therapy is remarkably similar to mindfulness as described in Buddhist literature.

Design

In the original study, 22 subjects who met the criteria for DSM-111-R generalized anxiety disorder or panic disorder participated in a pretest post-test one-group design assessing an intervention based on mindfulness meditation. This study reported clinically and statistically significant reductions on all measures, such as frequency and severity of panic attacks, during the intervention period, and these results were maintained at 3-month follow-up. In this 3-year follow-up study, 18 of the original 22 subjects participated, 10 of whom were interviewed in person, and 8 by telephone.

Critique: It is possible that those who chose to participate in the follow-up study are not representative. Although only 4 subjects did not participate, these 4 may have had particularly unfavorable responses to the intervention, and their exclusion in this study may bias the results. Also, the design suffers from lack of alternate treatment and control groups.

169

(continued)

Miller, J. J., Fletcher, K., & Kabat-Zinn, J. (1995). Three-year follow-up and clinical implcations of a mindfulness meditation-based stress reduction intervention in the treatment of anxiety disorders. Gen Hosp Psychiatry. 17 (3), 192-200.

Measurement

The assessment battery included Hamilton Rating Scale for Anxiety, Hamilton Rating Scale for Panic Attacks, Hamilton Rating Scale for Depression, Beck Anxiety Inventory, Beck Depression Inventory, Mobility Inventory for Agoraphobia, Fear Survey Schedule, number of panic attacks in preceding week and severity of these attacks, current medications, amount of current practice of various formal mindfulness techniques, rating of subjective importance in their life of the interventive training, and types of additional treatment received. Each subject was also evaluated for current psychosocial stressors and current psychiatric and medical disorders.

Critique: Although validity and reliability information are not provided in the article, references are given where such data can be found. Considering the extensive battery of tests, and that several of the interviews were performed by phone, the accuracy of some of the data can be questioned. For instance, evaluation of current psychosocial stressors is a complex undertaking, and it may be difficult to obtain a valid assessment as part of a long phone interview.

Analysis

Repeated measures ANOVA compared pre-treatment, post-treatment and 3-year follow-up scores for all psychometric instruments. p values were calculated for each correlation.

Results

Means and standard deviations for all analyses are presented in two tables with F, df and p calculated for each ANOVA. Clinically and statistically significant improvements in subjective and objective symptoms of anxiety and depression demonstrated at posttreatment in the original study persisted at 3-year follow-up on the Hamilton and Beck scales for anxiety and depression. Also, posttreatment improvements in the Hamilton Panic Score and in the number and severity of panic attacks were also shown to be maintained at 3-year follow-up. Of the 18 subjects, 10 continued to practice a formal mindfulness technique at 3-year follow-up.

The researchers conclude that individuals with long-term chronic anxiety, whether undergoing other forms of treatment or not, can make substantial and long-lasting positive changes in their lives to reduce anxiety and panic by participating in a weekly mindfulness-based group stress reduction program. They suggest that mindfulness appears to give the individual a practical way to disentangle from reflexive behaviors and reactions that often have their roots in past experience.

Critique: There is a very helpful discussion of the results in relation to mindfulness theory toward the end of the article. Still, considering the lack of a control group, the researchers may be overstepping their bounds with their conclusions of

Miller, J. J., Fletcher, K., & Kabat-Zinn, J. (1995). Three-year follow-up and clinical implcations of a mindfulness meditation-based stress reduction intervention in the treatment of anxiety disorders. Gen Hosp Psychiatry, 17 (3), 192-200.

Results (continued)
the effectiveness of the intervention. The article ends with an interesting analysis of cost-effectiveness, comparing hospitalization and other costs for various interventions.

Generalizability
To support the potential generalizability of the results of this follow-up study, 58 nonstudy subjects reported on in the original study who had received identical treatment were contacted and retested. Thirty-nine responded. This provided an informal measure of generalizability, and results of this less rigorous group support results of the group of 18. This large sample size argues for greater reliability of the study.

Critique: Extensive screening was used to choose participants in the original study, and further selfscreening was evident in the follow-up. Therefore, the effects of the intervention can only be generalized, at most, to a rigorously screened clinical population. Methods of screening are not well-described, and researcher bias may be involved, especially considering that the researcher appears to be favorably inclined to this intervention.

Pearl, J. H., & Carlozzi, A. (1994). Effect of meditation on empathy and anxiety. <u>Perceptual and Motor Skills, 78 (1),</u> 297-298.

Purpose

To assess the effect of Clinically Standardized Meditation on anxiety and empathy.

Critique: The article provides a helpful literature review on prior studies evaluating the effect of meditation on empathy. No such studies have been performed since the 1970s.

Theory

Empathy is described as a desirable attribute for human service professionals, and the article theorizes, based on a few prior studies, that meditation is an effective technique for enhancing empathy.

Critique: Very little theory is provided, leaving the reader wondering about the nature of the meditative mechanism that supposedly increases empathy and decreases anxiety.

Design

This was a 2-group, post-test design utilizing random assignment with a self-selected convenience sample from the students, faculty and staff of a large public university in the southwestern United States, none of whom had ever meditated regularly. Of the sixty subjects who participated the study, 24 in the treatment group completed the study, as did 26 from the control group. The meditation intervention lasted for 8 weeks. After the intervention, both groups were administered the evaluation package.

Critique: A pre-test and follow-up testing session would have added to the rigor of this research. Also, at least a brief description of the meditative intervention would have been helpful. The article doesn't even mention how many minutes per day the subjects were engaged in the intervention.

172

(continued)

Pearl, J. H., & Carlozzi, A. (1994). Effect of meditation on empathy and anxiety. <u>Perceptual and Motor Skills, 78 (1),</u> 297-298.

Measurement

Capacity for empathy was measured by the Affective Sensitivity Scale. and anxiety level was measured using the Trait Anxiety scales of the Multiple Affect Adjective Check List and the State-Trait Anxiety Inventory.

Critique: Though references for these instruments are provided. no psychometric information is given in the article itself

Analysis

For both groups, means and standard deviations are calculated for all 3 inventories. For comparing the groups, multivariate analysis of variance is performed, and univariate Fs and significance levels are provided.

Critique: some power analysis, at least after the study was conducted, would have been valuable to understand the results.

Results

Data indicate that the meditation group's means differed significantly (p<.05) from the no-treatment group's means in the predicted direction on both anxiety measures. On the empathy measure, the intervention group showed greater empathy, but this result was not statistically significant (p=11). These data confirm the finding that meditation decreases anxiety but do not support the hypothesis that it also increases empathy.

(continued)

Pearl, J. H., & Carlozzi, A. (1994). Effect of meditation on empathy and anxiety. Perceptual and Motor Skills, 78 (1), 297-298.

Generalizability

With a small sample and no pretest, the initial similarity of groups on the key factors of empathy and anxiety is debatable. Therefore, the measured effects may be a product of sampling bias, and the results therefore may not be generalizable even to the sample, what to speak of a larger population.

Smith, W. P., Compton, W. C., & West, W. B. (1995). Meditation as an adjunct to a happiness enhancement program. Journal of Clinical Psychology, 51 (2), 269-273.

Purpose

To determine whether meditation increases happiness. The hypotheses tested were 1) a group that learned meditation in addition to Fordyce's Personal Happiness Enhancement Program (PHEP) would show significant changes in happiness, anxiety, and depression over a PHEP-only group as well as 2) over a control group and that 3) a PHEP-only group would show significant changes in happiness, anxiety, and depression over a control group.

Theory

Research on happiness, life satisfaction and subjective well-being has consistently found personality factors to be more important than situational factors in the prediction of these variables. The most important personality factors include positive self-esteem, optimism, the ability to form close relationships, an internal locus of control, and extraversion. Fordyce has developed a packaged training program for the enhancement of happiness that focuses on both cognitions and behaviors, and has summarized the literature on subjective well-being by delineating 14 fundamentals of happiness. He has found that his PHEP can improve significantly scores on scales that measure happiness. Meditation also has been used as a method of increasing well-being and has been practiced for centuries. Modem research has found meditation to be effective for stress management, increasing internal locus of control, decreasing anxiety, and increasing self-actualization. It is theorized, therefore, that meditation could be a useful adjunct to the PHEP, both by facilitating changes on variables impacted by both techniques, such as internal locus of control, and by adding new benefits to the PHEP, such as anxiety reduction.

Critique: This section provides a succinct and practical literature review on the fields of meditation and well-being research.

Design

This was a 3-group pre-test post-test design, using 36 undergraduate volunteers as subjects. Subjects whose schedules did not conflict with weekly instruction times were randomly assigned to either the Meditation plus PHEP group (MEDP) or the PHEP only group. Subjects whose schedules did conflict with weekly instruction times were assigned to the control group (n= 1 2). Demographic sheets and pretests were administered to all subjects prior to PHEP and meditation instruction. PHEP training consisted of 12 sessions of 1.5 hours each over a period of 6 weeks. Subjects in the MEDP group attended a separate session and were taught a concentrative form of meditation, combining Benson's Relaxation Response technique and concentration on the word "peace".

Critique: The article does not describe the amount of time involvement required on a daily basis for the meditation group. Also, a follow-up testing session would have been beneficial to evaluate durability of effects.

(continued)

Smith, W. P., Compton, W. C., & West, W. B. (1995). Meditation as an adjunct to a happiness enhancement program. Journal of Clinical Psychology, 51 (2), 269-273.

Measurement

The package included the Happiness Measure (HM), the Psychap Inventory (PHI), The State-Trait Anxiety Inventory (STAI), and the Beck Depression Inventory (BDI). Also, the authors developed a Frequency of Practice Log, designed to measure participation in the interventions. The HM combines both intensity and frequency of happiness, and has test-retest coefficients between .98 and 81 [or up to 1 month, and .62 for 4 months. Strong construct validity is also reported. The PHI is an 80-item questionnaire designed to measure happiness according to Fordyce's theory. Convergent validity appears to be strong, and reliability coefficients have ranged from .95 for test-retest periods of I week to .74 for 3 months. The STAI consists of two separate scales for measurement, anxiety. One scale measures the intensity of feelings of nervousness. tension, apprehension, and worry that the examinee is experiencing, and the other measures the apprehension and tension that the person normally experiences. Test-retest coefficients for the current state scale range from .16 (I hour) to .33 (104 days), and for the long-term trait scale they range from 76 (1 hour) to .77 (104 days). Strong validity is also reported. The BDI consists of 2 1 multiple-choice items that measure depression. Average internal consistency coefficients are .86 for clinical samples and .81 for non-clinical samples.

Critique: It is worth mentioning that all the research on these happiness measures has been done by Fordyce. In addition, the low reliability of the current state anxiety measure stands out, thous4h the authors explain that this is explained by the influence of situational factors. Still, the Usefulness of such a scale is arguable. I(is helpful that psychometric data are included in the article.

Smith, W. P., Compton, W. C., & West, W. B. (1995). Meditation as an adjunct to a happiness enhancement program. Journal of Clinical Psychology, 51 (2), 269-273.

Analysis
Based on the Frequency of Practice Log, the meditation group was divided into 2 subgroups, those who meditated at least 3 times per week (n=7), and those who meditated less than 3 times per week (n=5). This was done in accord with the research of Delmonte, who found that those who practice meditation less than three times a week receive little or no benefit. One-way ANOVAs on pretest scores for all groups were performed on all dependent measures to test for initial differences. ANOVAs were calculated for the pre-test post-test difference of means for all groups on all dependent measures. Student Newman-Keuls was used for all post-hoc tests between cell means.

Correlations between practice frequency and pre-post change scores were also calculated.

Results
t-tests between the PHEP only group and the low meditation subgroup on pre-post change scores were nonsignificant on all measures. Therefore, the PHEP only group and the low meditation subgroup were combined into a single group and compared with the high meditation subgroup. Pre-test ANOVAs were not significant for any dependent measure, indicating that the groups were not significantly different at pre-test on anxiety, depression or happiness. Significant differences (p<.05) in the hypothesized directions were found between the MEDP group and the PHEP only group on all dependent measures, and significant differences in the expected directions were also found between the MEDP group and the control group. On all measures except current state anxiety, significant differences in the theorized directions were found between the PHEP only group and the control group. Hypotheses 1 and 2 are supported by the data, and hypothesis 3 is partially supported. For most tests, significance is reported at p<.001. The results suggest that a program to enhance happiness can be significantly improved by the addition of a simple form of concentrative meditation.

Generalizability
Samples were small, though mean differences of scores were consistent with hypotheses are large enough to deserve attention. Still, replication with diverse samples is necessary to more clearly ascertain the generalizability and practical meaning of these results.

Stern, R. C., Canda, E.R., & Doershuk, C. F. (1992). Use of nonmedical treatment by cystic fibrosis patients. Journal of Adolescent Health, 13, 612-615.

Purpose

To assess use and perceived benefit of nonmedical treatments among patients with cystic fibrosis.

Theory

Often, physicians' interactions with practitioners and consumers of nonmedical treatment are adversarial. The authors suggest that by studying and better understanding these treatments, openness and empathy by doctors toward patients' beliefs might enhance rapport and facilitate discussion of possible helpful or adverse effects of nonmedical treatment.

Design

This is a cross-sectional survey design. All cystic fibrosis (CF) patients seen at a Cleveland hospital during 1989-1990 participated in this study (n=402; males, 225). None refused to participate. The patients were interviewed at an outpatient appointment or during hospitalization. Information on patients under 16 years was obtained from or confirmed by a parent. Subjects ranged in age from 0-45, with a mean of 17.5 and median of 18. Ninety-six percent were white and 94% were Christian. Mean educational attainment of parent was 14 years.

(continued)

Stern, R. C., Canda, E.R., & Doershuk, C. F. (1992). Use of nonmedical treatment by cystic fibrosis patients. Journal of Adolescent Health, 13, 612-615.

Measurement

Predictor variables included denomination and faith intensity (using a 0-3 scale). Demographic characteristics assessed included age, gender, race, and parents' highest educational level. Use of non-medical treatment was the outcome variable. This was defined as frequent (more than 5 times). occasional (3-5 times), or infrequent (I -2 times). Nonmedical treatments assessed included religion (e.g., visiting faith healers, making a pilgrimage, using a healing article. use of group prayer), chiropractic, folk remedies (e.g., nutritional modalities, external applications, sun lamp, use of spa), and other practices (e.g., acupuncture, meditation, hypnosis, homeopathy, medical seance, use of shaman, voodoo, or witch doctor, astrological advice, psychic surgery). For positive responses, the age of patient at first use, frequency of use, cost, and perceived benefit of nonmedical treatment was recorded.

Critique: The range of "nonmedical treatment" may be too broad, and the study may have been more effective had it looked at only part of this range. For instance, to lump nutritional modalities, faith healing, meditation and chiropractic into one category risks missing, substantial components of each. Focusing, for example. on nonmedical religious healing alternatives may have been a more manageable endeavor.

Analysis

Statistical analyses utilized the Systat Program, Alpha was set prior to analyses at .05. Analysis of variance was used to compare demographic categories, such as denomination, and an independent sample student t test was performed to determine correlation between intensity of faith and use of nonmedical treatment. A Pearson correlation was used to examine the relationship between parental education and use of non-medical treatment. Table I provides all demographic data, including average cost spent on nonmedical treatments. Correlation data are provided in the text.

Critique: Correlation data could have been presented in a separate table.

Results

Nonmedical treatment was used by 66% of patients. Fifty-seven percent used at least I religious treatment, while 27% used at least I nonreligious treatment, and 3% used both forms of treatment. Group prayer was employed by 48% of patients, and 65% of these used group prayer frequently. Ninety-two percent of those who used group prayer frequently believed it to be beneficial, primarily in maintaining health and demonstrating family and community support. Fourteen percent visited faith healers, and 70% of these perceived benefit from this activity. Twelve percent used religious objects and 4% made pilgrimages. The most common nonreligious treatments were chiropractic (14%), nutritional modalities (I I%) and meditation (5%). Catholics were the most likely denomination to use religious treatments. Neither intensity of faith, gender, or parental education was significantly associated with use of non-medical treatment.

The authors acknowledge that physicians often worry that nonmedical treatment will adversely affect standard treatment, and they report that in this study only .7% rejected medical treatment in favor of a nonmedical approach. Also, nonmedical costs were rarely more than those of medical interventions. Only 17 patients spent more than $200, as most nonmedical interventions were very inexpensive, or sometimes free. Though nonmedical treatment may pose a

(continued)

Stern, R. C., Canda, E.R., & Doershuk, C. F. (1992). Use of nonmedical treatment by cystic fibrosis patients. Journal of Adolescent Health, 13, 612-615.

Results (continued)

risk of injury, only 5 patients ever incurred such a risk, and none was actually injured. Perceived benefit of nonmedical treatment was very high, especially for group prayer (94%) and meditation (92%). The authors conclude that physicians should at least be understanding about use of nonmedical treatment.

Critique: The authors present a useful discussion of the results, focusing on practical considerations surrounding the issue of nonmedical treatment. This discussion includes considerations of time investment and potential benefit of nonmedical treatments. Moreover, the article contains a helpful literature review of other studies on this topic, and this review is appropriately related to the results of this study.

Generalizability

The authors state "We believe our findings in CF patients might apply to other serious illnesses, particularly those affecting children and young adults."

Critique: Considering that the entire sampling frame was used in the study, and that the sample size was impressive, the results can be applied to a larger population, though it's doubtful whether they can be applied, without further investigation, to a population other than white Christians. Still, the finding that religious healing interventions are utilized more than is generally acknowledged by the medical profession is worth noting. Evaluation of effects of these interventions was not rigorous, and therefore not generalizable.

Kaye, V. G. (1985). An innovative treatment modality for elderly residents of a nursing home. Clinical Gerontologist, 3 (4), 45-51.

Purpose

This is a report on an attempt to assist depressed residents of a geriatric nursing home in the Eastern United States by initiating an 8-week yoga program for residents.

Theory

There is no theory in this article. It is simply a narration of the author's experiences while teaching yoga in a nursing home. These experiences focus on the processes taught and the results reported by the residents, as well as the reactions of the author.

Critique: No theory is better than bad theory.

Design

Residents ranged in age from 65 to 92. The researcher/teacher/author spent several weeks at the home prior to beginning the yoga program. During this pre-intervention period she gleaned many important understandings about the environment. For instance, she learned that yoga had a negative connotation, and therefore the yoga exercises were presented as relaxation techniques, and mantra chanting was presented as singing. The content of all 8 sessions is described, with a lot of detail provided. Basically, the procedures involved progressively complex combinations of yoga relaxation, including breathing and muscle work, and chanting OM.

Critique: The written presentation is pleasant, interesting and informative, as the author convinces the reader that this experience is worth reporting. Still, since the presentation is in the form of a qualitative research report, some additional details, such as number of participants and length of sessions, should have been included. Also, the author describes the mantra chanting at the initial session, before OM was introduced, by writing "I was careful to keep the language to a common framework." It's not clear what this means, and therefore future researchers could not replicate this technique.

Kaye, V. G. (1985). An innovative treatment modality for elderly residents of a nursing home. Clinical Gerontologist, 3 (4), 45-51.

Analysis / Results

Residents responded marvelously to these sessions. During the first session they felt their relaxation therapy would be an invaluable too] for them. Some reported that after the progressive relaxation exercise they felt as if they had had a good night's sleep. After the first session, some who favorably responded to the chanting felt as if they had had a lullaby sung to them. Many reported relieved depression and happy memories. During the second session, all were asked to remove their glasses, and all complied. The author cites this as evidence that rapport and trust had been established. By the third session, some participants were incorporating breathing techniques into other aspects of their therapy, Such as physical therapy, with reports of increased mobility. By the fourth session participants were very enthusiastic about the chanting. During this session they were instructed in the use of the OM chant. They were asked to pronounce the word "home" without the "h". Many residents asked for extra chanting. All agreed that the chanting was a valuable experience for them. By the end of the fourth session all participants were responding well to all techniques and to the structure of the sessions, which consisted of progressive relaxation, deep breathing, and chanting. At the fifth session one resident reported that she felt herself exercise as a result of the progressive relaxation techniques The simple motion of lifting the leg and contracting provided exercise for those who are limited in there physical activities. At the seventh session, residents were visibly shaken upon hearing that this was their next to last session. The eighth session was poorly attended, and the author suggests that this was due to anger and resentment over the termination of the meetings. Those who did attend were very grateful and felt that th e techniques would be valuable tools for them.

Gereralizability

The techniques and approach presented in this article should be considered seriously by helping professionals in geriatric settings. Except for one procedure mentioned in the Design section, the sessions are outlined in sufficient detail to adequate replication. Also, the mode of presentation seems appropriate, based on results, for the time, persons and circumstance.

Nakhaima, J. M., & Dicks, B. H. (1995). Social work practice with religious families. Families in Society, 76 (6), 360-368.

Purpose

Study presents three case studies for purpose of providing support for a model of social work practice with religious families. More specifically, the case illustrations seek to show how religious counselors and clergy can be brought into the social work process, and to demonstrate how the religious support network can play an important role in resolving family problems.

Theory

The underlying principle of the proposed model is empowerment of the family's network or natural support system. Also, the approach is based on the socialization model of religious development in families. Additionally, there is discussion of the debate in social work over the past three decades regarding involvement of religious content and spirituality in practice and education. This model draws upon the rich network of emotional and tangible resources typically possessed by religious communities. The authors caution against the potentially destructive isolation of religious families from their belief system in the social work process.

Critique: The theory section and related references may be helpful in dealing with communities from a spiritual, social work perspective.

Design

The authors chose three cases from their practice that illustrate methodology and results relevant to the aims of the study.

Critique: More cases could have been presented, depicting a wider variety of obstacles. Also, cases were chosen for inclusion in the article in order to illustrate salient points about the model. In this sense, the article is not truly a report of a qualitative experiment, but rather a narration of a few case studies to demonstrate the usefulness and practicality of a community-based model that focuses on religious resources.

(continued)

Nakhaima, J. M., & Dicks, B. H. (1995). Social work practice with religious families. Families in Society, 76 (6), 360-368.

Analysis / Results

Results are presented in narrative form in an appealing and educational manner. Though this is explorative research, considerable detail is given regarding implementation of the described model, including instructions on assessing resources and strengths, approaching members of the religious community to become involved. and considerations of generational and organizational sensitivity. There is pertinent discussion of bias, confidentiality and trust issues. Also, potential obstacles to implementation of this model are addressed.

Gereralizability

Some aspects of the cases may be applied to other situations. However, there is some very nuanced material, and future researchers and practitioners should be cautious about inappropriately applying the findings of this study. Sufficient detail is provided for this research to be replicated, allowing for individual client and support group variation.

Sweet, M., & Johnson, C. (1990). Enhancing empathy: The interpersonal implications of a Buddhist meditation technique. Psychotherapy, 27 (1), 19-29.

Purpose

To assess the effectiveness of the Meditation Enhanced Empathy Training (MEET) with regard to increasing abilities to relate to others in a friendly and noncontrolling manner while retaining autonomous identity. More specifically, the aim of MEET is to facilitate the development of a well integrated personality with stable self-esteem and the ability to relate toward others in an empathic, compassionate and accepting manner.

Theory

Western literature dealing with meditation has principally been concerned with arousal-reducing concentrative meditation practices, rather than exploring the social psychological side of the meditative experience. This social component of meditation is important in the Buddhist tradition, and has as its aim the generation of empathic concern and other prosocial attitudes. Such attitudes have analogues in the Judeo-Christian ethic, Kant's categorical imperative, and the benevolence of universal love prominent in Chinese philosophy.

The authors present a theory, based on pathological responses of early social environments, of unfriendly personality styles. Also, Kohut's conceptualization of empathy as both an affective and cognitive skill is described. Further, the authors explain several points of convergence between MEET and contemporary psychological frameworks. For example, research in developmental psychology indicates the development of empathic and prosocial behavior to be an innate process. Mahayana Buddhism on which MEET is based, holds a similar view of the innate potential of all humans to develop universally empathic attitudes.

It is suggested, based on theory, that MEET can be especially effective for personality disordered individuals who have deficits in empathic ability, including those with narcissistic, compulsive, paranoid, schizoid and antisocial personality disorders or features.

Critique: The theory section is rich and informative. However, the authors state that MEET is an adapted form of the Buddhist meditation practice known as "the four boundless meditative states," with the changes involving linguistic considerations to accommodate the Western mentality. It should be noted that techniques such as this one are carefully passed down through a system of disciplic succession, and changes that an uninformed researcher may consider to be essentially inconsequential may actually be very substantial.

Sweet, M., & Johnson, C. (1990). Enhancing empathy: The interpersonal implications of a Buddhist meditation technique. Psychotherapy, 27 (1), 19-29.

Design

Three case studies are described, subjects being chosen from the clinical practice of the authors. These cases were chosen to illustrate situations where MEET can he effective, as well as to show an instance where caution must be exercised in applying the technique. Choice of cases for inclusion in the article was made after intervention In one case there was a 3-year follow-up, and in another case there was a 1-year follow-up. The meditative technique, based on silent repetition of self-statements accompanied by appropriate mental imagery, is outlined in some detail.

Measurement

The Structural Analysis of Social Behavior (SASB), a system for coding dyadic interpersonal behavior. is described as an instrument for measuring the effects of MEET. The authors write "The effectiveness of SASB as an analytical tool is based on its clinical sensitivity and the empirical corroboration of its reliability and validity."

Critique: Although references for this instrument are provided, no psychometrics are given in the article itself. Also, the case study descriptions don't describe the use or results of this assessment tool.

Results / Discussion

In one case (1 7 year old male), the client apparently demonstrated some positive effects from MEET. Two weeks later, however, he attempted suicide as a result of fury stemming from his parents' divorce. The authors conclude that the method has potential to suppress negative affects, leading to future symptom formation, rather than to resolution and growth. In this case, anger issues should have been worked through more thoroughly before beginning the meditative intervention. In the two other cases described, the clients, after several months involvement with MEET, displayed significant improvement. In one case (59 year old male), violent fantasies were greatly reduced in frequency and intensity. Three-year follow-up indicated an acceptable and comfortable level of psychological functioning. In another case (24 year old male), the client achieved higher self-esteem, greater comfort in social situations, and more friendliness, acceptance and sensitivity toward others, which he ascribed to the meditation practice. Follow-up one year later found this man, who had suffered from drug abuse and avoidant, dependent and passive-aggressive personality traits, to be functioning well in graduate school, drug-free, and involved in a long-term relationship.

In addition to clinical use, the authors suggest that MEET has potential as a tool in training program for mental health professionals.

(continued)

Sweet, M., & Johnson, C. (1990). Enhancing empathy: The interpersonal implications of a Buddhist meditation technique. Psychotherapy, 27 (1), 19-29.

Replicability

The technique is described in interesting detail, though not sufficiently for another researcher to reproduce the intervention. However, by accessing the references given in the article, the MEET therapy could probably be reproduced.

Generalizability

A sample size of 3, with only one gender represented, is clearly not generalizable to a larger population. The purpose of this qualitative report, however, was to foster interest in the technique, perhaps spawning rigorous research. Still, a caution is warranted due to the suggestions of the authors regarding the potential populations that can be served by MEET They suggest that those with severe personality disorders may be benefited. One of the cases, however, illustrated the potential dangers of the method. Therefore, practitioners and researchers should be wary about applying this method to persons with severe mental imbalances.

Urbanowski, F. B., & Miller, J .J. (1996). Trauma, psychotherapy, and meditation. Journal of Transpersonal Psychology. 28 (1), 31-48.

Purpose

To explore the process of healing past trauma and increasing client awareness of how the past affects the present through a combination of psychotherapy and meditation techniques. The therapeutic alliance of these two approaches is stressed in this model. The meditation techniques include Mindfulness Meditation (MM), Concentration Meditation (CM), and Body Scan (BS). Five case reports are presented to demonstrate the integration of meditation with traditional psychotherapy and the diverse ways the therapy may evolve based upon the circumstances of the individual.

Theory

A literature review of the research on meditation as used with trauma survivors is presented, with the results indicating that meditative techniques can be useful with this population. The authors dispel stereotypical conceptions of meditation as an escape from reality, or as merely a form of relaxation. They describe it as "a courageous and sometimes painful exploration of an individual's inner world and can greatly facilitate psychological development in ways that traditional psychotherapy cannot." Further, they assert that meditation can facilitate the process of guiding individuals through childhood pain, allowing them to relive past trauma in a safe environment. Two broad types of meditation are described concentration and mindfulness. CM develops a laser beam type of attention, on an object such as breath, a mantra, a flame, etc. In MM, attention can be compared to a spotlight, and any passing object in the mind can become the object of attention. Many techniques, such as BS, incorporate CM and MM. Walking meditation is also described. Common frustrations of novice meditators are expounded, as are psychological symptoms and defenses that characterize a traumatized individual. A common experience for trauma survivors during meditation is the unveiling of the past trauma which had been suppressed. Initially this often results in an increase in psychological distress. Within this turmoil, however, is the potential to heal the trauma and continue the growth process. Effective meditation is incompatible with active use of drugs or alcohol, and therefore trauma survivors who have selfmedicated their pain with substance abuse must establish sustained sobriety before engaging in meditation therapy. The authors emphasize the person of the therapist in meditation therapy. Specifically, it is suggested that "the therapist must draw upon his or her in-depth experience with meditation ... to skillfully decide when, what meditative techniques, and what frequency of practice will be appropriate for a particular client."

Critique: This is an interesting attempt at integrating Eastern and Western psychological approaches. in particular, this model seeks to simultaneously strengthen ego, as in psychotherapy, and provide opportunities for egolessness, as is common in meditative strategies.

(continued)

Urbanowski, F. B., & Miller, J .J. (1996). Trauma, psychotherapy, and meditation. Journal of Transpersonal Psychology, 28 (1), 31-48.

Design

Five cases are presented and analyzed. All 5 involve Western clients in their 20s or 30s, 4 of whom had prior meditation experience. Four of the subjects are female, and one of the female clients had a strong religious (Catholic) orientation.

Critique: Representative or saturating sampling is obviously not possible in such a qualitative design incorporating so few cases. Still, more diversity, especially with regard to age range, may have enhanced the external validity of the design. As it is, the design allows some generalizability to young Western adults, especially those with meditation experience. Cases are presented in sufficient detail for understanding the process of integrating meditation and psychotherapy, though the complex and individualized nature of the intervention would make it difficult to directly apply the procedure of any one case. Duration of therapy in these cases ranges from 3 months to 2 years.

The authors write "The five cases described here demonstrate the wide range of clinical presentations which can benefit from the addition of a meditation practice to traditional psychotherapy." Actually, the cases didn't vary substantially enough, as each one dealt with uncovering childhood memories of abuse. The study might benefit, for example, from cases involving other types of trauma, such as traumas from war or accident.

Analysis / Results

All 5 cases demonstrated success over varying time periods, with the subject resolving childhood abuse and manifesting a happier, more productive life as a result of therapy combining meditation and traditional psychotherapy. Potential dangers of the method were also revealed and discussed. For instance, one subject entered into a flashback and experienced severe terror. Fortunately, the therapist successfully handled the situation. For traumatized persons, the experience of egolessness can be horrifying, creating a sense of emptiness and disintegration of whatever sense of self had existed. The authors caution that this can even lead to psychosis. Therefore, the article frequently emphasizes that it is important for the therapist to have an intimate knowledge of the client and the meditative techniques. They state "This practice cannot be approached as a cookbook treatment learned by reading about it, attending a seminar on it, and then using it in one's psychotherapy practice. ...these practices need to be an integral part of the therapist's own personal life..." (p. 41).

The authors conclude that there are many instances where psychotherapy combined with meditation is potentially more effective in helping traumatized patients than either method alone. Also, meditation techniques provide a person with powerful tools to utilize throughout their lives. Moreover, this technique provides a flexible framework for a client to progress at an individualized pace, and acknowledges and provides for the incorporation of a number of treatment modalities. This can reduce treatment cost. Additionally, this therapy is empowering for the client, as one learns a practice which enables her/him to be present with whatever mental content presents itself. In some instances, the trauma survivor may meet with the psychotherapist weekly, and then may engage in self-directed meditation with less frequent contact with the therapist, though it is important for the client to know that the therapist is available at all phases of therapy. The article concludes with advantages of this model in a managed care environment.

Critique: Results of each case are appropriately analyzed with regard to benefits and limitations. Still, it is clear that the authors are attempting to promote this model, and there may be inferential leaps regarding therapeutic effects that are more than the evidence can bear. Findings must be considered in light of the fact that there are no control or alternate treatment groups.

In one case, prior to treatment the subject was accustomed to praying to the Virgin Mary for shelter. Though the authors claim "this case provides a good example of integrating an individual's religious belief system with CM and MM" (p. 39), the case description implied that the particular focus of meditation may

(continued)

Urbanowski, F. B., & Miller, J .J. (1996). Trauma, psychotherapy, and meditation. Journal of Transpersonal Psychology, 28 (1), 31-48.

Analysis/Results (continued) have been imposed on the subject. A more genuine integration could have incorporated the client's existing prayer as an object of meditation.

Generalizability
Despite design limitations that are inherent in this type of qualitative investigation, the intervention is thoroughly described and therefore adequately replicable. Also, the authors sufficiently explicate caveats that define when this modality should be used. Still, much is left to the discretion of the therapist, and the potential for effective or irresponsible utilization remains. Specifically, therapists with experience and knowledge of meditation techniques who are working with victims of childhood abuse can seriously consider implementing the integrative intervention described in this article.

Delmonte, M. M. (1983). Mantras and meditation: A literature review. Perceptual & Motor Skills, 57 (1), 64-66.

Purpose

To review the literature on mantra and meditation interventions in order to determine whether the "mantra-person fit" is of central importance, as claimed by many teachers of meditation. Also, the author sought to examine the research on exercises based on meditation, but lacking the cultural or spiritual connotations that are usually associated with meditation traditions.

Critique: Especially in its focus on mantra research, this literature review is unique and significantly contributes to the topic.

Theory

At introductory talks on meditation, especially those given by teachers of transcendental Meditation (TM), the importance of using the correct mantra, that is, the individual mantra match, is stressed. Different mantras purportedly have different effects. However, Benson has suggested that any mental device that minimizes one's attention to other stimuli would suffice during meditation. Additionally, the author cites Festinger's theory of cognitive dissonance, which postulates that the process of cognitive organization generates pressures that induce individuals to make overt or covert efforts to achieve maximum cognitive consistency by decreasing cognitive inconsistency, to explain the positive effects of personal mantras and meditative techniques. For instance, a novice meditator, having paid a considerable amount of money for a personal mantra, as is the case with TM, may experience cognitive pressure to find mantra practice rewarding.

Critique: The theory section is appropriately skeptical about the success of so-called meditational and mantra practices that have become popular in the West. However, the article would benefit by some exposition of authentic Vedic theory on which mantra meditation is based. Such an explanation would enhance the credibility of this literature review.

Design

This is a literature review that examines and synthesizes the results of 10 studies on mantra meditation and 4 studies on other meditative techniques. These studies were published between 1972 and 198 1. The studies included in this review involved designs that compare a meditation or mantra practice with a pseudo-meditation or pseudo-mantra practice, in order to isolate and identify the effects of the supposedly genuine technique.

Critique: Based on the computer search conducted by the author of this specialization paper, the studies selected for inclusion in this literature review, especially in the area of mantra, are representative, though not exhaustively, of the research in the field from 1972-1981.

(continued)

Delmonte, M. M. (1983). Mantras and meditation: A literature review. <u>Perceptual & Motor Skills, 57 (1),</u> 64-66.

Analysis/Results

In text form, the author summarizes the main results of each study, and presents these results in the context of TM theory and the theory of cognitive dissonance. To summarize, every study that evaluated mantras compared to a treatment group of mock-mantras found that any mental device onto which the attention can be focused is equally effective in terms of measurable outcomes. Measurable outcomes in these studies included physiological indicators such as heart rate, EEG alpha, respiration rate, and blood pressure, and psychometric measures of anxiety. Also, the studies have generally reported effective use of meditation techniques that are devoid of the cultural or spiritual connotations which are usually associated with either the Eastern or Western meditation traditions. The author emphasizes the role of reduction in cognitive dissonance in regards to the effects of meditation and mantra chanting.

Critique: A more quantitative analysis and presentation of data would have enhanced this literature review. Still, the article effectively conveys the gist of the research in this area.

Gemeralizability

This article succeeds to represent the research on the topic of effectiveness of mantra and meditation techniques, as compared with mock-mantras and pseudo-meditation techniques, for 1972-1981. Prior to 1982, the research in this area focused on physiological effects. since then there have been several studies that concentrate on psychological and spiritual indicators, such as stress, empathy, spirituality, and happiness. It should be noted that, while the results of this literature review adequately represents the research in the field in many ways, the research on this topic generally does not examine genuine mantra or meditative techniques, as the techniques in the form that they have come to the West tend not to conform to original Vedic descriptions.

Delmonte, M. M., & Kenny, V. (1985). An overview of the therapeutic effect of meditation. Psychologia: An International Journal of Psychology in the Orient, 28 (4), 189-202.

Purpose

This literature review seeks to address the usefulness of meditation as a therapeutic intervention in the framework of conceptual models of the meditation experience. In the West, integrative meditation, as opposed to mindfulness meditation or concentrative meditation, is most widely practiced, and therefore this review focuses on this meditative form.

Theory

Shapiro described 3 groupings of attentional strategies in meditation: wide angle lens attention, which focuses on a broad field, represented by mindfulness meditation, zoom lens attention, which focuses on a specific object, as in concentrative meditation, and a shifting back and forth between the two as in integrated meditation. The author describes the effects of mantra meditation with reference to the primary process of psychodynamic theory, Freudian dream theory, and preverbal construing of personal construct theory. Further, the trancelike influence of mantras are analyzed with regard to the effects of various sounds on state of mind, and compared to practices such as Rosary and repetition of Latin prayers. The process of stress relief through mantra meditation is analyzed, as are the phenomena of loosening, tightening and creativity, within the eclectic framework of psychodynamic theory, cognitive models of thought processing, and neurophysiological conceptualizations.

According to the studies reviewed by the authors, prospective meditators tend to be more anxious and neurotic than the average person, and they report a greater number of problems in general. A major reported benefit of meditation is reduced anxiety, with self-paced desensitization postulated as the mechanism leading to the anxiety decrease. Related to anxiety relief is the benefit, often attributed to meditation, of improved steep. Other reported benefits include self-actualization, improved respiration, decreased blood pressure and decreased drug dependence. The article briefly discusses proposed mechanisms for these effects as offered by various schools, including behaviorism, classical conditioning, and psychodynamic. The authors conclude "This plethora of hypothetical pathways accounting for therapeutic gain from meditation practice is rather confusing" (p. 195). They then proceed to attempt a complex, synthesized model that integrates behavioral and psychoanalytic concepts.

Critique: This is an interesting, sophisticated analysis of integrative meditation from the vantage point of several Western psychological perspectives. Unfortunately, the authors have not given adequate attention to the intrinsic paradigm of mantra meditation in attempting to explain the process and its effects. For example, the Vedas are a prime source of genuine mantra meditation, and there is no mention of Vedic psychology. It's as if one sought to analyze, say, the Bowenian model, and the analysis were performed with reference to the philosophies of Vyasa, Kanada, Kapila, and Gautama, with no regard to Bowen or any other Western theorist, such as Freud, Haley or Maslow.

(continued)

Delmonte, M. M., & Kenny, V. (1985). An overview of the therapeutic effect of meditation. Psychologia: An International Journal of Psychology in the Orient, 28 (4), 189-202.

Design

This literature review covers several aspects of research in the field, including studies that have investigated reported benefits of meditation, the predisposition of meditators, comparative studies of meditation and other techniques. and meditation as relaxation. Twelve studies and I literature review are evaluated to assess reported benefits. 7 studies on meditator predisposition are included, 12 research articles on comparative evidence are included, and the section on meditation and relaxation contains 4 articles.

Critique: In the predisposition and relaxation sections. an inordinate proportion of the studies are by Delmonte. this leads to some doubt about the objectivity of the literature review. Otherwise. based on the computer search by the author of this specialization paper, the selected articles appear representative of research in the area.

Analysis / Results

Research supports the claim that meditation practice reduces anxiety, or is at least associated with this result. Improved sleep has also been associated with meditation practice. In addition, evidence exists that meditation is more successful in reducing neuroticism, introversion and drug usage than progressive relaxation, although both techniques appear to be equally effective in reducing anxiety and insomnia. Meditation appears to be associated with lower physiological arousal than simple eyes-closed rest, though the difference is "not striking". Overall, relative to established relaxation procedures, meditation does not produce special physiological effects. Several studies indicate that a tendency to discontinue practice and to meditate infrequently is related to an unhealthy psychological profile, including high levels of neuroticism, low self-esteem, external locus of control, and low social desirability, Response to meditation was not related to gender. Relatively neurotic or anxious subjects may have problems too severe to benefit from a technique such as meditation.

The authors emphasize that meditation was not originally conceived as a relaxation technique, but rather it is part of a holistic approach to self-development. Relaxation and peacefulness are derivative effects. It is concluded that meditation may be a helpful adjunct to psychotherapy, though it is pointed out that the long-term objectives of meditation appear to be more ambitious than most forms of psychotherapy. The authors assert that the final goal of meditation is "to transcend the ego" (p. 198). They acknowledge that some therapists may share this philosophy, as opposed to conventional psychotherapeutic approaches which strive to strengthen the ego, though they caution that such art approach to therapy may not be practical, "as self-exploration and personal development through meditation is usually envisaged as taking many years of dedicated application under careful supervision" (p. 198). It is suggested that if meditation has therapeutic value, then it is limited to those who are already reasonably well-integrated.

Critique: Presentation of results would have been aided by charts, tables or figures. Also, some quantitative analysis, rather than merely narrative description, would have added to the significance and substance of the literature review. It is appreciated that the results section attempts to analyze meditation with regard for the philosophy upon which mantra meditation is based. Still, it should be mentioned that the Vedic literatures describe the goal of mantra meditation as realizing one's spiritual ego, not abandoning ego altogether or strengthening one's material ego (Prabhupada, 1976).

Delmonte, M. M., & Kenny, V. (1985). An overview of the therapeutic effect of meditation. <u>Psychologia: An International Journal of Psychology in the Orient, 28 (4),</u> 189-202.

Generalizability

Despite the caveats mentioned in the Design section, this literature review adequately represent the research on the topic, and is the most comprehensive review in the field. There have been many studies performed since this literature review was conducted, and researchers would benefit from an updated version. Still, based on the findings of the author of this specialization paper, more recent research does not contradict the main results of the article under discussion.

APPENDIX B: Pilot Study

Pilot Study: Single System Design

In March and April of 1998 the author conducted a single-system design pilot study experiment on the efficacy of chanting the *hare krsna maha mantra*. As described previously, mantra science, according to the Vedas, is based on sound vibration that is capable of extricating the mind from the modes of material nature, and especially from the modes of *rajas* and *tamas*. Attentive concentration on a genuine mantra, such as the *hare krsna maha mantra*, which, according to Vedic description, is purely in the mode of *sattva*, will help us to develop *sattvic* qualities, such as satisfaction and contentment. Effects of mantra chanting are hypothesized in the Vedas, and can be operationalized in accord with *guna* theory, as was done in this single-system design and the group study described in this dissertation. *Guna* theory is explained in the section of chapter 1 of this dissertation entitled material science and the Vedas.

Appendix A presents a systematic synthesis of research literature on spiritual interventions, and includes several studies on Eastern techniques, including mantra chanting. A brief summary of the research on chanting is provided below.

Janowiak and Hackman (1994) conducted a three-group pretest-posttest experimental design with random assignment, with one group being a mantra-chanting group. This group showed a significant ($p<.01$) increase in self-actualization and a significant reduction ($p<.01$) in stress. For stress, which was a dependent variable in the group design maha mantra experiment described later in this dissertation, Janowiak and Hackman obtained an effect size of 2.38, which indicates the magnitude of difference between pretest and posttest mean scores for the mantra chanting group, divided by the pretest standard deviation . Further, r^2 for the correlation between stress reduction and chanting compliance was .42. Both of these effect sizes are larger than the effect sizes obtained for the group that practiced a yoga relaxation technique. Rosenthal (1997) reports that a mean difference of 2.38 and an r^2 of .42 both reflect very large effect sizes.

Kaye (1985) included chanting of the mantra "om" in an intervention package with a group of elderly clients. In this qualitative study, Kaye reports that response to the chanting was very enthusiastic, and that the clients were enlivened by and looked forward to the chanting sessions. Delmonte (1983) conducted a literature review on meditative and mantra interventions. He concluded that the supposed "mantra-person fit" advocated by some proponents of mantra meditation is not supported by empirical evidence. That is, the literature suggested that any sort of mental device, or mock-mantra, was as effective as the so-called genuine mantras. Outcome measures in his literature review included physiological indicators such as heart rate and blood pressure, as well as measures of anxiety.

Methods of Pilot Study

Sampling for Pilot Study

The researcher placed advertisements in a student newspaper in a mid-sized town in the Southeastern section of the United States. These ads announced that a study is being conducted on an Eastern-style intervention for relieving stress and depression, and that participants would be monetarily reimbursed. Twelve persons responded to the ads. Of these 12, five did not respond to the researcher's attempts to contact them, after the initial discussion about their participation in the study. Another respondent explained that he was already chanting the *hare krsna maha mantra*. As it would be unethical to ask him to discontinue the chanting in order to obtain baseline data, this respondent did not participate in the experiment. Of the six remaining respondents, one filled out the packet of pretest surveys, but did not respond to any further attempts at contact, leaving five participants in the study. All respondents read and signed a consent form for participating in research.

Design and Procedures

This was an A-B-A withdrawal design, with the baseline and follow-up periods each about one week in length, and the intervention period lasting for approximately four weeks. Subjects completed survey packages on Day 1, and at weekly intervals after that, for a total of seven data points during a six-week period. The second survey package was completed at the beginning of Week 2, just before the subject was instructed in the chanting intervention. One outcome measure, the Self-Rated Well Being Scale, is a self-anchored scale, and was completed on every day of the study, from the beginning of baseline through the end of follow-up. Each participant received $25 at the beginning of the study, and $25 after the follow-up session.

The intervention is described as follows. The subject was given a string of 109 beads, known as *japa* beads, with one bead markedly larger than the others. The researcher instructed the client to chant mantras while counting the number of mantras with the set of beads. Specifically, this method entails holding the bead on either side of the large bead with the thumb and middle finger of the right hand. While holding the bead, one should chant the maha mantra, which is composed of the following 32 syllables: *hare krishna, hare krishna, krishna krishna, hare hare, hare rama, hare rama, rama rama, hare hare*. After the mantra is completed, one should move one bead through the fingers so that the second bead from the large bead is now being held. Again one should chant the maha mantra. In this way, chanting one mantra per bead, 108 mantras should be chanted. This constitutes one "round" of *japa*. *Japa* can be performed in any circumstance. For instance, one may be sitting or walking. The essential factor is that one is fully attentive to the chanting. After teaching the subjects how to chant, the researcher instructed them to chant three rounds of *japa* every day for the duration of the intervention period.

Outcome Measures for Pilot Study

Subjects daily completed a Self-Rated Well Being Scale, with "Worst I've Ever Felt" and "Best I've Ever Felt" at the extremes of an 11-point continuum.

In addition to the self-anchored scale, subjects completed a packet of six surveys at weekly intervals.These surveys included the Vedic Personality Inventory (VPI) (Wolf, 1998), the Spiritual Involvement and Beliefs Scale (SIBS) (Hatch, Hellmich, Naberhaus, & Berg, 1995), the Generalized Contentment Scale (GCS) (Hudson, & Proctor, 1977), the Index of Clinical Stress (ICS) (Abell, 1991), The Verbal Aggressiveness Scale (VAS) (Infante, & Wigley, 1986), and the Satisfaction with Life Scale (SWLS) (Diener, et. al., 1985). All measuring instruments used in this study are found in Appendix D. The VPI, GCS, and ICS are all described in the measurement section of Chapter 3. Also, the VPI and SIBS are described in the measurement of spirituality section of Chapter 2. An 80-item version of the VPI was used for the pilot study. This version consisted of 28 *sattva* items, 24 *rajas* items, and 28 *tamas* items. This 80-item version, after statistical analysis, was later reduced to the 56-item version used in the group *japa* study.

The Verbal Aggressiveness Scale
Infante and Wigley (1986) describe verbal aggressiveness as a personality trait that inclines persons to attack the self-concept of other people. They developed a scale of 20 items, half worded positively and half stated negatively, to assess the construct of verbal aggressiveness. The rating format is a five-point linear scale with "almost never true" and "almost always true" as endpoints.

Reliability and factorial validity for the scale were tested on a sample of 636 students enrolled in introductory communication courses at large Midwestern state university. Alpha for the scale was .81, and test-retest reliability was .82. Factor analysis indicated that the scale is unidimensional (Infante and Wigley, 1986).

To test construct validity the VAS was administered, along with seven other trait measures, to 104 students. Results for all scales, compared with the VAS, were in the direction predicted by theory. Scales included the Social Desirability Scale, the Hostility-Guilt Inventory, and the Feelings of Inadequacy Subscale (Infante and Wigley, 1986).

The Satisfaction With Life Scale (SWLS)
This scale, which consists of five items and a linear response range with "strongly disagree" and "strongly agree" as the endpoints, measures global life satisfaction, which is an important component in subjective well-being. Factorial validity and reliability for the SWLS were assessed on a sample of 176 undergraduates at a large Midwestern university. Two months after testing, 76 of the students were readministered the scale. Test-retest reliability was .82, and coefficient alpha was .87. Factor analysis indicated a single factor that accounted for 66% of the variance in the scores. Eleven measures were administered to a sample of 339 undergraduates to test the construct validity of the scale. All results were in the direction predicted by theory, suggesting strong construct validity. This instrument has also been tested with a geriatric population, and this testing revealed strong known-instruments criterion validity for the SWLS (Diener, et. al., 1985).

Compliance Log
Subjects filled out a Chanting Compliance Log, noting on the log the number of rounds that they chanted each day. Though they were instructed to chant three rounds per day, the log indicated the actual frequency of chanting.

Results of Pilot Study
For the five subjects who completed the study, Table 28 shows their mean scores for each outcome measure, as well as the Compliance Log score, which indicates the average number of rounds chanted per day. Average scores for each measure are listed for baseline, treatment, and follow-up phases.

Table 28

Mean Scores on Dependent Measures by Subject for Baseline, Treatment, and Follow-up

Subject A (chanted for 30 days)

	Sattva	Rajas	Tamas	VAS	SWLS	ICS	GCS	SIBS	SWBS	CL
Baseline	5.36	3.35	3.18	53.50	17.00	30.00	40.00	97.50	5.43	
Treatment	5.29	3.44	2.79	55.50	18.25	26.84	47.91	93.50	5.82	2.20
Follow-up	5.11	3.00	3.00	55.00	18.00	30.00	48.23	94.00	6.00	

Subject B (chanted for 29 days)

	Sattva	Rajas	Tamas	VAS	SWLS	ICS	GCS	SIBS	SWBS	CL
Baseline	5.21	3.63	2.23	32.50	18.00	33.00	23.34	93.00	3.57	
Treatment	5.41	3.47	2.21	31.25	24.00	27.67	26.33	91.00	7.52	2.38
Follow-up	5.29	3.71	2.26	32.00	24.00	24.67	26.67	91.00	6.83	

Subject C (Chanted for 30 days)

	Sattva	Rajas	Tamas	VAS	SWLS	ICS	GCS	SIBS	SWBS	CL
Baseline	5.18	3.48	2.61	31.50	24.50	28.50	23.50	90.50	5.29	
Treatment	5.48	3.48	2.46	28.25	26.25	25.50	22.00	97.25	7.58	2.93
Follow-up	5.48	3.42	2.61	30.00	22.00	30.00	24.00	91.00	6.17	

Subject D (Chanted for 30 days)

	Sattva	Rajas	Tamas	VAS	SWLS	ICS	GCS	SIBS	SWBS	CL
Baseline	5.48	3.38	3.13	32.00	20.50	21.50	23.00	86.00	6.17	
Treatment	5.72	3.26	2.77	26.75	25.75	23.00	21.83	93.75	7.10	2.93
Follow-up	5.61	3.25	2.21	26.00	26.00	25.00	23.00	98.00	4.00	

Subject E (Chanted for 30 days)

	Sattva	Rajas	Tamas	VAS	SWLS	ICS	GCS	SIBS	SWBS	CL
Baseline	5.21	3.83	3.16	34.00	20.50	34.00	31.34	83.00	4.00	
Treatment	5.52	3.28	2.67	27.75	25.25	27.25	26.00	95.50	7.76	2.77
Follow-up	5.64	3.25	2.21	25.00	25.00	24.33	25.00	96.00	6.33	

VAS- Verbal Aggressiveness Scale
SWLS- Satisfaction with Life Scale
ICS- Index of Clinical Stress
GCS- Generalized Contentment Scale
SIBS- The Spiritual Involvement and Beliefs Scale
SWBS- Self-rated Well-Being Scale
CL- Compliance Log

Analysis of Pilot Study

To restate the research hypotheses, it was predicted that *japa* intervention will increase *sattva*, satisfaction with life, spirituality, and well-being, and will decrease *rajas*, *tamas*, verbal aggressiveness, stress, and depression. Effects of *japa* were hypothesized to carry over to the follow-up period, though there is predicted to be some loss of effects. Therefore, follow-up scores were hypothesized to reverse direction. For instance, *japa* intervention would predict an increase in *sattva* from baseline to intervention, and then a decrease from intervention to follow-up, although the final score at the end of follow-up would not be expected to be as low as the mean baseline score. Follow-up scores were not analyzed in instances where baseline to treatment scores did not change according to the hypotheses. The reason for this is that if baseline to treatment scores did not behave as hypothesized, it is not reasonable to predict, according to Vedic theory, the direction of treatment to follow-up scores. For the following analysis of results, refer to Table 28.

Subject A

Analyzing mean scores, with regards to research hypotheses, from baseline to treatment phases, subject A went in the predicted direction on measures of *tamas*, satisfaction with life, stress, and well-being, and in a direction contrary to the research hypotheses for measures of *sattva, rajas*, verbal aggressiveness, depression, and spirituality. For those measures that behaved in a way in accord with Vedic theory, follow-up measures also behaved in the predicted manner for three of four scales, with the exception being the self-rated well-being scale.

Subject A was a middle-aged female undergoing intensive treatments for an illness. During our first phone discussion she mentioned that she really needs the money, though she also expressed interest in meditation. I gave her the packet of surveys at her home a few days after we spoke on the phone. At this meeting I also described to her the nature and procedures of the study, though I didn't describe what the details of the chanting intervention. We also filled out necessary paper work, including the consent form. The next week, at her home, I gave her the first 25$ and showed her how to chant. After chanting one round (108 mantras) together, she seemed to have a good feel for the process. We again met one week later, as I wanted to check on her chanting and collect the surveys. She greeted me by requesting the remainder of the payment, as she had an electric bill due. To encourage her continued participation in the study, I gave her $20 of the $25 still owed, in the hope that she would complete the study for the 5$ still remaining. At the session where I gave her the $20, we chanted one round together, and the fluency of her chanting indicated to me that she had been following the process in earnest. When I met with her again the next week, I collected the surveys and we chanted one round together. We met again about 2 weeks later, when she gave back the *japa* beads (after the required 4 weeks of chanting). A week later I collected the follow-up survey packet.

Subject B

From baseline to treatment, subject B's scores moved in the direction predicted by Vedic theory for measures of *sattva, rajas, tamas*, verbal aggressiveness, satisfaction with life, stress, and well-being, and in a direction contrary to research hypotheses for measures of depression and spirituality. For baseline to treatment measures that were in agreement with theory, the only follow-up mean score that was in the opposite direction from that predicted by theory was the measure for stress.

Subject B was a female undergraduate university student in her early twenties. During our first phone conversation she mentioned that she's experiencing a great amount of stress, and was interested to participate in the study in hopes that it would relieve her stress. About two weeks after this phone discussion the researcher this author gave her the baseline survey packet and explained to her the nature of the study. When we met again the next week to begin the intervention she was very happy, largely because she was about to begin some process meant to relieve her stress. This young woman quickly learned how to chant properly. We met every week during the intervention phase, except for one week when she was out of town. At the meetings she would submit the completed survey packets, and we would chant one round together. Her clear and fairly rapid chanting indicated that she was practicing the chanting on a regular basis. This woman was noticeably stressed during finals week, which corresponded with the last days of the intervention phase and the first days of the follow-up phase.

Subject C

From baseline to intervention, Subject C showed change in the direction predicted by the research hypotheses for all measures except *rajas*, which did not change. Follow-up scores were also in the direction predicted by theory.

Subject C was a female university graduate student in her mid-twenties. During the initial phone conversation she stated that the reimbursement of $50 was low, as she had been in studies where she earned hundreds of dollars. Anyhow, she agreed to participate. At the first meeting with this subject she was given the packet of surveys and the researcher explained to her the nature of the study, and necessary paperwork was completed. After a week we met again, and the researcher showed her how to chant. She seemed to like the idea of chanting this specific mantra. We met once a week for the duration of the study, and chanted one round together.

Subject D

From baseline to intervention, Subject D showed change in the predicted direction for measures of *sattva, rajas, tamas*, verbal aggressiveness, satisfaction with life, depression, spirituality, and well-being. Follow-up scores showed change in the predicted direction for *sattva*, and well-being, but not for *rajas, tamas*, verbal aggressiveness, satisfaction with life, depression and spirituality. Also, for well-being, the average follow-up score was below the baseline score, and thus the drop in mean score was greater than that predicted by theory.

Subject D was a female university graduate student in her mid-twenties. During the second week of intervention (3rd week of the study) with this subject she began a full-time job, the first of her life. She was excited about this, though it also caused anxiety. This subject quickly learned to chant properly. We met for the first 3 weeks of the study, and then she no-showed for 2 weeks in a row. On the phone she apologized, and explained that with her work and school responsibilities she was very busy and forgot about our meetings. She emphasized that she is chanting, and that she likes the chanting. Our next meeting was after follow-up, when she gave me the completed surveys. I cautioned Subject D not to chant during the follow-up phase, and she said that she didn't.

Subject E

Scores for subject E, from baseline to treatment, went in the predicted direction for all measures. Follow-up scores did not move in the predicted direction for any of the measures.

Subject E was a female university undergraduate in her early 20s. During our initial phone discussion she reported that she does silent meditation. About two weeks after this phone discussion the researcher gave her the baseline survey packet and described the study, and necessary paperwork was completed. A week later the researcher showed her the chanting intervention. She complained that the mantra was too long, and described her experience with a shorter mantra. In any case, she agreed to participate in the experiment, and quickly learned how to chant correctly on beads. After the introductory chanting meeting, we met again a week later, and again after 3 weeks of intervention. She no-showed for the meeting of the 2nd week of intervention, and for the meeting at the end of the intervention period. After follow-up we met again, and she submitted the completed survey packets.

Analyses of Results in Relation to Measures

Sattva.
The *sattva* scale behaved in accord with theory for four of the five subjects, from baseline to intervention. Of these four subjects, three showed *sattva* follow-up scores that concurred with predictions.

Rajas.
Rajas scores, from baseline to intervention, behaved according to theory for three of five subjects, with one subject showing no change. Only in one subject did follow-up scores move in the direction predicted by theory.

Tamas.
Tamas scores moved in accord with research predictions for every subject from baseline to intervention, and with three of five subjects from intervention to follow-up.

Verbal Aggressiveness.
The measure for verbal aggressiveness moved in the predicted direction for four of five subjects from baseline to intervention, and for two subjects from intervention to follow-up.

Satisfaction with Life.
Satisfaction with Life changed in the predicted direction for all five subjects from baseline to intervention, and for two subjects from intervention to follow-up.

Stress.
Stress scores changed in the predicted direction for four out of five subjects from baseline to intervention, and for two subjects from intervention to follow-up.

Depression.
Measures for depression behaved according to theory in three of five cases from baseline to intervention, and in one case from intervention to follow-up.

Spirituality.
Spirituality scores moved in the predicted direction in three cases from baseline to intervention, and in one case from intervention to follow-up.

Well-Being.
Self-rated well-being scores moved in the predicted direction for all subjects from baseline to intervention, and for three subjects from intervention to follow-up, though one

of these follow-up scores moved too far in the predicted direction, with regards to the research hypothesis.

Altogether, from the baseline phase to the intervention phase, 36 out of 45 measures (80%) moved in the direction predicted by theory. Of the 36 scores that behaved in accord with Vedic predictions from baseline to intervention, 19 (52.7%) responded according to the research hypotheses from the intervention period to the follow-up period.

Discussion of Pilot Study

With 80% of the measures responding according to the research hypotheses from baseline to intervention phases, this study provides some preliminary evidence for the efficacy of chanting the *hare krsna maha mantra* on *japa* beads. Measures of well-being, satisfaction with life, and *tamas* responded particularly well to the intervention, though all measures behaved according to theoretical predictions in at least three of five cases. With regard to follow-up scores, only 52.7% of the measures responded in accord with the research hypotheses, indicating that the research hypotheses were not successful in predicting directionality of scores one week after cessation of the intervention. The baseline to intervention results represent the main effects that this study attempted to examine, with intervention to follow-up data included primarily for exploratory purposes.

According to Vedic theory, which is the conceptual framework for this study, all sound vibrations are permeated by various combinations of the three modes of nature-*sattva, rajas and tamas*. A person's consciousness is affected by the types of sound vibrations to which one is exposed. Thus, a person who regularly associates with sound in the mode of *rajas* (passion) will develop *rajasic* consciousness, which might be characterized by qualities such as intense activity and high stress. The *hare krsna maha mantra*, according to Vedic theory, is completely in the mode of *sattva*. Therefore, one who chants this mantra will exhibit *sattvic* symptoms, which include a decrease in *rajas* and *tamas*, as well as reduced verbal aggressiveness, stress and depression, and increased spirituality, satisfaction with life, and sense of well-being. Thus, Vedic *guna* theory provides a possible explanation for the results of this study (Prabhupada, 1976).

Cook and Campbell (1979) delineate threats to external validity, construct validity and internal validity. Based on the validity considerations of Cook and Campbell, it can be concluded that internal, construct and external validity of this study are not strong. Clients were not sampled randomly, and therefore the results cannot necessarily be applied to any population outside of the participants in the study. Also, the sample size was very small, further reducing generalizability of results. Another threat to external validity that was not controlled with this design was the interaction of selection and treatment. That is, those who chose to participate in the experiment may not be representative of any particular population, with regards to their response to chanting. This is particularly relevant because the newspaper advertisement that initially attracted participants mentioned an "Eastern-style intervention". Also, the monetary reimbursement is another threat to generalizability of results.

Construct validity refers to the extent that the design allows the researcher to study the effects of the intervention, rather than some artifact of the procedures. In this study, experimenter expectancies and biases, as described earlier in this dissertation, could be perceived as a threat to construct validity of the design. Specifically, the experimenter expected the research hypotheses to be validated, and therefore researcher-subject interaction may have influenced the results towards verification of the research hypotheses.

Internal validity relates to the extent to which the design allows assessment of the causal relationship between the dependent and independent variables. In this study, there were no control, alternative treatment or placebo treatment groups, and thus there is very little comparative basis for the results of the subjects who chanted the maha mantra. Due to lack of controls, it is difficult to conclude with assurance that the intervention was the cause of change. For instance, each of the five subjects had histories during the course of the study. Factors such as individual relationships, academic pressures, and many other stressors could have influenced scores on outcome measures. Another uncontrolled threat to internal validity was maturation, meaning that scores on outcome measures may have changed simply due to the maturation of the subjects that occurred because of the passage of time. This is especially significant considering that several of the participants were young college students who were at a stage in life where their cognitions, emotions and perceptions tend to change relatively rapidly. Testing is another threat to internal validity. Subjects completed the same measures many times throughout the study, and subsequent scores may have been influenced by prior scores. Lack of any sort of random procedure for subject selection is a major threat to external validity, as is the unpredictable effects of monetary compensation. The researcher did attempt to minimize the effects of diffusion, as each subject was dealt with individually, not in a group, and subjects did not know the identity of other subjects.

Other shortcomings of the study include the unequal length of phases and the insufficiency of baseline points for most measures. Bloom, Fischer, and Orme (1995) recommend that phases of a single-system design should be of equal length, to allow internal factors to influence phases equally. In this study, the baseline lasted for about a week, as did the follow-up phase, though the intervention period lasted for about four weeks. Also, Bloom, Fischer, and Orme emphasize that baseline data should include enough data points to indicate stability. Except for the Self-rated Well Being Scale, which included seven or eight data points, the other measures included only two data points. From the graphs of the results of the study, it is clear in many cases that baseline data was not stable for many measures. In some cases, baseline data was going in the direction predicted by theory before intervention began, and therefore it is not certain whether the intervention caused the effects, or if the effects would have continued in the same direction as suggested by the trend of the baseline. Data was not analyzed with inferential statistics, and the method used, visual inspection, is subject to many deficiencies. From visual inspection of graphs it is apparent that many of the changes, though they were in the predicted direction, were only slight, and therefore the results are suggestive, but far from conclusive. Further, no effect sizes were calculated in this pilot study.

Replication studies with various populations and in different settings could help to clarify the generalizability of the results of this study. Further, studies on the hare krsna maha mantra that include random assignment and control groups will increase internal validity and help to assess the effects of this chanting intervention. This dissertation describes such a study.

APPENDIX C: Pilot Study Graphs

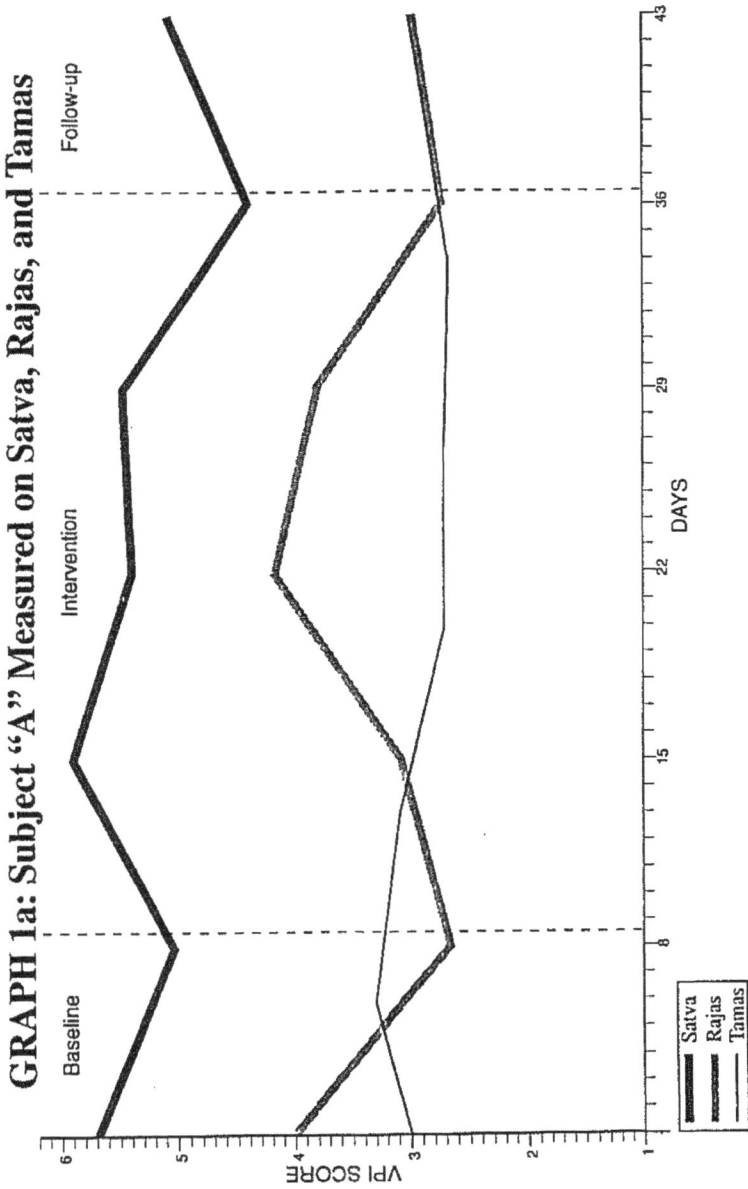

GRAPH 1a: Subject "A" Measured on Satva, Rajas, and Tamas

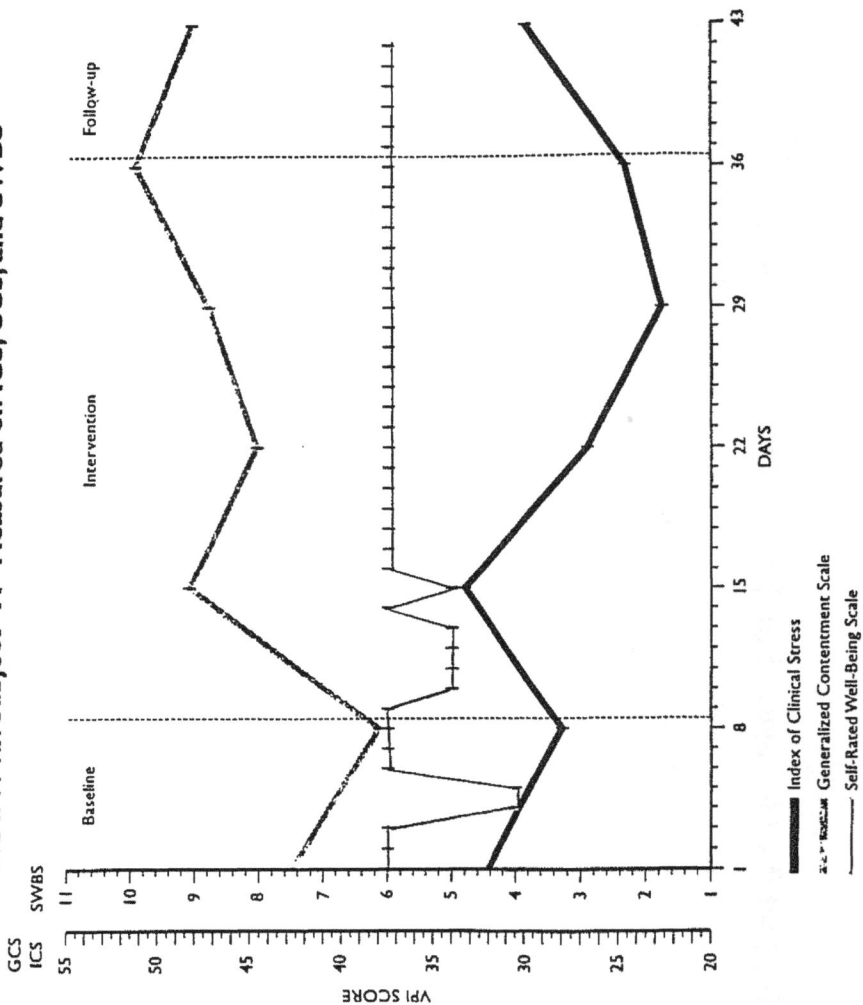

GRAPH Ib: Subject "A" Measured on ICS, GCS, and SWBS

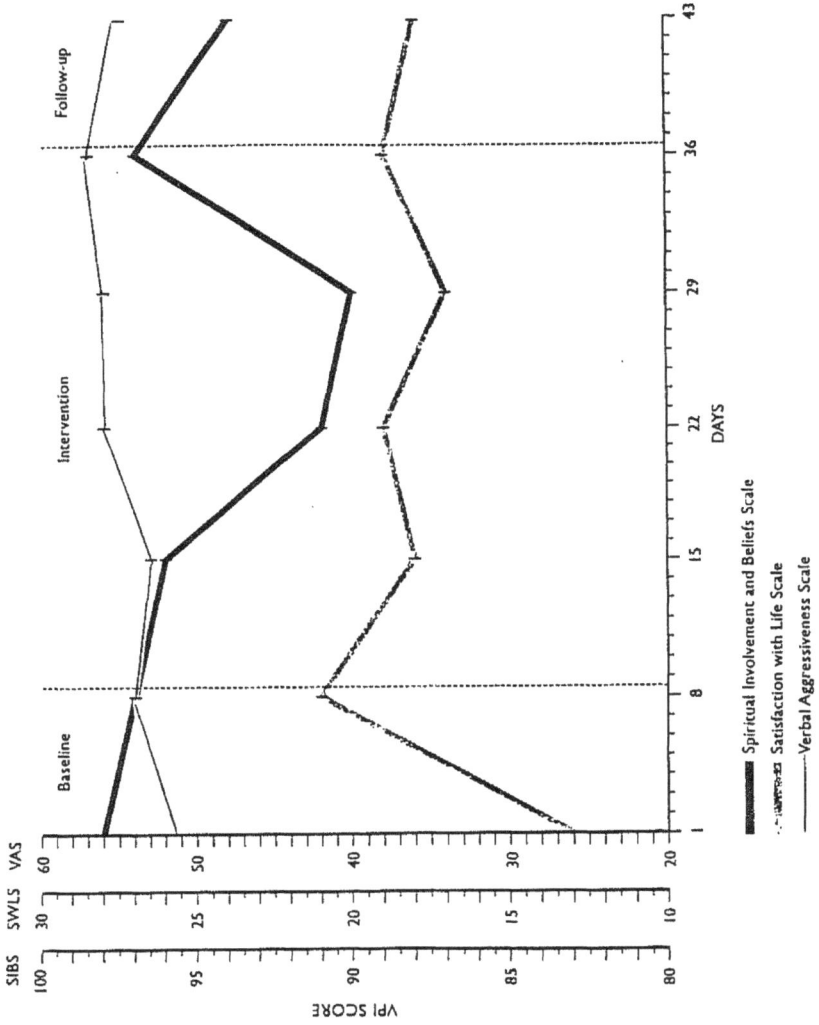

GRAPH 1c: Subject "A" Measured on SIBS, SWLS, and VAS

209

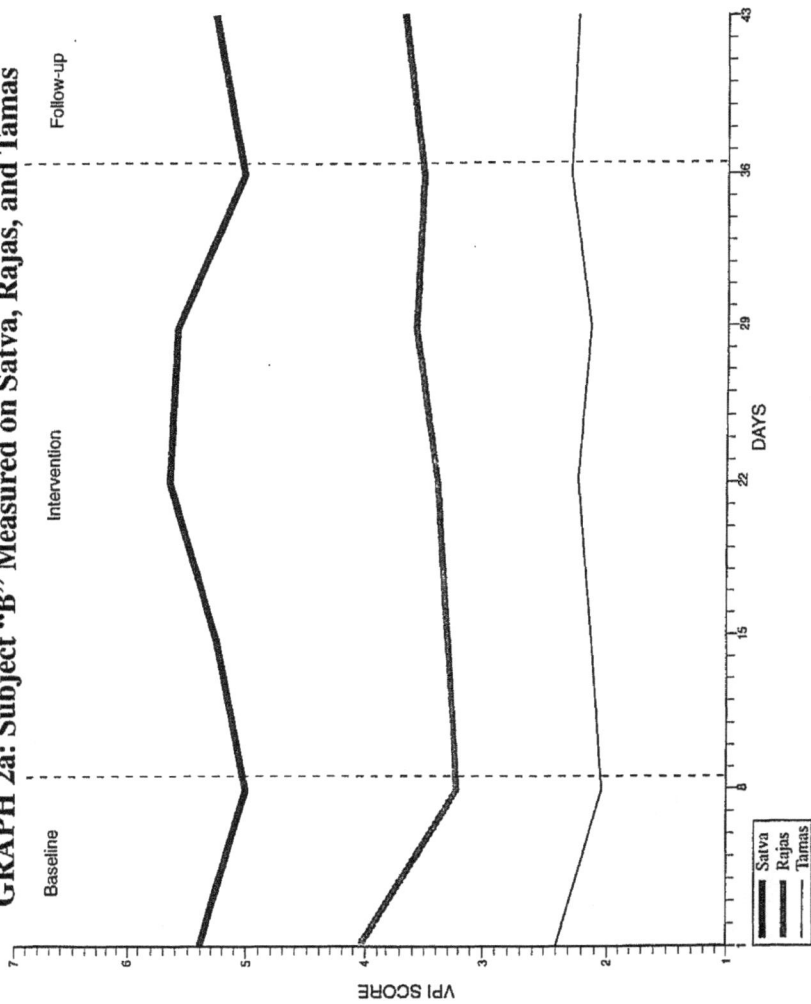

GRAPH 2a: Subject "B" Measured on Satva, Rajas, and Tamas

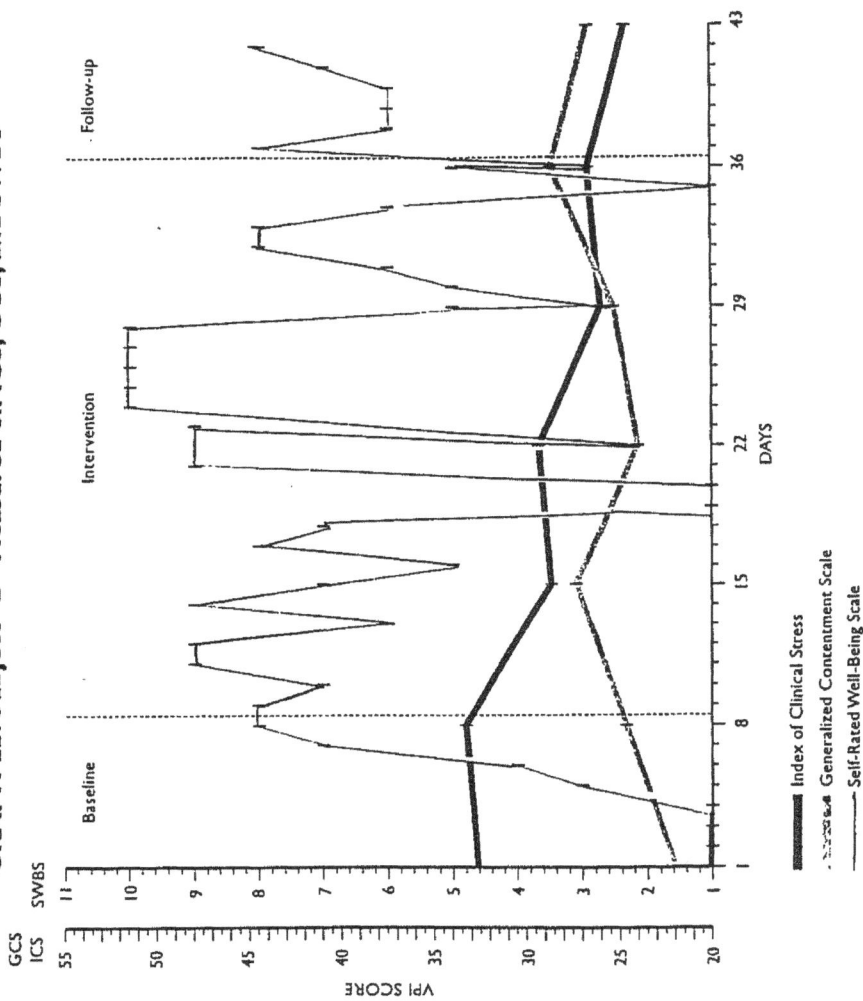

GRAPH 2b: Subject "B" Measured on ICS, GCS, and SWBS

Index of Clinical Stress
Generalized Contentment Scale
Self-Rated Well-Being Scale

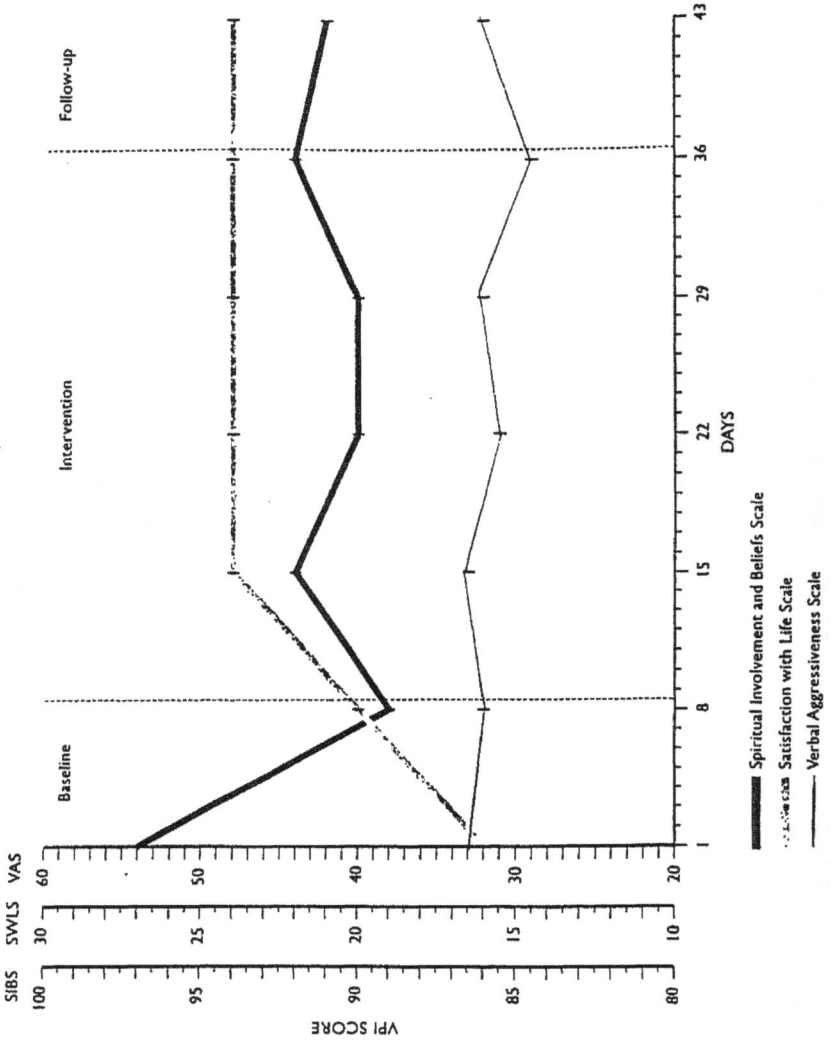

GRAPH 2c: Subject "B" Measured on SIBS, SWLS, and VAS

Spiritual Involvement and Beliefs Scale
Satisfaction with Life Scale
Verbal Aggressiveness Scale

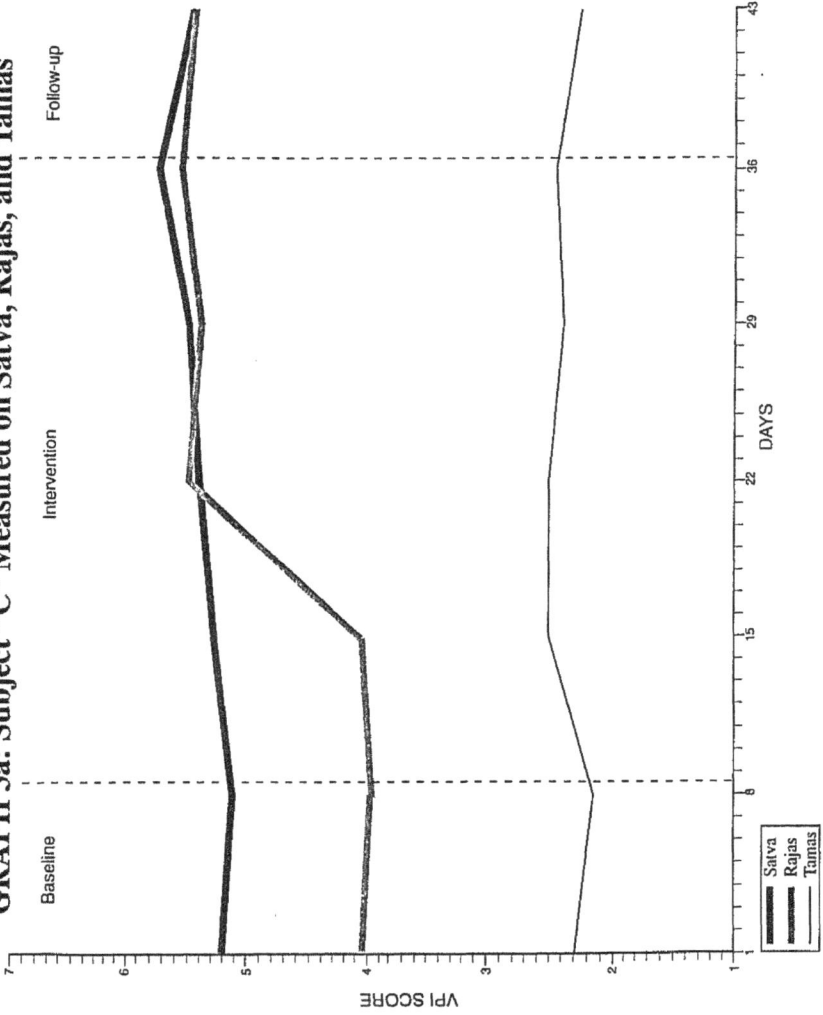

GRAPH 3a: Subject "C" Measured on Satva, Rajas, and Tamas

213

GRAPH 3b: Subject "C" Measured on ICS, GCS, and SWBS

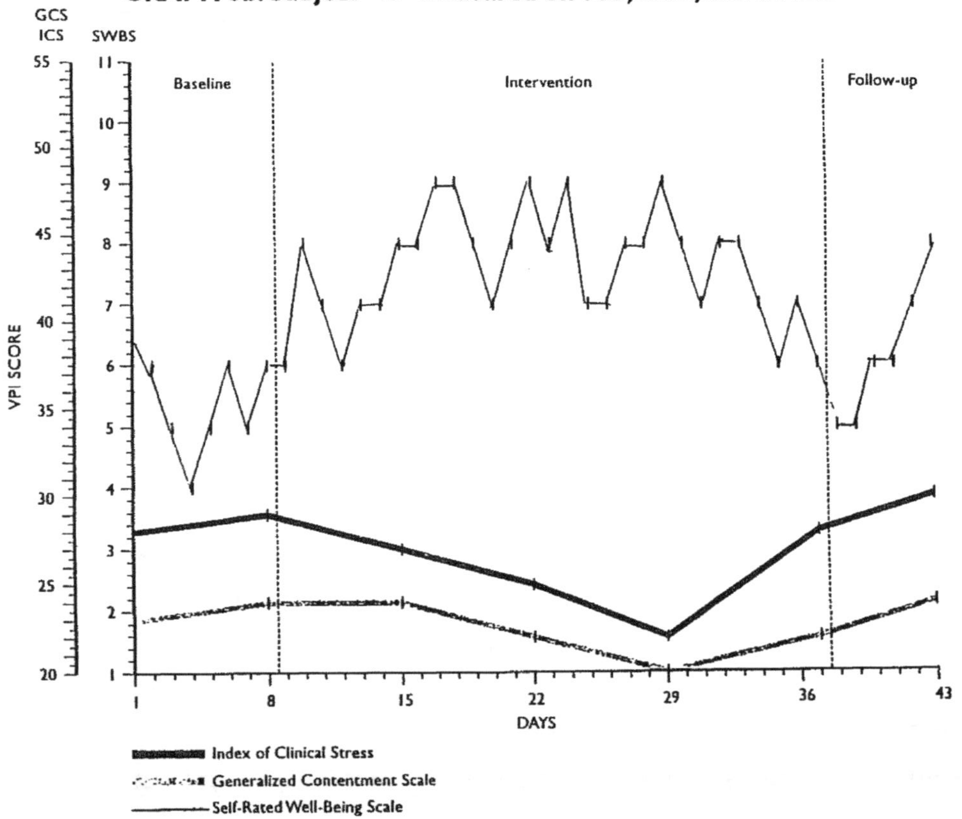
GCS
ICS
SWBS
VPI SCORE
55
50
45
40
35
30
25
20
11
10
9
8
7
6
5
4
3
2
1
Baseline
Intervention
Follow-up
1
8
15
22
29
36
43
DAYS
Index of Clinical Stress
Generalized Contentment Scale
Self-Rated Well-Being Scale

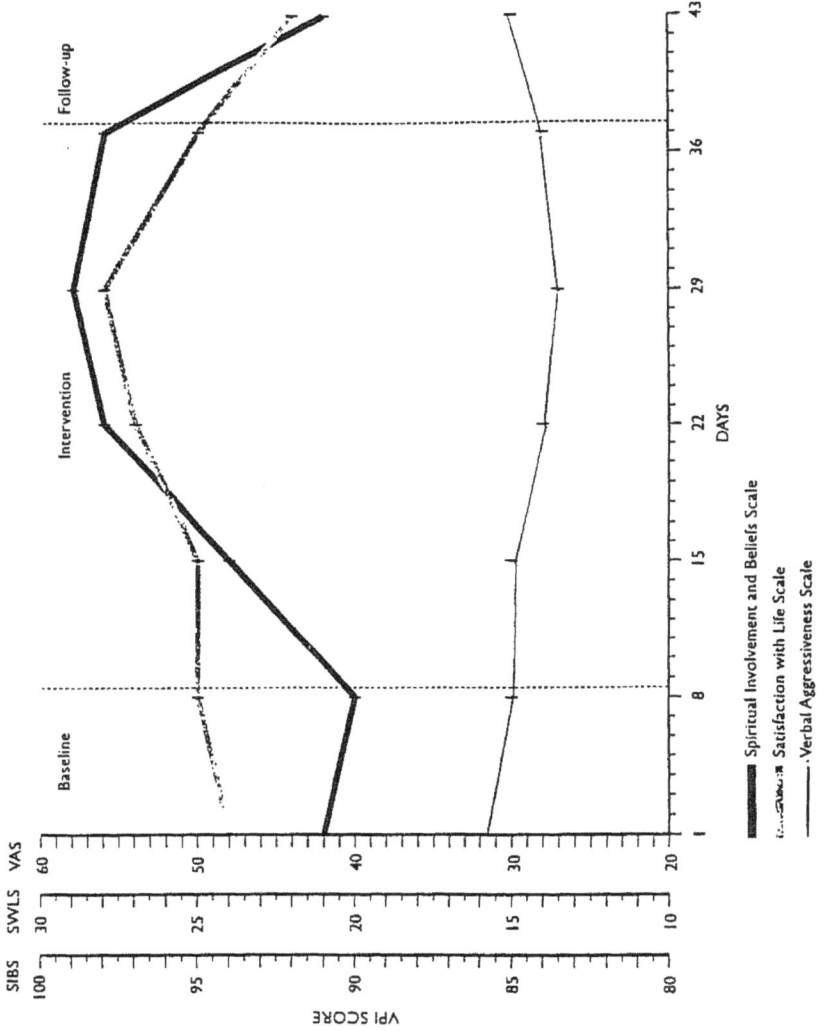

GRAPH 3c: Subject "C" Measured on SIBS, SWLS, and VAS

215

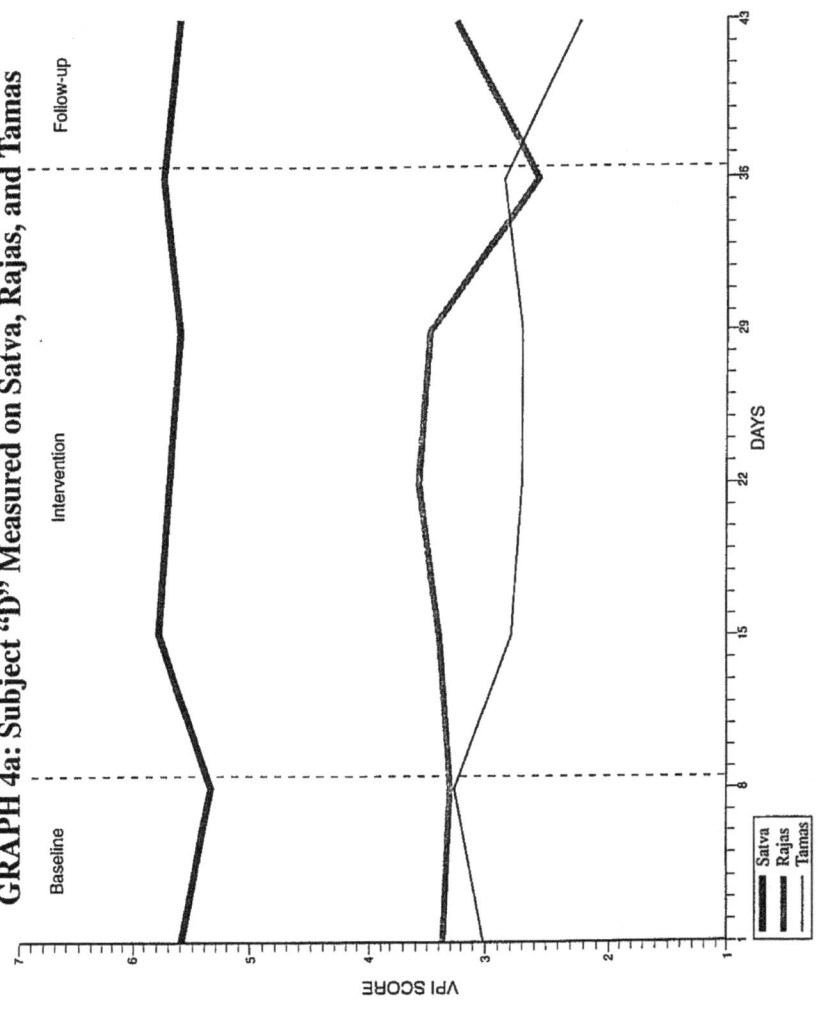

GRAPH 4a: Subject "D" Measured on Satva, Rajas, and Tamas

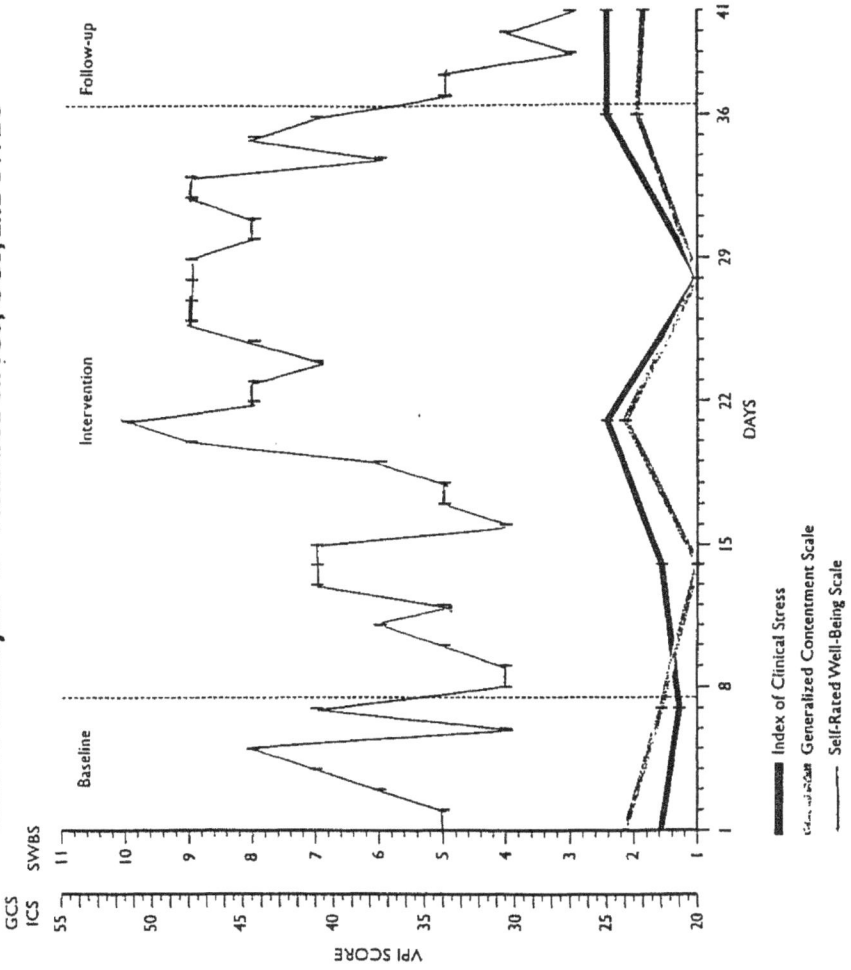

GRAPH 4b: Subject "D" Measured on ICS, GCS, and SWBS

Index of Clinical Stress
Generalized Contentment Scale
Self-Rated Well-Being Scale

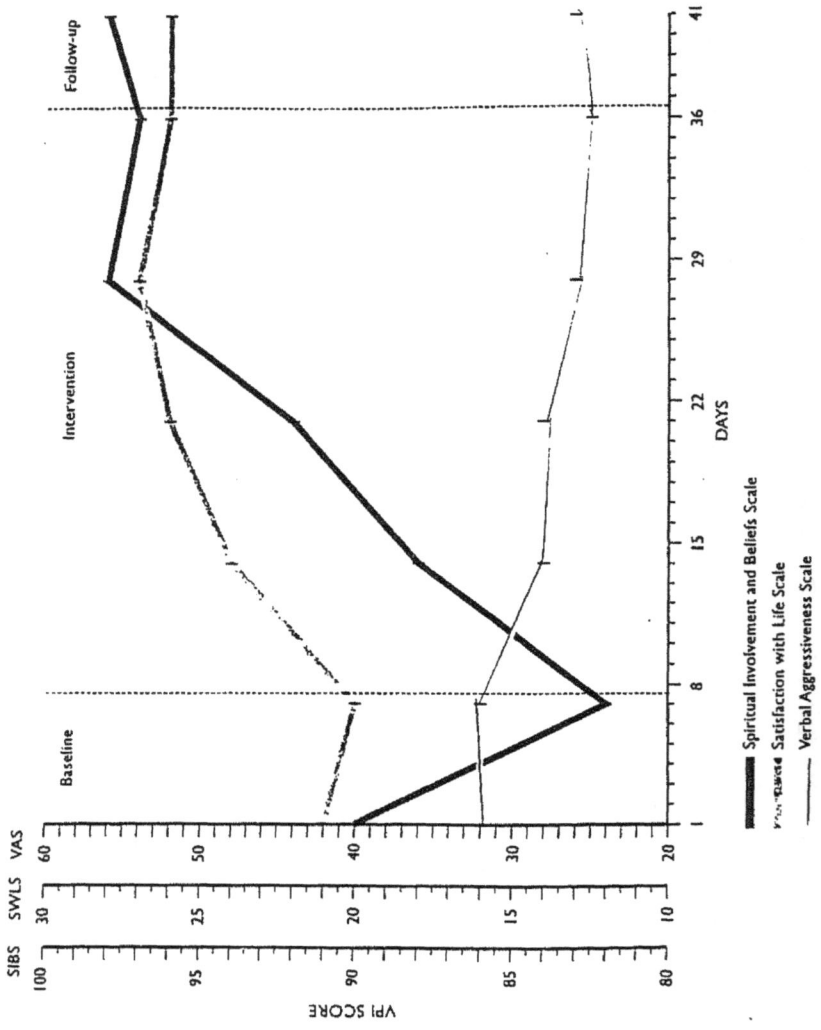

GRAPH 4c: Subject "D" Measured on SIBS, SWLS, and VAS

Spiritual Involvement and Beliefs Scale
Satisfaction with Life Scale
Verbal Aggressiveness Scale

218

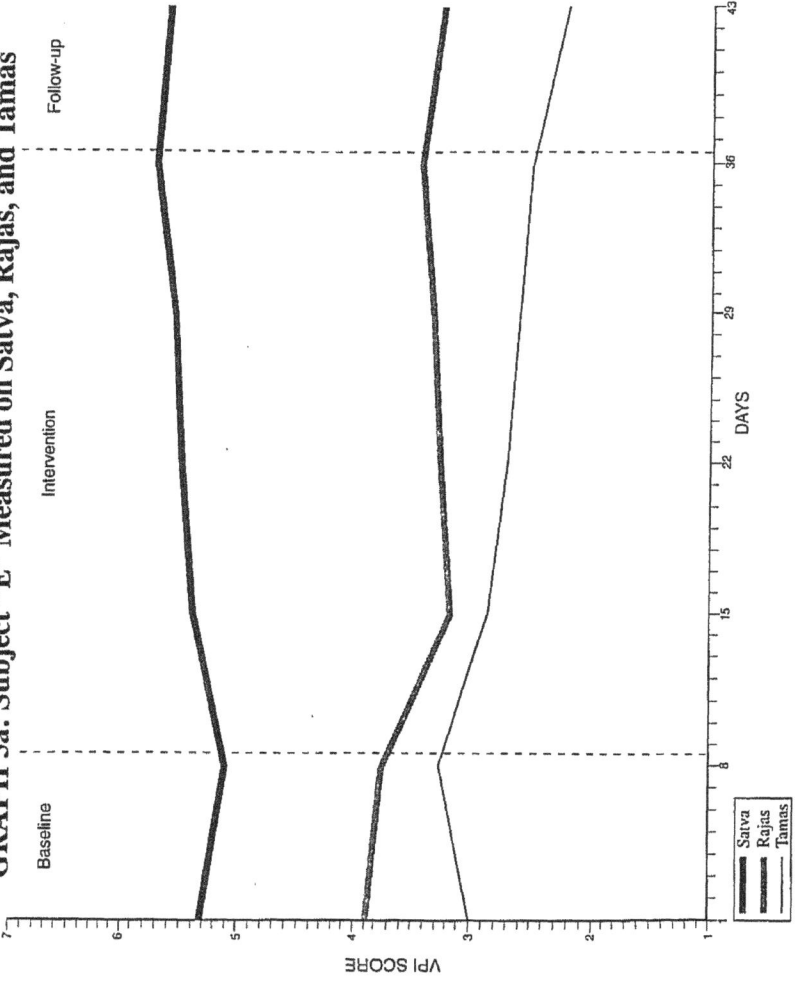

GRAPH 5a: Subject "E" Measured on Satva, Rajas, and Tamas

219

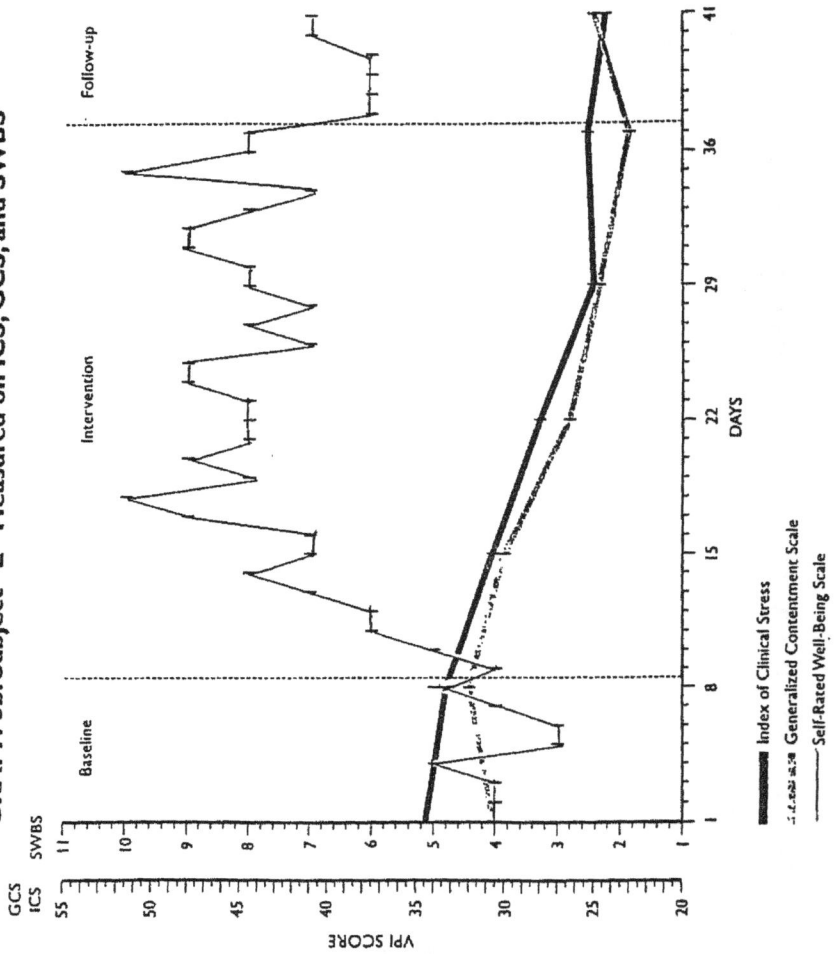

GRAPH 5b: Subject "E" Measured on ICS, GCS, and SWBS

220

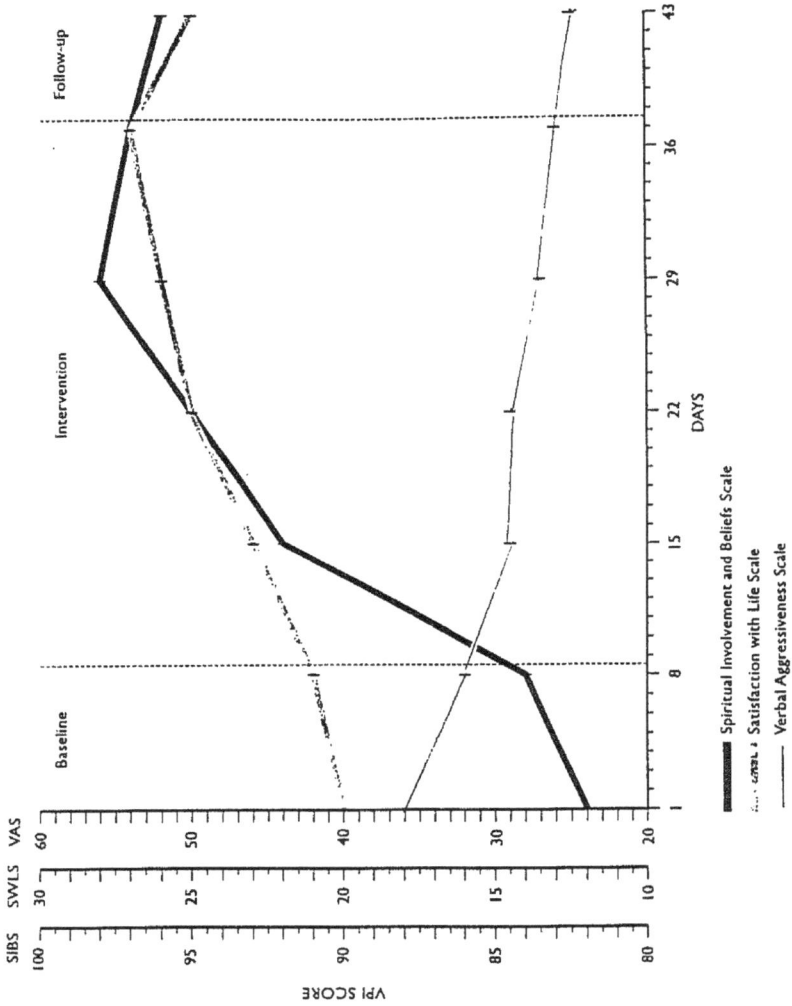

GRAPH 5c: Subject "E" Measured on SIBS, SWLS, and VAS

Spiritual Involvement and Beliefs Scale
Satisfaction with Life Scale
Verbal Aggressiveness Scale

APPENDIX D

Florida State
UNIVERSITY

Office of the Vice President
for Research
Tallahassee, Florida 32306-2811
(850) 644-5260 • FAX (850) 644-4392

APPROVAL MEMORANDUM
from the Human Subjects Committee

Date: February 18, 1998

From: Jack Brigham, Chair

To: David B. Wolf
17303 NW 112th Blvd.
Alachua, Florida 32615
Dept: Social Work
Re: Use of Human subjects in Research
Project entitled: Japa Studies: Experiments in Applied Vedic Science

---

The forms that you submitted to this office in regard to the use of human subjects in the proposal referenced above have been reviewed by the Secretary, the Chair, and two members of the Human Subjects Committee. Your project is determined to be exempt per 45 CFR § 46.101(b)2 and has been approved by an accelerated review process.

The Human Subjects Committee has not evaluated your proposal for scientific merit, except to weigh the risk to the human participants and the aspects of the proposal related to potential risk and benefit. This approval does not replace any departmental or other approvals which may be required.

If the project has not been completed by February 18, 1999 you must request renewed approval for continuation of the project.

You are advised that any change in protocol in this project must be approved by resubmission of the project to the Committee for approval. Also, the principal investigator must promptly report, in writing, any unexpected problems causing risks to research subjects or others.

By copy of this memorandum, the chairman of your department and/or your major professor is reminded that he/she is responsible for being informed concerning research projects involving human subjects in the department, and should review protocols of such investigations as often as needed to insure that the project is being conducted in compliance with our institution and with DHHS regulations.

This institution has an Assurance on file with the Office for Protection from Research Risks. The Assurance Number is M1339.

cc: N. Abell
human/newapp.doc
APPLICATION NO. 98.010

The Vedic Personality Inventory

1	2	3	4	5	6	7
Very Strongly Disagree	Strongly Disagree	Somewhat Disagree	Neutral	Somewhat Agree	Strongly Agree	Very Strongly Agree

1.	I am straightforward in my dealings with other people.	1	2	3	4	5	6	7
2.	I have very little interest in spiritual understanding.	1	2	3	4	5	6	7
3.	I am satisfied with my life.	1	2	3	4	5	6	7
4.	Fruits and vegetables are among my favorite foods.	1	2	3	4	5	6	7
5.	All living entities are essentially spiritual.	1	2	3	4	5	6	7
6.	In conducting my activities, I do not consider traditional wisdom.	1	2	3	4	5	6	7
7.	I often act without considering the future consequences of my actions.	1	2	3	4	5	6	7
8.	I usually feel discontented with life.	1	2	3	4	5	6	7
9.	I become happy when I think about the material assets that I possess.	1	2	3	4	5	6	7
10.	I am good at using willpower to achieve goals.	1	2	3	4	5	6	7
11.	I enjoy spending time in bars.	1	2	3	4	5	6	7
12.	Cleanliness is very important to me.	1	2	3	4	5	6	7
13.	Others say that my intelligence is very sharp.	1	2	3	4	5	6	7
14.	I often feel depressed.	1	2	3	4	5	6	7
15.	I often put off or delay my responsibilities.	1	2	3	4	5	6	7
16.	I greatly admire materially successful people.	1	2	3	4	5	6	7
17.	When I speak, I really try not to irritate others.	1	2	3	4	5	6	7
18.	I believe life is over when the body dies.	1	2	3	4	5	6	7
19.	I often feel helpless.	1	2	3	4	5	6	7
20.	I enjoy foods with strong tastes.	1	2	3	4	5	6	7
21.	I am constantly dissatisfied with my position in life.	1	2	3	4	5	6	7
22.	Having possessions is very important to me.	1	2	3	4	5	6	7
23.	When things are tough, I often bail out.	1	2	3	4	5	6	7
24.	I often feel like a victim.	1	2	3	4	5	6	7
25.	I feel that my knowledge is always increasing.	1	2	3	4	5	6	7
26.	I prefer city night life to a walk in the forest.	1	2	3	4	5	6	7
27.	For me, sex life is a major source of happiness.	1	2	3	4	5	6	7
28.	I take guidance from higher ethical and moral laws before I act.	1	2	3	4	5	6	7
29.	I enjoy intoxicating substances (including coffee, cigarettes and alcohol).	1	2	3	4	5	6	7
30.	I often feel greedy.	1	2	3	4	5	6	7
31.	I become greatly distressed when things don't work out for me.	1	2	3	4	5	6	7
32.	I am often angry.	1	2	3	4	5	6	7
33.	I often feel fearful.	1	2	3	4	5	6	7
34.	I do not have doubts about my responsibilities in life.	1	2	3	4	5	6	7
35.	I often feel emotionally unbalanced.	1	2	3	4	5	6	7
36.	I enjoy eating meat.	1	2	3	4	5	6	7
37.	I am self-controlled.	1	2	3	4	5	6	7

38.	I am very dutiful.	1	2	3	4	5	6	7
39.	When I give charity, I often do it grudgingly.1	2	3	4	5	6	7	
40.	Self-realization is not important for me.	1	2	3	4	5	6	7
41.	I often feel dejected.	1	2	3	4	5	6	7
42.	I carry out my responsibilities regardless of whether there is success or failure.	1	2	3	4	5	6	7
43.	I often neglect my responsibilities to my family.	1	2	3	4	5	6	7
44.	I am easily affected by the joys and sorrows of life.	1	2	3	4	5	6	7
45.	I often whine.	1	2	3	4	5	6	7
46.	Regardless of what I acquire or achieve, I have an uncontrollable desire to obtain more.	1	2	3	4	5	6	7
47.	I am currently struggling with an addiction, physical or psychological, to some type of intoxicant (including caffeine, cigarettes and alcohol).	1	2	3	4	5	6	7
48.	I often envy others.	1	2	3	4	5	6	7
49.	My job is a source of anxiety.	1	2	3	4	5	6	7
50.	I never think about giving up my wealth and position for a simpler life.	1	2	3	4	5	6	7
51.	It often happens that those things that brought me happiness later become the source of my suffering.	1	2	3	4	5	6	7
52.	I often feel mentally unbalanced.	1	2	3	4	5	6	7
53.	I don't have much will power.	1	2	3	4	5	6	
54.	I often neglect my responsibilities to my friends.	1	2	3	4	5	6	7
55.	I often act violently towards others.	1	2	3	4	5	6	7
56.	I am good at controlling my senses and emotions.	1	2	3	4	5	6	7

Gender: _____ Female _____ Male

Age: _____

VPI Scoring Key

Sattva- 1, 3, 4, 5, 10, 12, 13, 17, 25, 28, 34, 37, 38, 42, 56

Rajas- 8, 9, 16, 18, 20, 21, 22, 23, 26, 27, 30, 31, 39, 44, 46, 48, 49, 50, 51

Tamas- 2, 6, 7, 11, 14, 15, 19, 24, 29, 32, 33, 35, 36, 40, 41, 43, 45, 47, 52, 53, 54, 55

Scoring Instructions: Sum all the responses for a guna, then divide this sum by the total possible score for the guna. This will give the guna score in the form of a percentage. Then, to obtain a standardized score for a guna, sum the three guna percentage scores and divide it into the the guna percentage scores. The three standardized scores form the guna profile for a person.

Example:

For the 15 sattva items a respondent scores 60, or an average of 4.0. This converts to a guna percentage score of 57.14% (60/105 or 4/7).

For the 19 rajas items a respondent scores 57, or an average of 3.0. This converts to a guna percentage score of 42.86% (57/133 or 3/7).

For the 22 tamas items a respondent scores 55, or an average of 2.5. This converts to a guna percentage score of 35.71% (55/154 or 2.5/7).

The sum of the three guna percentage scores is $57.14 + 42.86 + 35.71 = 135.71$

The standardized sattva score is $57.14/135.71 = 42.10\%$

The standardized rajas score is $42.86/135.71 = 31.58\%$

The standardized tamas score is $35.71/135.71 = 26.31\%$

The Index of Clinical Stress

Name:_____   Today's Date:_____

Gender: _____Female   _____Male Age (in years): _____

Do you have prior experience with chanting mantras, meditation, yoga, or biofeedback?

This questionnaire is designed to measure the way you feel about the amount of personal stress that you experience. It is not a test, so there are no right or wrong answers. Answer each item carefully and as accurately as you can by placing a number beside each one as follows.

    1 = None of the time
    2 = Very rarely
    3 = A little of the time
    4 = Some of the time
    5 = A good part of the time
    6 = Most of the time
    7 = All of the time

1.____I feel extremely tense.
2.____I feel very jittery.
3.____I feel like I want to scream.
4.____I feel overwhelmed.
5.____I feel very relaxed.
6.____I feel so anxious I want to cry.
7.____I feel so stressed that I'd like to hit something.
8.____I feel very calm and peaceful.
9.____I feel like I am stretched to the breaking point.
10.____It is very hard for me to relax.
11.____It is very easy for me to fall asleep at night.
12.____I feel an enormous sense of pressure on me.
13.____I feel like my life is going very smoothly.
14.____I feel very panicked.
15.____I feel like I am on the verge of a total collapse.
16.____I feel that I am losing control of my life.
17.____I feel that I am near a breaking point.
18.____I feel wound up like a coiled spring.
19.____I feel that I can't keep up with all the demands on me.
20.____I feel very much behind in my work.
21.____I feel tense and angry with those around me.
22.____I feel I must race from one task to the next.
23.____I feel that I just can't keep up with everything.
24.____I feel as tight as a drum.
25.____I feel very much on edge.

227

Generalized Contentment Scale

Name:_____ Today's Date:_____

This questionnaire is designed to measure the way you feel about your life and surroundings. It is not a test, so there are no right or wrong answers. Answer each item carefully and as accurately as you can by placing a number beside each one as follows.

   1 = None of the time
   2 = Very rarely
   3 = A little of the time
   4 = Some of the time
   5 = A good part of the time
   6 = Most of the time
   7 = All of the time

1.____I feel powerless to do anything about my life.
2.____I feel blue.
3.____I think about ending my life.
4.____I have crying spells.
5.____It is easy for me to enjoy myself.
6.____I have a hard time getting started on things that I need to do.
7.____I get very depressed.
8.____I feel there is always someone I can depend on when things get tough.
9.____I feel that the future looks bright for me.
10.____I feel downhearted.
11.____I feel that I am needed.
12.____I feel that I am appreciated by others.
13.____I enjoy being active and busy.
14.____I feel that others would be better off without me.
15.____I enjoy being with other people.
16.____I feel that it is easy for me to make decisions.
17.____I feel downtrodden.
18.____I feel terribly lonely.
19.____I get upset easily.
20.____I feel that nobody really cares about me.
21.____I have a full life.
22.____I feel that people really care about me.
23.____I have a great deal of fun.
24.____I feel great in the morning.
25.____I feel that my situation is hopeless.

Verbal Aggressiveness Scale

The following twenty questions are concerned with how we try to get people to comply with our wishes. Indicate how often each statement is true for you personally when you try to influence other persons. Use the following scale:

1 = Almost never true
2 = Rarely true
3 = Occasionally true
4 = Often true
5 = Almost always true

1. I am extremely careful to avoid attacking individuals' intelligence when I attack their ideas.

    1   2   3   4   5

2. When individuals are very stubborn, I use insults to soften the stubbornness.

    1   2   3   4   5

3. I try very hard to avoid having other people feel bad about themselves when I try to influence them.

    1   2   3   4   5

4. When people refuse to do a task I know is important, without good reason, I tell them they are unreasonable.

    1   2   3   4   5

5. When others do things I regard as stupid, I try to be extremely gentle with them.

    1   2   3   4   5

6. If individuals I am trying to influence really deserve it, I attack their character.

    1   2   3   4   5

7. When people behave in ways that are in very poor taste, I insult them in order to shock them into proper behavior.

    1   2   3   4   5

8. I try to make people feel good about themselves even when their ideas are stupid.

    1   2   3   4   5

9. When people simply will not budge on a matter of importance I lose my temper and say rather strong things to them.

    1   2   3   4   5

10. When people criticize my shortcomings, I take it in good humor and do not try to get back at them.

    1   2   3   4   5

11. When individuals insult me, I get a lot of pleasure out of really telling them off.

    1   2   3   4   5

12. When I dislike individuals greatly, I try not to show it in what I say or how I say it.

    1   2   3   4   5

13. I like poking fun at people who do things that are very stupid in order to stimulate their intelligence.

    1   2   3   4   5

14. When I attack peoples' ideas, I try not to damage their self-concepts.

              1   2   3   4   5

15. When I try to influence people, I make a great effort not to offend them.

              1   2   3   4   5

16. When people do things that are mean or cruel, I attack their character in order to help correct their behavior.

              1   2   3   4   5

17. I refuse to participate in arguments when they involve personal attacks.

              1   2   3   4   5

18. When nothing seems to work in trying to influence others, I yell and scream in order to get some movement from them.

              1   2   3   4   5

19. When I am not able to refute others' positions, I try to make them feel defensive in order to weaken their positions.

              1   2   3   4   5

20. When an argument shifts to personal attacks, I try very hard to change the subject.

              1   2   3   4   5

Spiritual Involvement and Beliefs Scale

Please answer the following questions by circling your response.

1) In the future, science will be able to explain everything.

Strongly Agree Neutral Disagree Strongly
Agree Disagree

2) I can find meaning in times of hardship.

Strongly Agree Neutral Disagree Strongly
Agree Disagree

3) A person can be fulfilled without pursuing an active spiritual life.

Strongly Agree Neutral Disagree Strongly
Agree Disagree

4) I am thankful for all that has happened to me.

Strongly Agree Neutral Disagree Strongly
Agree Disagree

5) Spiritual activities have not helped me become closer to other people.

Strongly Agree Neutral Disagree Strongly
Agree Disagree

6) Some experiences can be understood only through ones' spiritual beliefs.

Strongly Agree Neutral Disagree Strongly
Agree Disagree

7) A spiritual force influences the events in my life.

Strongly Agree Neutral Disagree Strongly
Agree Disagree

8) My life has a purpose.

Strongly Agree Neutral Disagree Strongly
Agree Disagree

9) Prayers do not really change what happens.

Strongly Agree Neutral Disagree Strongly
Agree Disagree

10) Participating in spiritual activities helps me forgive other people.

Strongly Agree Neutral Disagree Strongly
Agree Disagree

11) My spiritual beliefs continue to evolve.

Strongly Agree Neutral Disagree Strongly
Agree Disagree

12) I believe there is a power greater than myself.

Strongly Agree Neutral Disagree Strongly
Agree Disagree

13) I probably will not reexamine my spiritual beliefs.

Strongly Agree Neutral Disagree Strongly
Agree Disagree

14) My spiritual life fulfills me in ways that material possessions do not.

Strongly Agree Neutral Disagree Strongly
Agree Disagree

15) Spiritual activities have not helped me develop my identity.

Strongly Agree Neutral Disagree Strongly
Agree Disagree

16) Meditation does not help me feel more in in touch with my inner spirit.

Strongly Agree Neutral Disagree Strongly
Agree   Disagree

17) I have a personal relationship with a power greater than myself.

Strongly Agree Neutral Disagree Strongly
Agree   Disagree

18) I have felt pressured to accept spiritual beliefs that I do not agree with.

Strongly Agree Neutral Disagree Strongly
Agree   Disagree

19) Spiritual activities help me draw closer to a power greater than myself.

Strongly Agree Neutral Disagree Strongly
Agree   Disagree

Please indicate how often you do the following:

20) When I wrong someone, I make an effort to apologize.

Always Usually Sometimes Rarely Never

21) When I am ashamed of something I have done, I tell someone about it.

Always Usually Sometimes Rarely Never

22) I solve my problems without using spiritual resources.

Always Usually Sometimes Rarely Never

23) I examine my actions to see if they reflect my values.

Always Usually Sometimes Rarely Never

24) During the last WEEK, I prayed... (check one)
_____ 10 or more times.
_____ 7-9 times.   _____ 1-3 times.
_____ 4-6 times.   _____ 0 times.

25) During the last WEEK, I meditated... (check one)
_____ 10 or more times.
_____ 7-9 times.   _____ 1-3 times.
_____ 4-6 times.   _____ 0 times.

26) Last MONTH, I participated in spiritual activities with at least one other person... (check one)
_____ more than 15 times.
_____ 11-15 times.   _____ 1-5 times.
_____ 6-10 times.   _____ 0 times.

Satisfaction With Life Scale

The following five questions deal with life satisfaction. Please use the following scale to answer them.

1= Strongly disagree
2= Disagree
3= Slightly disagree
4= Neither agree nor disagree
5= Slightly agree
6= Agree
7= Strongly agree

1. In most ways my life is close to my ideal.	1	2	3	4	5	6	7
2. The conditions of my life are excellent.	1	2	3	4	5	6	7
3. I am satisfied with my life.	1	2	3	4	5	6	7
4. So far I have gotten the important things I want in my life.	1	2	3	4	5	6	7
5. If I could live my life over, I would change almost nothing.	1	2	3	4	5	6	7

Self-rated Well-Being Scale

1	2	3	4	5	6	7	8	9	10	11
Worse I've				Feeling Okay						Best I've
Ever Felt										Ever Felt

Date	Rating		Date	Rating		Date	Rating

Consent Form for Participating in Research

I, _____, agree to participate in this study entitled Japa Studies: An Experiment in Applied Vedic Science, conducted by David B. Wolf, a Ph.D. student in the School of Social Work of Florida State University. My participation in this experiment is completely voluntary. I understand that my participation in this experiment will last for _____ weeks, and that I am free to withdraw my participation at any time during the study. I agree that if, during the course of this experiment I learn the identity of other participants in the study, I will maintain complete confidentiality regarding their participation in this research project. In addition, By signing this consent form I am affirming that I am at least 18 years old of age. Further, it is agreed herein that David Wolf will pay me the sum of $_____ for participating in this study. Half of this sum will be received when I sign this consent form, and the other half will be received four weeks from today. I am under no obligation to refund this money for any reason.

I agree to the conditions of this Consent Form, as described above.

_____   _____
Print Name   Social Security #

_____   _____
Signature   Date

Payment Receipt

I. _____
 · Print Name

have received $_____ from _____
                                     Name of Research Team member

as reimbursement for participation in the research study entitled Japa Studies: Experiments in Applied Vedic Science.

_____
Signature

236

Japa Studies - Compliance Log

Date	Number of Round		Date	Number of Round

References

Abell, N. (1991). The Index of Clinical Stress: A brief measure of subjective stress for practice and research. *Social Work Research and Abstracts*, 27(2), 12-15.

Agresti, A., & Finlay, B. (1986). *Statistical Methods for the Social Sciences*, 2nd ed., Riverside, New Jersey: Dellen Publishing Company.

Albano, A. M., Morris, T. L. (1998). Childhood anxiety, obsessive-compulsive disorder, and depression. In Plaud, J. J., Ed. *From Behavior Theory to Behavior Therapy*. Boston, Allyn & Bacon. 203-222.

Alexander, C. N., Robinson, P., & Rainforth, M. (1995). Treating and preventing alcohol, nicotine, and drug abuse through transcendental meditation: A review and statistical meta-analysis. *Alcoholism Treatment Quarterly*, 13 (4), 97.

Alford, G. S., Koehler, R. A., & Leonard, J. (1991). Alcoholics Anonymous-Narcotics Anonymous model inpatient treatment of chemically-dependent adolescents: a two-year outcome study. *Journal of Studies on Alcohol*, 52(2), 118-126.

Alvarado, K. A., Templer, D. I., Bresler, C., Thomas-Dobson, S. (1995). The relationship of religious variables to death depression and death anxiety. *Journal of Clinical Psychology*, 51(2), 202-204.

American Psychiatric Association. (1994). *Diagnostic and statistical manual of mental disorders* (4th ed.). Washington, DC: American Psychiatric Association.

Benson, H. (1975). *The Relaxation Response*. New York: William Morrow & Company.

Berk, J. H. (1998). Trauma and resilience during war: A look at the children and humanitarian aid workers of Bosnia. *Psychoanalytic Review*, 85 (4), 639-658.

Bloom, M., Fischer, J., & Orme, J. G. (1995). *Evaluating Practice: Guidelines for the Accountable Professional* (2nd ed.). Needham Heights, Massachussets: Allyn & Bacon.

Bracht, G. H., & Glass, G. V. (1968). The external validity of experiments. *American Educational Research Journal*, 5, 437-474.

Bradley, D. E. (1995). Religious involvement and social resources: evidence from the data set "Americans' Changing Lives". *Journal for the Scientific Study of Religion*, 34(2), 259-267.

Bryant, S., & Rakowski, W. (1992). Predictors of mortality among elderly African-Americans. *Research on Aging*, 14(1), 50-67.

Bufford, R. K., Paloutzian, R. F., & Ellison, C. W. (1991). Norms for the Spiritual Well-Being Scale. *Journal of Psychology and Theology*, 19(1), 56-70.

Bullis, R. K. (1996). *Spirituality in Social Work Practice.* Washington, D. C.: Taylor and Francis.

Burgener, S. C. (1994). Caregiver religiosity and well-being in dealing with Alzheimer's dementia. *Journal of Religion and Health*, 33(2), 175-189.

Burkett, S. R., & Warren, B. O. (1987). Religiosity, peer associations, and adolescent marijuana use: a panel study of underlying causal structures. *Criminology*, 25(1), 109-131.

Burrell, G., & Morgan, G. (1979). *Sociological paradigms and organisational analysis-Elements of the sociology of corporate life.* London: Heinemann Educational Books Ltd.

Byrd, R. C. (1988). Positive therapeutic effects of intercessory prayer in a coronary care unit population. *South Med J*, 81(7), 826-829.

Canda, E. R. (1988). Spirituality, religious diversity, and social work practice. *Social Casework: The Journal of Contemporary Social Work*, 69(4), 238-247.

Canda, E. R., & Phaobtong, T. (1992). Buddhism as a support system for Southeast Asian refugees. *Social Work*, 37 (1), 61-67.

Carroll, S. (1991). Spirituality and purpose in life in addiction recovery. *J Stud Alcohol*, 54, 297-301.

Carson, V. B. (1993). Prayer, meditation, exercise, and special diets: Behaviors of the hardy person with HIV/AIDS. *Journal of the Association of Nurses in AIDS Care*, 4(3), 18-28.

Carson, V. B., & Green, H. (1992). Spiritual well-being: a predictor of hardiness in patients with Acquired Immunodeficiency Syndrome. *Journal of Professional Nursing*, 8(4), 209-220.

Chadwick, B. A., Top, B. L. (1993). Religiosity and delinquency among LDS adolescents. *Journal for the Scientific Study of Religion*, 32(1), 51-67.

Cochran, J. K., Wood, P. B., & Arneklev, B. J. (1994). Is the religiosity-delinquency relationship spurious? *Journal of Research in Crime and Delinquency*, 31(1), 92-123.

Cohen, J., & Cohen, P. (1983). *Applied multiple regression/Correlation analysis for the behavioral sciences* (2nd ed.). Hillsdale, New Jersey: Lawrence Erlbaum Associates.

Cook, T. D., & Campbell, D. T. (1979). *Quasi-experimentation: Design and analysis issues for field settings.* Chicago: Rand McNally Publishing.

Cormier, S., & Cormier, B. (1997). *Interviewing Strategies for Helpers: Fundamental Skills and Cognitive Behavioral Interventions*, 4th ed. Washington, D.C.: Taylor and Francis.

Dasa, K. (1994). *The nectar of discrimination: A treatise on the three modes of material nature.* New Delhi: Eye of the Bird Books.

Dasa, M. (1998). Good intentions. *Back to Godhead: The magazine of the Hare Krishna Movement*, 32(2), 42-43.

Dasgupta, S. (1961). *A history of Indian philosophy.* Great Britain: Cambridge University Press.

Dawson, P. J. (1997). A reply to Goddard's "spirituality as integrative energy". *Journal of Advanced Nursing*, 25(2), 282-289.

Delmonte, M. M., & Kenny, V. (1985). An overview of the therapeutic effect of meditation. *Psychologia: An International Journal of Psychology in the Orient*, 28(4), 189-202.

Delmonte, M. M. (1983). Mantras and meditation: A literature review. *Perceptual & Motor Skills*, 57(1), 64-66.

Derr, S., Shaikh, U., Rosen, A., & Guadagnimo, P. (1998). Medical students' attitudes toward, knowledge of, and experience with complementary medicine therapies. *Academic Medicine*, 73 (9), 1020.

Diener, E., Emmons, R. A., Larsen, R. J., & Griffin, S. (1985). The Satisfaction With Life Scale, *Journal of Personality Assessment*, 49(1), 71-75.

Dolgoff, R., Feldstein, D., & Skolnik, L. (1993). *Understanding social welfare* (3rd ed.). White Plains, New York: Longman Publishing Group.

Dossey, L. MD (1993). *Healing words- The power of prayer and the practice of medicine*. San Francisco: Harper Collins Publishers.

Dowdy, S., & Wearden, S. (1991). *Statistics for research* (2nd ed.). New York: John Wiley and Sons.

Ellis, G. A., & Corum, P. (1994). Removing the motivator: A holistic solution to substance abuse. *Alcoholism Treatment Quarterly*, 11 (3-4), 271-296.

Ellison, C. G. (1995). Race, religious involvement, and depressive symptomatology in a southeastern U.S. community. *Social Science and Medicine*, 40(11), 1561-1572.

Ellison, C. W., & Smith, J. (1991). Toward an integrative measure of health and well-being. *Journal of Psychology and Theology*, 19(1), 35-48.

Evans, T. D., Cullen, F. T., Dunaway, R. G., & Burton, Jr., V. S. (1995). Religion and crime reexamined: the impact of religion, secular controls, and social ecology on adult criminality. *Criminology*, 33(2), 195-217.

Fischer, J. (1971). A framework for the analysis and comparison of clinical theories of induced change. *Social Service Review*, 45, 110-130.

Foa, E. B. (1997). Trauma and women: Course, predictors, and treatment. *Journal of Clinical Psychiatry*, 58 (9), 25-28.

Foshee, V. A., & Hollinger, B. R. (1996). Maternal religiosity, adolescent social bonding, and adolescent alcohol use. *Journal of Early Adolescence*, 16(4), 451-468.

Freeston, M. H., Ladouceur, R., Provencher, M., Blais, F. (1995). Strategies used with intrusive thoughts: Context, appraisal, mood, and efficacy. *Journal of Anxiety Disorders*, 9 (3), 201-215.

Gallup, G., & Castelli, J. (1989). *The people's religion*. New York: MacMillan Publishing Co.

Gergen, K.J., Gulerce, A., Lock, A., & Misra, G. (1996). Psychological science in cultural context. *American Psychologist*, 51 (5), 496-503.

Ginsburg, M. L., Quirt, C., Ginsburg, A. D., & MacKillop, W. J. (1995). Psychiatric illness and psychosocial concerns of patients with newly diagnosed lung cancer. *Canadian Medical Association Journal*, 152(5), 701-708.

Goldbourt, U., Yaari, S., & Medalie, J. Ho. (1993). Factors predictive of long-term coronary heart disease mortality among 10,059 male Israeli civil servants and municipal employees. *Cardiology*, 82, 100-121.

Goswami, S. D. (1977). *Readings in Vedic literature- The tradition speaks for itself.* Los Angeles: The Bhaktivedanta Book Trust.

Green, E., & Green, A. (1977). *Beyond biofeedback*. New York: Dell Publishing Company.

Harris, R. C., Dew, M. A., Lee, A., Amaya, M., Buches, L, Reetz, D., & Coleman, C. (1995). The role of religion in heart-transplant recipients' long-term health and well-being. *Journal of Religion and Health*, 34(1), 17-32.

Hatch, R. L., Hellmich, L. K., Naberhaus, D. S., & Berg, M. A. (1995). *The Spiritual Involvement and Beliefs Scale: A New Instrument for Assessing Spirituality.* Presented at the 15th Annual Family in Family Medicine Conference, Society of Teachers of Family Medicine, Amelia Island, Fl., March, 1995.

Heineman, M. B. (1981). The Obsolete Scientific Imperative in Social Work Research. *In New foundations for scientific social and behavioral research: The heuristic paradigm,* ed. Tyson, K. Boston: Allyn and Bacon.

Hudson, T. (1996). Measuring the results of faith. *Hosp Health Netw,* 70(18), 22-28.

Hudson, W. W. (1982). A measurement package for clinical workers. *The Journal of Applied Behavioral Science,* 18(2), 229-238.

Hudson, W. W., & Proctor, E. K. (1977). Assessment of depressive affect in clinical practice. *Journal of Consulting and Clinical Psychology,* 45(6), 1206-1207.

Infante, D. A., & Wigley, C. J. (1986). *Communication Monographs,* 53, 61-68.

Jacobs, C. (1997). Essay: On spirituality and social work practice. *Smith College Studies in Social Work,* 67 (2), 171-175.

Janoff-Bulman, R., & Marshall, G. (1982). Mortality, well-being, and control: A study of a population of institutionalized aged. *Personality and Social Psychology Bulletin,* 8(4), 691-698.

Janowiak, J. J., & Hackman, R. (1994). Meditation and college students' self-actualization and rated stress. *Psychological Reports,* 75(2), 1007-1010.

Joiner, J. G., & Sawyer, H. W. (1992). Counseling strategies for adjustment services. *Vocational Evaluation & Work Adjustment Bulletin,* 25 (3), 97-99.

Joseph, M. V. (1988). Religion and social work practice. *Social Casework: The Journal of Contemporary Social Work,* 69(4), 443-452.

Kabat-Zinn, J., Massion, A. O., Kristeller, J., & Peterson, L. G. (1992). Effectiveness of a meditation-based stress reduction program in the treatment of anxiety disorders. *American Journal of Psychiatry,* 149 (7), 936-943.

Karel, N. (1993). Twelve years experience with yoga in psychiatry. *International Journal of Psychosomatics*, 40 (1-4), 105-107.

Kaye, V. G. (1985). An innovative treatment modality for elderly residents of a nursing home. *Clinical Gerontologist*, 3(4), 45-51.

Keefe, T. W. (1979). The development of empathic skill: A study. *Journal of Education for Social Work*, 15 (2), 30-37.

Keefe, T. (1996). *Meditation and Social Work Treatment*. In F. J. Turner (Ed.). Social work treatment- Interlocking theoretical approaches (pp. 434-460). New York: The Free Press.

Kehoe, N. C., & Gutheil, T. G. (1994). Neglect of religious issues in scale-based assessment of suicidal patients. *Hospital Community Psychiatry*, 45(4), 366-369.

Khumar, S. S., Kaur, P., & Kaur, S. (1993). Effectiveness of Shavasana on depression among university students. *Indian Journal of Clinical Psychology*, 20 (2), 82-87.

King, D. E., & Bushwick, B. (1994). Beliefs and attitudes of hospital inpatients about faith healing and prayer. *Journal of Family Practice*, 39(4), 349-352.

Klein, W. C., & Bloom, M. (1994). Social work as applied social science: A historical analysis. *Social Work*, 39(4), 421-431.

Krause, N. (1995). Religiosity and self-esteem among older adults. *Journal of Gerontology: Psychological Sciences*, 50B(5), P236-P246.

Kremer, D., Malkin, M. J., Benshoff, J. J. (1995). Physical activity programs offered in substance abuse treatment facilities. *Journal of Substance Abuse Treatment*, 12 (5), 327-333.

Kutz, I. (1985). Meditation as an adjunct to psychotherapy: An outcome study. *Psychotherapy & Psychosomatics*, 43(4), 209-218.

Landis, B. J. (1996). Uncertainty, spiritual well-being, and psychosocial adjustment to chronic illness. *Issues in Mental Health Nursing*, 17, 217-231.

Lane, D. J. (1994). What can alternative medicine offer for the treatment of asthma? *Journal of Asthma*, 31 (3), 153-160.

Laungani, P. (1993). Cultural differences in stress and its management. *Stress Medicine*, 9 (1), 37-43.

Levin, J. S., Larson, D. B., & Puchalski, C. M. (1997). Religion and spirituality in medicine: Research and education. *JAMA*, 278(9), 792-793.

Levin, J. S., Chatters, L. M., & Taylor, R. J. (1995). Religious effects on health status and life satisfaction among black Americans. *Journal of Gerontology: Social Sciences*, 50B(3), S154-S163.

Levinson, H. N., M.D. (1994). *Dyslexia: A Scientific Watergate*. Lake Success, New York: Stonebridge Publishing, Inc.

Lloyd, M. (1997). Dying and bereavement, spirituality and social work in a market economy of welfare. *British Journal of Social Work*, 27 (2), 175-190.

Lorch, B. R., & Hughes, R. H. (1985). Religion and youth substance use. *Journal of Religion and Health*, 24(3), 197-208.

Lukoff, D., Lu, F. G., & Turner, R. (1995). Cultural considerations in the assessment and treatment of religious and spiritual problems. *Psychiatr Clin North Am*, 18(3), 467-485.

Maugans, T. A., Wadland, W. C. (1991). Religion and family medicine: A survey of physicians and patients. *Journal of Family Practice*, 32(2), 210-213.

McKee, D. D., & Chappel, J. N. (1992). Spirituality and medical practice. *Journal of Family Practice*, 35(2), 201-208.

McNeil, K., Newman, I., & Kelly, F. J. (1996). *Testing research hypotheses with the general linear model*. Carbondale, Illinois: Southern Illinois University Press.

Mickley, J. R., Soeken, K., & Belcher, A. (1992). Spiritual well-being, religiousness, and hope among women with breast cancer. *Journal of Nursing Scholarship*, 24(4), 267-272.

Miller, T. W., & Basoglu, M. (1991). Posttraumatic stress disorder: The impact of life stress events on adjustment. *Integrative Psychiatry*, 7 (3-4), 207-215.

Miller, J. J., Fletcher, K., & Kabat-Zinn, J. (1995). Three-year follow-up and clinical implications of a mindfulness meditation-based stress reduction intervention in the treatment of anxiety disorders. *Gen Hosp Psychiatry*, 17(3), 192-200.

Millison, M. B. (1995). A review of the research on spiritual care and hospice. *Hospice Journal*, 10(4), 3-18.

Millison, M. B., & Dudley, J. R. (1990). The importance of spirituality in hospice work: A study of hospice professionals. *Hospice Journal*, 6(3), 63-78.

Montgomery, D. C. (1997). *Design and analysis of experiments* (4th ed.). New York: John Wiley and Sons.

Mook, D. G. (1983). In defense of external invalidity. *American Psychologist*, 38(4), 379-387.

Morgan, P. P., & Cohen, L. (1994). Spirituality slowly gaining recognition among North American psychiatrists. *Canadian Medical Association Journal*, 150(4), 582-585.

Nakhaima, J. M., & Dicks, B. H. (1995). Social work practice with religious families. *Families in Society*, 76(6), 360-368.

National Association of Social Workers, Inc. (1990). *NASW Code of Ethics*. Chicago: Nelson-Hall Inc.

Nunnally, J. C., & Bernstein, I. H. (1994). *Psychometric Theory*, 3rd ed., New York, McGraw-Hill, Inc.

Olton, D. S., & Noonberg, A. R. (1980). *Biofeedback: Clinical Applications in Behavioral Medicine*. Englewood Cliffs, New Jersey: Prentice-Hall, Inc.

Orme, J. G., & Combs-Orme, T. D. (1986). Statistical power and Type II errors in social work research. *Social Work Research & Abstracts*, 22, 3-10.

Pargament, K. I., Ishler, K., DuBow, E. F., Stanik, P., & Rouiller, R. (1994). Methods of religious coping with the Gulf War: cross-sectional and longitudinal analyses. *Journal for Scientific Study of Religion*, 33(4), 347-361.

Pathak, N. S., Bhatt, I. D., & Sharma, R. (1992). Manual for classifying personality on tridimensions of gunas- An Indian approach. *Indian Journal of Behaviour*, 16 (4), 1-14.

Payne, M. S. (1991). *Modern Social Work Theory: A Critical Introduction*. Chicago: Lyceum Books, Inc.

Pearl, J. H., & Carlozzi, A. (1994). Effect of meditation on empathy and anxiety. *Perceptual and Motor Skills*, 78(1), 297-298.

Peri, T. A. (1995). Promoting spirituality in persons with acquired immunodeficiency syndrome: A nursing intervention. *Holistic Nursing Practitioner*, 10(1), 68-76.

Pollner, M. (1989). Divine relations, social relations, and well-being. *Journal of Health & Social Behavior*, 30(1), 92-104.

Prabhupada, A. C. B. S. (1971). *Bhakti-rasamrta-sindhu*. Los Angeles: The Bhaktivedanta Book Trust.

Prabhupada, A. C. B. S. (1972). *Bhagavad-gita As It Is*. Hong Kong: Bhaktivedanta Book Trust.

Prabhupada, A. C. B. S. (1975). *Sri Caitanya-caritamrta*. Los Angeles: The Bhaktivedanta Book Trust.

Prabhupada, A. C. B. S. (1976). *Srimad-Bhagavatam*. Los Angeles: The Bhaktivedanta Book Trust.

Raskin, M., Johnson, G., & Rondestvedt, J. W. (1973). Chronic anxiety treated by feedback-induced muscle relaxation. *Archives of General Psychiatry*, 28, 263-267.

Rangaswami, K. (1996). Indian system of psychotherapy. *Indian Journal of Clinical Psychology*, 23 (1), 62-75.

Rao, P. V. K., & Harigopal, K. (1979). The three gunas and esp: An exploratory investigation. *Journal of Indian Psychology*, 2 (1), 63-68.

Rigdon, E. E., Schumacker, R. E., & Wothke, W. (1996). A Comparative Review of Interaction and Nonlinear Modeling. In *Interaction and nonlinear effects in structural equation modeling*, ed. Schumacker, R. E., & Marcoulides, G. A. London: Lawrence Erlbaum Associates.

Rochford, E. B. (1985). *Hare Krishna in America*. New Brunswick, N.J.: Rutgers University Press.

Rosenthal, J. A. (1997). Pragmatic concepts and tools for data interpretation: A balanced model. *Journal of Teaching in Social Work*, 15, 113-131.

Royse, D. (1995). *Research methods in social work* (2nd Ed.). Chicago: Nelson-Hall Publishers.

Rutledge, C. R., Levin, J. S., Larson, D. B., & Lyons, J. S. (1995). The importance of religion for parents coping with a chronically ill child. *Journal of Psychology and Christianity*, 14(1), 50-57.

Ryan, T. P. (1997). *Modern regression methods*. New York: John Wiley & Sons, Inc.

Sands, D. Introducing Maharishi Ayur-Veda into clinical practice. *Alcoholism Treatment Quarterly*, 11 (3-4), 335-365.

Sen, A., & Srivastava, M. (1990). *Regression Analysis: Theory, Methods, and Applications*. New York: Springer-Verlag.

Shapiro, S. L., Schwartz, G. E., & Bonner, G. (1998). Effects of mindfulness-based stress reduction on medical and premedical students. *Journal of Behavioral Medicine*, 21 (6), 581-599.

Sherril, K. A., Larson, D. B. Adult burn patients: The role of religion in recovery. *South Med J*, 81(7), 821-825.

Sheskin, D. J. (1997). *Handbook of Parametric and Nonparametric Statistical Procedures.* Boston: CRC Press.

Smith, W. P., Compton, W. C., & West, W. B. (1995). Meditation as an adjunct to a happiness enhancement program. *Journal of Clinical Psychology*, 51(2), 269-273.

Snaith, R. P., Owens, D., & Kennedy, E. (1992). An outcome study of a brief anxiety management programme: Anxiety Control Training. *Irish Journal of Psychological Medicine*, 9 (2), 111-114.

Solfvin, J. (1984). Mental healing. *Advances in Parapsychological Research*, 4, 55-56.

Spencer, S. W. (1957). Religious and spiritual values in social casework practice. *Social Casework*, 38, 519-526.

Spiegler, M. D., & Guevremont, D. C. (1993). *Contemporary Behavior Therapy* (2nd ed.).Belmont, California: Wadsworth, Inc.

Stern, R. C., Canda, E. R., & Doershuk, C. F. (1992). Use of nonmedical treatment by cystic fibrosis patients. *Journal of Adolescent Health*, 13, 612-615.

Sweet, M., & Johnson, C. (1990). Enhancing empathy: The interpersonal implications of a Buddhist meditation technique. *Psychotherapy*, 27(1), 19-29.

Thyer, B. A. (1991). Guidelines for evaluating outcome studies on social work practice. *Research on Social Work Practice*, 1(1), 76-91.

Turk, D. C., Meichenbaur, D., & Genest, M. (1983). *Pain and Behavioral Medicine.* New York: Guilford.

Turner, N. H., Ramirez, G. Y., Higginbotham, J. C., Markides, K., Wygant, A. C., & Black, S. (1994). Tri-ethnic alcohol use and religion, family, and gender. *Journal of Religion and Health*, 33(4), 341-351.

Urbanowski, F. B., & Miller, J. J. (1996). Trauma, psychotherapy, and meditation. *Journal of Transpersonal Psychology*, 28(1), 31-48.

Valentine, L., & Feinauer, L. L. (1993). Resilience factors associated with female survivors of childhood sexual abuse. *American Journal of Family Therapy*, 21 (3), 216-224.

Wardlaw, F. (1994). Hypnosis in the treatment of bruxism. *Australian Journal of Clinical & Experimental Hypnosis*, 22 (2), 97-107.

Westgate, C. E. (1996). Spiritual wellness and depression. *Journal of Counseling & Development*, 75(1), 26-35.

Williams, R. B., & Gentry, W. D. (1977). *Behavioral Approaches to Medical Treatment.* Cambridge, Mass.: Ballinger Publishing Company.

Wolf, D. B. (1998). The Vedic Personality Inventory: A Study of the Gunas. *Journal of Indian Psychology*, 16(1), 26-43.

Biographical Sketch

[from 1999, as it appeared in the original dissertation]

David Brian Wolf was born in Philadelphia, Pennsylvania, on December 3, 1960. He earned a Bachelor of Science degree in Psychology from Pennsylvania State University in 1983, and a Master of Social Work degree from Florida State University in 1997. In 1994 he authored a book, published by the Florida Vedic College Press, entitled *Krsna, Israel, and the Druze: an Interreligious Odyssey*. Also, in 1998 he published an article in the Journal of Indian Psychology entitled The Vedic Personality Inventory: A Study of the Gunas. Other writings include dozens of articles in various Vaisnava journals around the world. He has more than eight years of experience in Pennsylvania and Florida in various social service and mental health fields, including crisis-intervention and short-term counseling, children and family counseling, foster care, and medical social work. Additionally, he has extensively lectured and conducted seminars internationally on topics including child protection in spiritual institutions, communication skills, and Vaisnava philosophy. Currently David Brian Wolf serves as Director of the Central Office of Child Protection for the International Society for Krishna Consciousness, Social Services Program Manager for eleven counties in north Florida for Children's Medical Services, and on the Board of Directors of several community and educational organizations in Alachua County, Florida.

A Selection of Publications
Related to the Maha Mantra Studies

Abell, N. and Wolf, D. (2003). Implementing Intervention Research in Doctoral Education. *Journal of Teaching in Social Work*, vol. 23, numbers 1/2, 3-19.

Damerla, V. R., Goldstein, B., Wolf, D., Madhavan, K., and Patterson, N. (2018). *Integrative Medicine: A Clinician's Journal.* Novice Meditators of an Easily Learnable Audible Mantram Sound Self-Induce an Increase in Vagal Tone During Short-term Practice: A Preliminary Study, Vol. 17-5, 20-28.

Stempel, H. S., Cheston, S., Greer, J. M., Gillespie, C. K. (2006). Further exploration of the Vedic Personality Inventory: Validity, reliability and generalizability. *Psychological Reports*, 98 (1), pgs. 261-273.

Wolf, D. and Abell, N. (2003). Examining the Effects of Meditation Techniques on Psychosocial Functioning. *Research on Social Work Practice*, 13 (1), 752-766.

Wolf, D. (2017). *Relationships That Work: The Power of Conscious Living- A Transformative Communication Approach to Self-Realization.* 2nd edition. Alachua, Florida: Satvatove Institute.

Wolf, D. (2013). Stress Management and Mantra Meditation. *Milestone Education Review (The Journal of Ideas on Educational and Social Transformation)*, 4 (2), 4-19.

Wolf, D. B. (2013). Jacuzzi for the Mind: Effects of the Maha Mantra on Mental Health. *Integral Yoga Magazine* (Fall, 2013), 40-41.

Wolf, D. (2003). The Vedic Theory of Social Work, *The Indian Journal of Social Work*, 64 (3), July, 2003, 64 (3).

Wolf, D. (2002). Vaisnavism and the Social and Mental Health Sciences. *The Journal of Indian Psychology*, 20 (1), 1-12.

Wolf, D. (2001). Effects of the Hare Krsna Maha Mantra on Some Mental Health Indicators, *The Indian Journal of Social Work*, April, 2001, 151-168.

Wolf, D. (2000). Social Work and Speciesism. *Social Work*, 45 (1), 88-93.

Wolf, D. (1999). A Psychometric Analysis of the Three Gunas, *Psychological Reports*, 84, 1379-1390.

Wolf, D. (1999). Effects of the Hare Krsna Maha Mantra on Stress, Depression and the Three Gunas, Doctoral dissertation, Florida State University, 1999.

Wolf, D. (1998). The Vedic Personality Inventory- A Study of the Gunas. *The Journal of Indian Psychology*, 16 (1), 26-43.

About the Author

Since the early 1980s David B. Wolf has served in diverse social and mental health service fields, including counselor training, crisis-intervention, medical social work, children and family counseling, spiritual life coaching and developing and leading personal transformation seminars.

In 1998 he started the Association for the Protection of Children (APC), an international child protection agency, and served as director of the APC for six years. As part of his doctoral studies he developed the Vedic Personality Inventory (VPI), a personality assessment tool based on Vedic psychology, and researched the effects of *mantra* meditation. He is a world leader in the field of *mantra* meditation research.

In the 1990s David Wolf began developing and conducting workshops and seminars on Transformative Communication, a communication-based approach to self-realization. These seminars became the foundational programs of Satvatove Institute, a non-profit organization based in North Florida, dedicated to educate people in transformative communication and principles of self-realization and spiritual empowerment, which David has co-directed with Marie Glasheen since 2003. In 2004 David established the Satvatove Institute School of Transformative Coaching.

David has conducted transformational seminars in more than a dozen countries (including India, Russia, New Zealand, Guyana, and throughout Western Europe and North America), and has coached and counseled thousands of people, groups, and organizations. He is the author of *Relationships That Work: The Power of Conscious Living*, and has been featured as a communications expert on media outlets such as Fox News and CNN News.

Dr. Wolf has been practicing and teaching *bhakti-yoga* around the world for more than 35 years. He is an aspiring follower of A.C. Bhaktivedanta Swami Prabhupāda, and an avid reader of the books of Bhaktivedanta Swami Prabhupāda.